SLAVERY
IN THE
SOUTH

FIRST-HAND ACCOUNTS
OF THE
ANTE-BELLUM
AMERICAN SOUTHLAND
FROM
NORTHERN & SOUTHERN WHITES, NEGROES, & FOREIGN OBSERVERS

Edited with an Introduction by

HARVEY WISH

Professor of History, Western Reserve University

New York
FARRAR, STRAUS AND COMPANY

CONTENTS

III THE VIEW OF THE SOUTHERN WHITE

SLAVERY
AND THE
SOUTHERN PLANTATION
SYSTEM

The ancient custom of slavery, practised by Africans, biblical patri-
archs, Greek mineowners, Roman landlords, and others, drew its
vitality throughout history from labor scarcity, intertribal wars, élit-
ist aspirations, and the profit motive. Spain, Portugal, England, Hol-
land, and other expansionist nations once regarded the slave trade as
a major source of revenue and power. Colonial New England—so the
antebellum Southerners reminded the Yankees—was a pioneer in the
African slave trade. By 1700, Rhode Island merchants were sending
out eighteen slave ships annually, each equipped with the necessary
chains, handcuffs, vinegar, and rum to trap or otherwise acquire Africans to be sold to the plantations of the American South and the
West Indies.

Although New England's climate and soil discouraged the rise of a
plantation system, Massachusetts alone had over 5200 slaves in 1763,
and all New England is estimated to have had three times as many.
These slaves were employed as seamen, lumberjacks, farmhands,
craftsmen, and domestic servants. Occasionally a New Englander
wrote proslavery propaganda in an attempt to reconcile slavery with
the tenets of Christianity. However, economic conditions as well as
the antislavery efforts of Quakers, Moravians, and eighteenth century liberals insured the abolition of human bondage in New England.

While Jefferson, Washington, and other eighteenth-century Southern liberals hated slavery and urged its abolition, they hesitated too
long over the means of freeing the 700,000 Negroes enslaved in
1776. They feared that sudden emancipation would not only endan-
ger the plantation economy but engender a race war; therefore, they
insisted upon prerequisites to emancipation such as Negro education
—a condition that the next generation of Southerners was to reject as

an incendiary step. By that time the plantation system was in full flower, stimulated by the growing world demand for tobacco, sea-island cotton, indigo, rice, and other semi-tropical products. Virginia tobacco lands, it is true, suffered from soil exhaustion for several decades, and this condition encouraged many planters to emancipate slaves in their wills despite their uneasiness over the existence of free Negroes. But it had long been evident that the labor shortage could not be easily solved by the white (and sometimes black) in-dentured-servant system, because it permitted white workers to ac-quire small farms at the end of the contract period. Aspiring South-ern aristocrats with political influence in London could easily get title to vast empty acreages, but the abundance of cheap fertile lands quickly attracted the newly freed indentured servants. Compulsory Negro labor insured the growth of the large plantation. Although the plantation actually preceded the slave system, the profits of expan-sion through perpetual slavery proved irresistible.

The sensational growth of British textile manufacturing, a leading phase of the Industrial Revolution, brought about such a demand for raw cotton as to stimulate plantation inventiveness greatly. Thus Eli Whitney's cotton gin was the most successful of an array of in-ventions that made commercially feasible the cultivation of the low-priced short-staple green-seed cotton. Hitherto, the costly hand-process of separating the seed from the plant could be justified only in the cultivation of sea-island cotton, a silk-like long-staple black-seed variety, because prices often rose as high as two dollars a pound for it, while the price for short-staple cotton rarely rose above thirty cents. As a result, planters and slave-traders recruited slave gangs from among the surplus slaves of the Upper South, taking them to the frontier lands of the Deep South along the Gulf.

An observer in 1839 saw traders from Virginia riding on horseback armed with long whips as they drove their slaves ahead chained to-gether in pairs. Even Indian tribes like the Cherokee of Georgia be-came slaveholders before they were themselves evicted and transported across the Mississippi into the future Indian Territory (or Oklahoma). By 1860 the Cotton Kingdom had moved so far westward as to absorb the eastern part of Texas.

While England and France, in response to strong antislavery pressures, abolished slavery in their colonies during the 1830's, and even Czarist Russia considered the emancipation of her serfs, the American South clung to slavery not only as profitable but as an indispensable method of racial control. By 1860, one third of the Southern population of twelve million consisted of Negroes, including 250,-000 free blacks. Since Negroes made up large majorities in numerous counties of the Deep South and outnumbered whites altogether in South Carolina and Mississippi, the issue of white-man supremacy was always in the air. Evidence indicates that racial feeling below the Mason-Dixon Line was exacerbated by slave insurrections, real and fancied, and by the militant abolitionist propaganda after 1831, the date that the abolitionist (but Christian Non-Resistant) William Lloyd Garrison founded the uncompromising *Liberator* and Nat Turner precipitated his bloody insurrection in Virginia. Southerners generally regarded these two events as interrelated.

The story of the plantation system as seen by slaves constitutes a large part of the first-hand narratives published here. Most of them show an understandable bitterness toward their former masters, but here and there are tributes to kindly slaveowners. They are far more outspoken than the Negroes whom Frederick Law Olmsted interviewed in his journey through the South. The Negro writings vary in literacy, ranging from the attractive prose of Charlotte Forten—who was never a slave—to the dictated narrative of Nat Turner, and in none of the narratives can the slightest support or justification for the proslavery arguments and alleged facts about the plantation system given by Professor Thomas R. Dew of Virginia be found. Although a minority of slaves, largely those employed as domestics in the Big House, showed docility and even affection toward their masters, the predominant number of field hands, it is clearly evident, persevered in resisting slavery. Such slaves frequently plotted uprisings and would occasionally organize violence, if the domestic servants did not first betray them. Southern newspapers and contemporary handbills reveal the frequency of slave escapes, although the successful fugitives were usually those from the border states where contact with such refugee institutions as the Underground Railway could be made. The reiteration by Southern politicians of the need for an effective federal Fugitive Slave Law testifies to the fear of escaping slaves. Furthermore, if the declaration that slave labor was given unwillingly needs proof, the state of affairs may be inferred also from the studies and contemporary accounts of dawdling over tasks, feigning of illness, destruction of machinery and expensive tools, abuse of plantation animals, and attempts of personal violence toward masters and overseers. Olmsted indicates that masters might become brutal or callous because their experience would lead them to believe that slaves habitually lied about being ill or incapable of continuing work.

Slave resistance had begun even before plantation times, for during the early and notorious Middle Passage, kidnapped Africans had frequently mutinied on the slave ship and sometimes even succeeded in forcing the pilots to steer a return course to West Africa. The Gabriel Prosser insurrection of 1800 in Virginia had frightened Southern leaders, initiated debates over emancipation, and encouraged a movement for colonization of slaves in Africa. Thoughtful free Negroes like James Forten of Massachusetts denounced colonization and few showed any enthusiasm for it. Jefferson, who had proposed colonization as early as 1776, was supported by Virginia liberals like Monroe, Madison, and John Marshall, and by the transplanted Virginian Henry Clay, but the results were not impressive. By 1860, only 15,000 Negroes had been colonized in Africa; much of this result was due to the efforts of Southern liberals and their American Colonization Society founded in 1817.

Slave insurrections inspired a variety of reactions among white Southerners and their legislatures. New laws and strict regulations of the plantation regime followed the startling Nat Turner revolt of

1831 in Virginia and the movement led by Denmark Vesey of South Carolina. Legislatures forbade anyone to teach Negroes to read or write or to permit slaves to congregate off the plantation without the presence of a white man. Able-bodied whites were expected to join or assist slave-patrols in watching for any signs of rebellion or lack of discipline among the slaves. Vigilance committees, California-style, were in evidence by 1856 at the time when the new Republican Party began their first presidential canvass. These extra-legal groups tracked down suspected rebels, held informal trials, used force to extricate confessions, and even executed their judgments. These elaborate preparations for trouble give evidence of a continuing Southern nervousness about the docility of their charges, so it is not surprising that so many Southern newspapers immediately interpreted the small-scale John Brown raid on Harper's Ferry in 1859 as proof of an abolitionist-inspired effort to set off a race war in the South. (Actually, the slaves, as usual, lacked any effective organization and did not lend any appreciable aid to Brown.)

Proslavery propagandists like George Fitzhugh, Thomas R. Dew, and James Henry Hammond tried to assure worried Southerners that their fears of insurrection were exaggerated. Fitzhugh admitted privately that he saw many evils in slavery but thought that when replying to the charges of the abolitionists none of them should be admitted. Instead he and others built up a romantic plantation image in which slaves loved their masters and were utterly dependent upon them in a child-like fashion. Besides, they argued, things were worse with the exploited wage-slave of the North or in Europe. Dew concluded that slavery was the finest basis for a civilization. John Calhoun even believed that planters and Northern industrialists should unite in order to avoid any uprising by either slaves or wage workers. Pseudo-anthropologists like Nott, Glidden, and others won surprisingly respectful attention as far away as the London anthropological societies and encouraged the belief that slavery must be perpetual because of the inferiority of the Negro. A southern maverick like Hinton Rowan Helper, author of *The Impending Crisis in the South,*

who severely arraigned slavery as the chief cause for the backwardness of the plantation states—as Olmsted also implied—did not
argue for the equality of the slave; he actually hated Negroes as
much as did any proslavery man.

The publication and amazing sale of Harriet Beecher Stowe's *Uncle Tom's Cabin* (1852) embittered the national debate over slavery,
particularly over the brutalities of the slave system. The testimony
of ex-slaves such as Frederick Douglass, Josiah Henson, and Solomon Northup are quite detailed in their description of plantation
abuses. Most of the distinguished British visitors like Fanny Kemble,
Captain Basil Hall, and Charles MacKay are no less emphatic in
denouncing what they saw of plantation life. An earlier visitor from
Dublin, Isaac Weld, an honored topographer of Ireland who had
entrée into aristocratic plantations such as Mount Vernon, offered a
rather tolerant estimate of slavery on the large estates, but severely
condemned it on the small farms and among the poorer masters. The
Free-Soiler Frederick Law Olmsted, who was trying to create a free
state in West Texas just as other antislavery men were aiming at the
same goal for Bleeding Kansas, hoped to convince planters that
slavery did not pay. All of these views are explicit in the selections of
this book.

Historians have noted that the lot of the slave differed somewhat
from region to region, from plantation to plantation, as well as from
plantation to small farm. They have noted that the rapidly rising
prices of slaves, soaring from an early $300 to over $2000 by 1860,
might be expected to offer a strong incentive for kindly treatment of
slaves among practical-minded planters. Other writers, using sources
such as those included here, have recognized the psychological factor
in which absolute power offers irresistible temptations to authoritar-
ian personalities. Since Negro testimony against whites counted for
very little in the South, complaints would worsen conditions. Therefore, as the accompanying selections illustrate, the system required
whippings, fettering, stocks, slave pens, and frequent cuts in rations.

Public auctions, as Captain Hall and others observed, exposed human beings to close and intimate scrutiny like horses. Families were separated, except where explicit laws or a master's will forbade it, and were a frequent occurrence when a large estate had to be disposed of.

The presence of numerous mulattoes among the slave population reflected the sexual habits of many planters and their sons and overseers. Rape of a female slave by a white was not a capital crime, although a Negro rape of a white woman certainly was. It is difficult to know to what extent these inter-racial unions were based on affection rather than force; not infrequently, the planter did show such attachment and provided for his mistress and offspring in his will; others preferred to avoid embarrassing acknowledgments of paternity. Furthermore, slavery left an abiding influence on the Negro family by greatly reducing the responsibility and authority of the male, minimizing the sanctity of slave marriage, encouraging promiscuity, and affording no penalties for desertion. The matriarchal Negro family, which had some roots in African societies, took even stronger hold under the plantation system. However, planters indignantly denied the abolitionist charge that they practised slave-breeding for profit, although some contemporary evidence for the existence of this practise exists.

The idyllic picture of the slave system as described by Fitzhugh, Simms, Dew, and other proslavery writers was marred not only by the well-known stringent methods of control, which included occasional use of bloodhounds in Uncle Tom style, but by the deliberate practice of discouraging self-reliance and independent habits. Olmsted affords many such examples of the childlike dependence of slaves and their exasperating habit of pestering masters with questions about every detail of an operation. Again, in this atmosphere of distrust and irresponsibility, overseers regularly scrutinized slave cabins for weapons of any kind and for stolen goods, enforced the curfew and pass system, punished runaways harshly or threatened to sell recalcitrant slaves "down the river" to mythical masters who were naturally much worse than the local variety. Overseers, always strictly accountable for a high output, might resort to tough Negro slave-drivers to apply the needed pressure to the labor gangs. While the average Negro did not require prodding to go to church, this institution too could serve the system by sermons on obedience, docility, and patience for the ultimate spiritual reward in heaven. At all times, the Negro was kept in his place and forbidden contact with free Negroes who set a bad example to men in bondage.

Yet there were many masters who acted humanely as far as the peculiar institution permitted and offered substantial incentives to their people which might very well have prolonged slavery had not war intervened. Coercion, the planters understood, would not grow cotton, and severe punishments injured valuable property. Any master, in fact, was unhappy to see the valuable time of his slave wasted by long jail sentences even for confirmed rascals. Slaves frequently could use the little plots of ground around their cabins to raise chickens, pigs, and vegetables to vary their diet or to earn extra money at the village market. Quite commonly, slaves like Frederick Douglass were permitted to hire themselves out to individuals or local factories and to keep part of their earnings. Hard workers—Stakhanovites, Dixie-style—often received special incentive payments.

Olmsted learned that planters preferred to use Irish or German workers, when available, for dangerous tasks which might injure costly slave property. They also pointed out the absence in the South of that physical aversion to race displayed by Northerners and dwelt on the picture of the affectionate slave mammy tenderly suckling the white babe. Jim Crow did not, in fact, exist as strongly in antebellum times as it did in the era of the Dixie demagogues when Negroes were excluded from trades that they had pursued even in slavery days. Progressive planters boasted of their slave hospitals, their devoted home-style medical services, and perhaps of the plantation doctor. But the testimony of Fanny Kemble, wife of a Georgia planter, is not reassuring on this point. Slave clothing, if crudely simple, was usually adequate for everyday work in a warm climate, and it might be supplemented by the cast-off finery of the Big House or the wares offered by the German-Jewish peddlers. Food, as already noted, could be varied not only by home-raised products but by occasional hunting, trapping, or fishing.

Frederick Douglass and other ex-slaves took issue with the impression of plantation visitors that the slaves must have been contented, judging from the constant outbreak of hearty Negro laughter, the improvised singing, and the vigorous dancing. One heard their rhythmic shouts, the clapping of hands, the concern with African superstitions, and watched the dramatic leaps of men reliving an unforgotten African pattern. All this *did* show an impressive zest for life and a level of existence undoubtedly higher than that of the inmates of a twentieth-century concentration camp. Visitors concerned with being fair to both sides liked to mention the house servants who were in daily personal contact with the planter and his family and who commonly spoke with sincere affection of their "folks." These domestic servants, as noted, might look down on the lowly field hands and would hasten to expose any rumored uprising. A hasty visitor could easily forget that these people, who included so many gifted individuals—judging from the escapees alone—were denied normal outlet for their natural abilities and inclinations, suffered daily humiliations, were refused free expression, and lived an insecure family life that was inferior to the level of their African ancestors.

As Olmsted and other keen observers maintained, slavery (and they should have added race feeling) injured Southern whites as well as Negroes. They doubted whether slavery paid economically and felt that it produced the cultural backwardness of the rural communities. Furthermore, as Southerners themselves complained, slavery cheapened the value of free labor, for the racial caste system discouraged white workers from working "like a nigger" or toiling alongside slaves, except as supervisors. Besides, too many useful tasks were apt to be consigned to "nigger work" and lose their attractiveness for Southern whites.

Nonslaveholders like Hinton Rowan Helper of North Carolina saw no benefits in the peculiar institution for their class. Some like Fitzhugh and James D. B. De Bow, editor of *De Bow's Review* of New Orleans, sought to increase the stake in slavery of nonslaveholders by reviving the African slave trade and thus making available a host of cheap slaves for deprived small farmers and "highlanders." But this movement fell afoul of Virginia's desire to sell her large surplus of slaves at high current prices. What united the nonslaveholders and the planters was the color of their skin and the fear of becoming an isolated racial minority in the huge black belts. Only one fourth or less of the whites were slaveholders or members of slaveholding families; 384,000 were counted by the Census of 1860 as slaveholders. Yet the Confederacy was to show an amazing degree of unity (there were of course great exceptions) during four years of struggle against overwhelming odds in men and resources.

Most of the causes given for the Civil War dwindle away alongside of the factor of the Southern insistence on white-man supremacy. Certainly the tariff factor was of mild importance in 1861, considering the major concessions won for lowered rates. Even less impressive is the theory of Charles Beard, following the Marxist version of Algie Simons, that planters and industrialists were arrayed against each other for economic motives—an explanation that has little monographic or documentary support. Many other explanations such as the factor of Southern nationalism, the abolitionist pressures, etc. do not necessarily exclude the overriding consideration of white-man supremacy. This psychology was fed on fears of slave insurrection and a growing suspicion that Yankee policy would provoke a race war or extinguish slavery upon which most whites of all classes depended as a basic method of policing Negroes.

The partial return of antebellum race relations came around 1876 with the withdrawal of Union troops, the entrenchment of the conservative Redeemers, and the Supreme Court's conservative interpretation of the equalitarian Fourteenth Amendment. When slavery disappeared, the South did not fight to restore it but resorted to newer forms of race control not too dissimilar from those used by modern colonial powers. The Redeemers or Bourbons were largely industrialists, merchants, and planters who permitted Negro suffrage wherever they could count on this vote and dealt with the Negro in the old paternalistic style. When they were overthrown by the small farmers and their "demagogic" leaders around 1890, the new ruling class crushed Negro political power as a tool of the Bourbons. By that time the victory of European imperialism gave sanction to a new racialism in the name of the white man's burden. Intimidation, lynchings, white primaries, grandfather clauses, and finally the introduction of Jim Crow in a rigid form gave racists the safeguards they had lost with emancipation and which they are now fighting to retain.

HARVEY WISH

January, 1964.

Editorial Note

These materials have, as a rule, been printed from the originals with only a few (silent) changes of punctuation. Unless otherwise noted, the footnotes are those of the original writer.

THE EDITORS

SELECT BIBLIOGRAPHY

Frederic Bancroft, *Slave Trading in the Old South* (Johns Hopkins, 1931)

H. Winston Coleman, Jr., *Slavery Times in Kentucky* (University of North Carolina, 1940)

E. Merton Coulter, *Thomas Spalding of Sapelo* (Louisiana State University, 1940)

Charles S. Davis, *The Cotton Kingdom in Alabama* (Montgomery, 1939)

Clement Eaton, *The Growth of Southern Civilization, 1790-1860* (Harper, 1961)

Stanley Elkins, *Slavery* (University of Chicago, 1959)

R. R. Flanders, *Plantation Slavery in Georgia* (University of North Carolina, 1933)

John Hope Franklin, *From Slavery to Freedom* (Knopf, 1948)

Lewis C. Gray, *History of Agriculture in the Southern United States to 1860* (Washington, D.C., 1933)

G. G. Johnson, *Ante-Bellum North Carolina, a Special History* (University of North Carolina, 1937)

Chase C. Mooney, *Slavery in Tennessee* (Indiana University, 1957)

Ulrich B. Phillips, *American Negro Slavery* (Appleton, 1918)

Joseph C. Robert, *The Tobacco Kingdom* (Duke, 1938)

James B. Sellers, *Slavery in Alabama* (University, Ala., 1950)

J. C. Sitterson, *Sugar Country, the Cane Sugar Industry in the South, 1753-1950* (Univ. of Kentucky, 1953)

Kenneth M. Stampp, *The Peculiar Institution* (Knopf, 1956)

Wendell H. Stephenson, *Isaac Franklin, Slave Trader and Planter of the Old South* (Louisiana State, 1938)

Charles S. Sydnor, *Slavery in Mississippi* (New York, 1933)

Orville Taylor, *Negro Slavery in Arkansas* (Duke, 1958)

Harrison A. Trexler, *Slavery in Missouri, 1804-1865* (Johns Hopkins, 1914)

Bell I. Wiley, *Southern Negroes, 1861-1865* (Yale, 1938)

PART ONE

THE NEGRO'S VIEW

NAT TURNER
(*1800-1831*)

In the most important and best-documented slave insurrection in Southern history, Nat Turner, son of an African-born slave mother in Southampton County, Virginia, led an uprising of sixty or seventy slaves. As his remarkable confession indicates, he was a precocious youth and became a preacher motivated by mystical voices to fulfill a dream to liberate his people. He admitted that his own master, Joseph Travis, was a kindly person; yet he and his family were the first to be slaughtered. At least 51— Gray says 55—were murdered the night of the uprising, August 21, 1831, The details are given in the *Confessions* below.

This event took on special significance to Southerners because the Southern press had reported insurrections in at least a half dozen places in the Caribbean or West Indies and one in North Carolina. (There is no proof of concerted conspiracy between Turner and the principals of the Carolina episode, however.) Following the massacre, the community tracked down suspects and killed an undetermined number, and the Court ordered sixteen executed and many more jailed or transported. Nat Turner went to the gallows, saying that he had nothing to add to his *Confession*.

The Nat Turner insurrection shocked the South and led most slave-state legislatures to pass stringent codes for policing. The flourishing emancipation movement in the South began to falter. Southerners came to believe that the revolt was connected with the rise of abolitionism, specifically with the publication of Garrison's *Liberator* in that same year of 1831, but this has never been proved. More tangible is the fact that Southerners never quite recovered from the fear of incipient slave insurrections despite the wordy reassurances of Thomas R. Dew and the proslavery propagandists that there was nothing to fear.

This edition of *The Confessions of Nat Turner* is complete. Only the appendices and prefatory material have been omitted. Punctuation and spelling have occasionally been silently corrected.

THE
CONFESSIONS
OF
NAT TURNER,
THE LEADER
OF
THE LATE INSURRECTION
IN SOUTHAMPTON, VA.

AS FULLY AND VOLUNTARILY MADE TO

THOMAS R. GRAY,

In the prison where he was confined, and acknowledged by him to be such,
when read before the Court of Southampton: with the
certificate, under seal of the Court convened at
Jerusalem, Nov. 5, 1831, for his trial.

ALSO,

AN AUTHENTIC ACCOUNT

OF THE

WHOLE INSURRECTION,

WITH

Lists of the Whites who were Murdered,

AND OF THE

*Negroes brought before the Court of Southampton,
and there sentenced, &c.*

———

RICHMOND:
PUBLISHED BY THOMAS R. GRAY.

T. W. WHITE, PRINTER.

....
1832.

CONFESSION

Agreeable to his own appointment, on the evening he was committed to prison, with permission of the Jailer, I visited NAT on Tuesday the 1st November, when, without being questioned at all, he commenced his narrative in the following words:—

SIR,—You have asked me to give a history of the motives which induced me to undertake the late insurrection, as you call it—To do so I must go back to the days of my infancy, and even before I was born. I was thirty-one years of age the 2d of October last, and born the property of Benj. Turner, of this county. In my childhood a circumstance occurred which made an indelible impression on my mind, and laid the ground work of that enthusiasm, which has terminated so fatally to many both white and black, and for which I am about to atone at the gallows. It is here necessary to relate this circumstance—trifling as it may seem, it was the commencement of that belief which has grown with time, and even now, sir, in this dungeon, helpless and forsaken as I am, I cannot divest myself of. Being at play with other children, when three or four years old, I was telling them something, which my mother overhearing, said it had happened before I was born—I stuck to my story, however, and related some things which went in her opinion to confirm it—others being called on were greatly astonished, knowing that these things had happened, and caused them to say in my hearing, I surely would be a prophet, as the Lord had shewn me things that had happened before my birth. And my father and mother strengthened me in this my first impression, saying in my presence, I was intended for some great purpose, which they had always thought from certain marks on my head and breast—[a pracel of excrescences which I believe are not at all uncommon, particularly among negroes, as I have seen several with the same. In this case he has either cut them off, or they have nearly disappeared]—My grand mother, who was very religious, and to whom I was much attached—my master, who belonged to the church, and other religious persons who visited the house, and whom I often saw at prayers, noticing the singularity of my manners, I suppose, and my uncommon intelligence for a child, remarked I had too much sense to be raised—and if I was, I would never be of any service to any one—as a slave—To a mind like mine, restless, inquisitive and observant of every thing that was passing, it is easy to suppose that religion was the subject to which it would be directed, and although this subject principally occupied my thoughts, there was nothing that I saw or heard of to which my attention was not directed—The manner in which I learned to read and write, not only had great influence on my own mind, as I acquired it with the most perfect ease, so much so, that I have no recollection whatever of learning the alphabet—but to the astonishment of the family, one day, when a book was shewn me to keep me from crying, I began spelling the names of different objects—this was a source of wonder to all in the neighborhood, particularly the blacks—and this learning was constantly improved at all opportunities—when I got large enough to go to work, while employed, I was reflecting on many things that would present themselves to my imagination, and whenever an opportunity occurred of looking at a book, when the school children were getting their lessons, I would find many things that the fertility of my own imagination had depicted to me before; all my time, not devoted to my master's service, was spent either in prayer, or in making experiments in casting different things in moulds made of earth, in attempting to make paper, gunpowder, and many other experiments, that although I could not perfect, yet convinced me of its practicability if I had the means.* I was not addicted to stealing in my youth, nor have ever been—Yet such was the confidence of the negroes in the neighborhood, even at this early period of my life, in my superior judgment, that they would often

---

* When questioned as to the manner of manufacturing those different articles, he was found well informed.

carry me with them when they were going on any roguery, to plan for them. Growing up among them, with this confidence in my superior judgment, and when this, in their opinions, was perfected by Divine inspiration, from the circumstances already alluded to in my infancy, and which belief was ever afterwards zealously inculcated by the austerity of my life and manners, which became the subject of remark by white and black.—Having soon discovered to be great, I must appear so, and therefore studiously avoided mixing in society, and wrapped myself in mystery, devoting my time to fasting and prayer. By this time, having arrived to man's estate, and hearing the scriptures commented on at meetings, I was struck with that particular passage which says: "Seek ye the kingdom of Heaven and all things shall be added unto you." I reflected much on this passage, and prayed daily for light on this subject—As I was praying one day at my plough, the spirit spoke to me, saying "Seek ye the kingdom of Heaven and all things shall be added unto you." *Question*—what do you mean by the Spirit. *Ans.* The Spirit that spoke to the prophets in former days—and I was greatly astonished, and for two years prayed continually, whenever my duty would permit—and then again I had the same revelation, which fully confirmed me in the impression that I was ordained for some great purpose in the hands of the Almighty. Several years rolled round, in which many events occurred to strengthen me in this my belief. At this time I reverted in my mind to the remarks made of me in my childhood, and the things that had been shewn me—and as it had been said of me in my childhood by those by whom I had been taught to pray, both white and black, and in whom I had the greatest confidence, that I had too much sense to be raised, and if I was I would never be of any use to any one as a slave. Now finding I had arrived to man's estate, and was a slave, and these revelations being made known to me, I began to direct my attention to this great object, to fulfil the purpose for which, by this time, I felt assured I was intended. Knowing the influence I had obtained over the minds of my fellow servants, (not by the means of conjuring and such like tricks—for to them I always spoke of such things with contempt) but by the communion of the Spirit whose revelations I often communicated to them, and they believed and said my wisdom came from God. I now began to prepare them for my purpose, by telling them something was about to happen that would terminate in fulfilling the great promise that had been made to me—About this time I was placed under an overseer, from whom I ran away—and after remaining in the woods thirty days, I returned, to the astonishment of the negroes on the plantation, who thought I had made my escape to some other part of the country, as my father had done before. But the reason of my return was, that the Spirit appeared to me and said I had my wishes directed to the things of this world, and not to the kingdom of Heaven, and that I should return to the service of my earthly master —"For he who knoweth his Master's will, and doeth it not, shall be beaten with many stripes, and thus have I chastened you." And the negroes found fault, and murmured against me, saying that if they had my sense they would not serve any master in the world. And about this time I had a vision—and I saw white spirits and black spirits engaged in battle, and the sun was darkened—the thunder rolled in the Heavens, and blood flowed in streams—and I heard a voice saying, "Such is your luck, such you are called to see, and let it come rough or smooth, you must surely bear it." I now withdrew myself as much as my situation would permit, from the intercourse of my fellow servants, for the avowed purpose of serving the Spirit more fully—and it appeared to me, and reminded me of the things it had already shown me, and that it would then reveal to me the knowledge of the elements, the revolution of the planets, the operation of tides, and changes of the seasons. After this revelation in the year 1825, and the knowledge of the elements being made known to me, I sought more than ever to obtain true holiness before the great day of judgment should appear, and then I began to receive the true knowledge of faith. And from the first steps of righteousness until the last, was I made perfect; and the Holy Ghost was with me, and said "Behold me as I stand in the Heavens"—and I looked and saw the forms of men in different attitudes—and there were lights in the sky to which the children of darkness gave other names than what they really were—for they were the lights of the Saviour's hands, stretched forth from east to west, even as they were extended on the cross on Calvary for the redemption of sinners. And I wondered greatly at these miracles, and prayed to be informed of a certainty of the meaning thereof—and shortly afterwards, while labouring in the field, I discovered drops of blood on the corn, as though it were dew from heaven—and I communicated it to many, both white and black, in the neighbourhood—and I then found on the leaves in the woods hieroglyphic characters and numbers, with the forms of men in different attitudes, portrayed in blood, and representing the figures I had seen before in the heavens.—And now the Holy Ghost had revealed itself to me, and made plain the miracles it had shown me—For as the blood of Christ had been shed on this earth, and had ascended to heaven for the salvation of sinners, and was now returning to earth again in the form of dew—and as the leaves on the trees bore the impression of the figures I had seen in the heavens, it was plain to me that the Saviour was about to lay down the yoke he had borne for the sins of men, and the great day of judgment was at hand.—About this time, I told these things to a white man, (Etheldred T. Brantley) on whom it had a wonderful effect—and he ceased from his wickedness, and was attacked immediately with a cutaneous eruption, and blood oozed from the pores of his skin, and after praying and fasting nine days, he was healed, and the Spirit appeared to me again, and said, as the Saviour had been baptised, so should we be also—and when the white people would not let us be baptised by the church, we went down into the water together, in the sight of many who reviled us, and were baptised by the Spirit—After this I rejoiced greatly, and gave thanks to God. And on the 12th of May, 1828, I heard a loud noise in the heavens, and the Spirit instantly appeared to me and said the Serpent was loosened, and Christ had laid down the yoke he had borne for the sins of men, and that I should take it on and fight against the Serpent, for the time was fast approaching, when the first should be last and the last should be first. *Ques.* Do you not find yourself mistaken now? *Ans.* Was not Christ crucified? And by signs in the heavens that it would make known to me when I should commence the great work—and until the first sign appeared, I should conceal it from the knowledge of men—And on the appearance of the sign, (the eclipse of the sun last February) I should arise and prepare myself, and slay my enemies with their own weapons. And immediately on the sign appearing in the heavens, the seal was removed from my lips, and I communicated the great work laid out for me to do, to four in whom I had the greatest confidence, (Henry, Hark, Nelson and Sam)—It was intended by us to have begun the work of death on the 4th of July last—Many were the plans formed and rejected by us, and it affected my mind to such a degree, that I fell sick, and the time passed without our coming to any determination how to commence—Still forming new schemes and rejecting them, when the sign appeared again, which determined me not to wait longer.

Since the commencement of 1830, I had been living with Mr. Joseph Travis, who was to me a kind master, and placed the greatest confidence in me; in fact, I had no cause to complain of his treatment to me. On Saturday evening, the 20th of August, it was agreed between Henry, Hark and myself, to prepare a dinner the next day for the men we expected, and then to concert a plan, as we had not yet determined on any. Hark on the following morning brought a pig, and Henry brandy, and being joined by Sam, Nelson, Will and Jack, they prepared in the woods a dinner, where, about three o'clock, I joined them.

Q. Why were you so backward in joining them.

A. The same reason that had caused me not to mix with them for years before.

I saluted them on coming up, and asked Will how came he there; he answered, his life was worth no more than others, and his liberty as dear to him. I asked him if he thought to obtain it? He said he would, or lose his life. This was enough to put him in full confidence. Jack, I knew, was only a tool in the hands of Hark, it was quickly agreed we should commence at home (Mr. J. Travis') on that night, and until we had armed and equipped ourselves, and gathered sufficient force, neither age nor sex was to be spared, (which was invariably adhered to.) We remained at the feast until about two hours in the night, when we went to the house and found Austin; they all went to the cider press and drank, except myself. On returning to the house, Hark went to the door with an axe, for the purpose of breaking it open, as we knew we were strong enough to murder the family, if they were awaked by the noise; but reflecting that it might create an alarm in the neighborhood, we determined to enter the house secretly, and murder them whilst sleeping. Hark got a ladder and set it against the chimney, on which I ascended, and hoisting a window, entered and came down stairs, unbarred the door, and removed the guns from their places. It was then observed that I must spill the first blood. On which armed with a hatchet, and accompanied by Will, I entered my master's chamber; it being dark, I could not give a death blow, the hatchet glanced from his head, he sprang from the bed and called his wife, it was his last word. Will laid him dead, with a blow of his axe, and Mrs. Travis shared the same fate, as she lay in bed. The murder of this family five in number, was the work of a moment, not one of them awoke; there was a little infant sleeping in a cradle, that was forgotten, until we had left the house and gone some distance, when Henry and Will returned and killed it; we got here, four guns that would shoot, and several old muskets, with a pound or two of powder. We remained some time at the barn, where we paraded; I formed them in a line as soldiers, and after carrying them through all the manœuvres I was master of, marched them off to Mr. Salathul Francis', about six hundred yards distant. Sam and Will went to the door and knocked. Mr. Francis asked who was there, Sam replied it was him, and he had a letter for him, on which he got up and came to the door; they immediately seized him, and dragging him out a little from the door, he was dispatched by repeated blows on the head;

there was no other white person in the family. We started from there for Mrs. Reese's, maintaining the most perfect silence on our march, where finding the door unlocked, we entered, and murdered Mrs. Reese in her bed, while sleeping; her son awoke, but it was only to sleep the sleep of death, he had only time to say who is that, and he was no more. From Mrs. Reese's we went to Mrs. Turner's, a mile distant, which we reached about sunrise, on Monday morning. Henry, Austin, and Sam, went to the still, where, finding Mr. Peebles, Austin shot him, and the rest of us went to the house; as we approached, the family discovered us, and shut the door. Vain hope! Will, with one stroke of his axe, opened it, and we entered and found Mrs. Turner and Mrs. Newsome in the middle of a room almost frightened to death. Will immediately killed Mrs. Turner, with one blow of his axe. I took Mrs. Newsome by the hand, and with the sword I had when I was apprehended, I struck her several blows over the head, but not being able to kill her, as the sword was dull. Will turning around and discovering it, dispatched her also. A general destruction of property and search for money and ammunition, always succeeded the murders. By this time my company amounted to fifteen, and nine men mounted, who started for Mrs. Whitehead's, (the other six were to go through a by way to Mr. Bryant's, and rejoin us at Mrs. White-head's,) as we approached the house we discovered Mr. Richard Whitehead standing in the cotton patch, near the lane fence; we called him over into the lane, and Will, the executioner, was near at hand, with his fatal axe, to send him to an untimely grave. As we pushed on to the house, I discovered some one run round the garden, and thinking it was some of the white family, I pursued them, but finding it was a servant girl belonging to the house, I returned to commence the work of death, but they whom I left, had not been idle; all the family were already murdered, but Mrs. Whitehead and her daughter Margaret. As I came round to the door I saw Will pulling Mrs. Whitehead out of the house, and at the step he nearly severed her head from her body, with his broad axe. Miss Margaret, when I discovered her, had concealed herself in the corner, formed by the projection of the cellar cap from the house; on my approach she fled, but was soon overtaken, and after repeated blows with a sword, I killed her by a blow on the head, with a fence rail. By this time, the six who had gone by Mr. Bryant's, rejoined us, and informed me they had done the work of death assigned them. We again divided, part going to Mr. Richard Porter's, and from thence to Nathaniel Francis', the others to Mr. Howell Harris', and Mr. T. Doyle's. On my reaching Mr. Porter's, he had escaped with his family. I understood there, that the alarm had already spread, and I immediately returned to bring up those sent to Mr. Doyle's, and Mr. Howell Harris'; the party I left going on to Mr. Francis', having told them I would join them in that neighborhood. I met these sent to Mr. Doyle's and Mr. Harris' returning, having met Mr. Doyle on the road and killed him; and learning from some who joined them, that Mr. Harris was from home, I immediately pursued the course taken by the party gone on before; but knowing they would complete the work of death and pillage, at Mr. Francis' before I could get there, I went to Mr. Peter Edwards', expecting to find them there, but they had been here also. I then went to Mr. John T. Barrow's, they had been here and murdered him. I pursued on their track to Capt. Newit Harris', where I found the greater part mounted, and ready to start; the men now amounting to about forty, shouted and hurraed as I rode up, some were in the yard, loading their guns, others drinking. They said Captain Harris and his family had escaped, the property in the house they destroyed, robbing him of money and other valuables. I ordered them to mount and march instantly, this was about nine or ten o'clock, Monday morning. I proceeded to Mr. Levi Waller's, two or three miles distant. I took my station in the rear, and as it was my object to carry terror and devastation wherever we went, I placed fifteen or twenty of the best armed and most to be relied on, in front, who generally approached the houses as fast as their horses could run; this was for two purposes, to prevent their escape and strike terror to the inhabitants—on this account I never got to the houses, after leaving Mrs. Whitehead's until the murders were committed, except in one case. I sometimes got in sight in time to see the work of death completed, viewed the mangled bodies as they lay, in silent satisfaction, and immediately started in quest of other victims—Having murdered Mrs. Waller and ten children, we started for Mr. William Williams'—having killed him and two little boys that were there; while engaged in this, Mrs. Williams fled and got some distance from the house, but she was pursued, overtaken, and compelled to get up behind one of the company, who brought her back, and after showing her the mangled body of her lifeless husband, she was told to get down and lay by his side, where she was shot dead. I then started for Mr. Jacob Williams', where the family were murdered—Here we found a young man named Drury, who had come on business with Mr. Williams— he was pursued, overtaken and shot. Mrs. Vaughan's was the next place we visited—and after murdering the family here, I determined on starting for Jerusalem—Our number amounted now to fifty or sixty, all mounted and armed with guns, axes, swords and clubs— On reaching Mr. James W. Parker's gate, immediately on the road leading to Jerusalem, and about three miles distant, it was proposed to me to call there, but I objected, as I knew he was gone to Jerusalem, and my object was to reach there as soon as possible; but some of the men having relations at Mr. Parker's it was agreed that they might call and get his people. I remained at the gate on the road, with seven or eight; the others going across the field to the house, about half a mile off. After waiting some time for them, I became impatient, and started to the house for them, and on our return we were met by a party of white men, who had pursued our blood-stained track, and who had fired on those at the gate, and dispersed them, which I knew nothing of, not having been at that time rejoined by any of them—Immediately on discovering the whites, I ordered my men to halt and form, as they appeared to be alarmed—The white men eighteen in number, approached us in about one hundred yards, when one of them fired, (this was against the positive orders of Captain Alexander P. Peete, who commanded, and who had directed the men to reserve their fire until within thirty paces.) And I discovered about half of them retreating, I then ordered my men to fire and rush on them; the few remaining stood their ground until we approached within fifty yards, when they fired and retreated. We pursued and overtook some of them who we thought we left dead; (they were not killed) after pursuing them about two hundred yards, and rising a little hill, I discovered they were met by another party, and had halted, and were re-loading their guns, (this was a small party from Jerusalem who knew the negroes were in the field, and had just tied their horses to await their return to the road, knowing that Mr. Parker and family were in Jerusalem, but knew nothing of the party that had gone in with Captain Peete; on hearing the firing they immediately rushed to the spot and arrived just in time to arrest the progress of these barbarous villains, and save the lives of their friends and fellow citizens.) Thinking that those who retreated first, and the party who fired on us at fifty or sixty yards distant, had all only fallen back to meet others with ammunition. As I saw them re-loading their guns, and more coming up than I saw at first, and several of my bravest men being wounded, the others became panic struck and squandered over the field; the white men pursued and fired on us several times. Hark had his horse shot under him, and I caught another for him as it was running by me; five or six of my men were wounded, but none left on the field; finding myself defeated here I instantly determined to go through a private way, and cross the Nottoway river at the Cypress Bridge, three miles below Jerusalem, and attack that place in the rear, as I expected they would look for me on the other road, and I had a great desire to get there to procure arms and ammunition. After going a short distance in this private way, accompanied by about twenty men, I overtook two or three who told me the others were dispersed in every direction. After trying in vain to collect a sufficient force to proceed to Jerusalem, I determined to return, as I was sure they would make back to their old neighborhood, where they would rejoin me, make new recruits, and come down again. On my way back,

I called at Mrs. Thomas's, Mrs. Spencer's, and several other places, the white families having fled, we found no more victims to gratify our thirst for blood, we stopped at Majr. Ridley's quarter for the night, and being joined by four of his men, with the recruits made since my defeat, we mustered now about forty strong. After placing out sentinels, I laid down to sleep, but was quickly roused by a great racket; starting up, I found some mounted, and others in great confusion; one of the sentinels having given the alarm that we were about to be attacked, I ordered some to ride round and reconnoiter, and on their return the others being more alarmed, not knowing who they were, fled in different ways, so that I was reduced to about twenty again; with this I determined to attempt to recruit, and proceed on to rally in the neighborhood, I had left. Dr. Blunt's was the nearest house, which we reached just before day; on riding up the yard, Hark fired a gun. We expected Dr. Blunt and his family were at Maj. Ridley's, as I knew there was a company of men there; the gun was fired to ascertain if any of the family were at home; we were immediately fired upon and retreated leaving several of my men. I do not know what became of them, as I never saw them afterwards. Pursuing our course back, and coming in sight of Captain Harris's, where we had been the day before, we discovered a party of white men at the house, on which all deserted me but two, (Jacob and Nat,) we concealed ourselves in the woods until near night, when I sent them in search of Henry, Sam, Nelson and Hark, and directed them to rally all they could, at the place we had had our dinner the Sunday before, where they would find me, and I accordingly returned there as soon as it was dark, and remained until Wednesday evening, when discovering white men riding around the place as though they were looking for some one, and none of my men joining me, I concluded Jacob and Nat had been taken, and compelled to betray me.—On this I gave up all hope for the present; and on Thursday night, after having supplied myself with provisions from Mr. Travis's, I scratched a hole under a pile of fence rails in a field, where I concealed myself for six weeks, never leaving my hiding place but for a few minutes in the dead of night to get water, which was very near; thinking by this time I could venture out, I began to go about in the night and eaves drop the houses in the neighborhood; pursuing this course for about a fortnight and gathering little or no intelligence, afraid of speaking to any human being, and returning every morning to my cave before the dawn of day. I know not how long I might have led this life, if accident had not betrayed me, a dog in the neighborhood passing by my hiding place one night while I was out, was attracted by some meat I had in my cave, and crawled in and stole it, and was coming out just as I returned. A few nights after, two negroes having started to go hunting with the same dog, and passed that way, the dog came again to the place, and having just gone out to walk about, discovered me and barked, on which thinking myself discovered, I spoke to them to beg concealment. On making myself known, they fled from me. Knowing then they would betray me, I immediately left my hiding place, and was pursued almost incessantly until I was taken a fortnight afterwards by Mr. Benjamin Phipps, in a little hole I had dug out with my sword, for the purpose of concealment, under the top of a fallen tree. On Mr. Phipps discovering the place of my concealment, he cocked his gun and aimed at me. I requested him not to shoot, and I would give up, upon which he demanded my sword. I delivered it to him, and he brought me to prison. During the time I was pursued, I had many hair breadth escapes, which your time will not permit you to relate. I am here loaded with chains, and willing to suffer the fate that awaits me.

I here proceeded to make some inquiries of him, after assuring him of the certain death that awaited him, and that concealment would only bring destruction on the innocent as well as guilty, of his own color, if he knew of any extensive or concerted plan. His answer was, I do not. When I questioned him as to the insurrection in North Carolina happening about the same time, he denied any knowledge of it; and when I looked him in the face as though I would search his inmost thoughts, he replied, "I see sir, you doubt my word; but can you not think the same ideas, and strange appearances about this time in the heavens might prompt others, as well as myself, to this undertaking." I now had much conversation with and asked him many questions, having forborne to do so previously, except in the cases noted in parentheses; but during his statement, I had, unnoticed by him, taken notes as to some particular circumstances, and having the advantage of his statement before me in writing, on the evening of the third day that I had been with him, I began a cross examination, and found his statement corroborated by every circumstance coming within my own knowledge, or the confessions of others whom had been either killed or executed, and whom he had not seen or had any knowledge since 22d of August last, he expressed himself fully satisfied as to the impracticability of his attempt. It has been said he was ignorant and cowardly, and that his object was to murder and rob for the purpose of obtaining money to make his escape. It is notorious, that he was never known to have a dollar in his life; to swear an oath, or drink a drop of spirits. As to his ignorance, he certainly never had the advantages of education, but he can read and write (it was taught him by his parents), and for natural intelligence and quickness of apprehension, is surpassed by few men I have ever seen.—As to his being a coward, his reason as given for not resisting Mr. Phipps, shews the decision of his character. When he saw Mr. Phipps present his gun, he said he knew it was impossible for him to escape, as the woods were full of men; he therefore thought it was better to surrender, and trust to fortune for his escape. He is a complete fanatic, or plays his part most admirably. On other subjects he possesses an uncommon share of intelligence, with a mind capable of attaining any thing; but warped and perverted by the influence of early impressions. He is below the ordinary stature, though strong and active, having the true negro face, every feature of which is strongly marked. I shall not attempt to describe the effect of his narrative, as told and commented on by himself, in the condemned hole of the prison. The calm, deliberate composure with which he spoke of his late deeds and intentions, the expression of his fiend-like face when excited by enthusiasm, still bearing the stains of the blood of helpless innocence about him; clothed with rags and covered with chains; yet daring to raise his manacled hands to heaven, with a spirit soaring above the attributes of man; I looked on him and my blood curdled in my veins.

I will not shock the feelings of humanity, nor wound afresh the bosoms of the disconsolate sufferers in this unparalleled and inhuman massacre, by detailing the deeds of their fiend-like barbarity. There were two or three who were in the power of these wretches, had they known it, and who escaped in the most providential manner. There were two whom they thought they had left dead on the field at Mr. Parker's, but who were only stunned by the blows of their guns, as they did not take time to reload when they charged on them. The escape of a little girl who went to school at Mr. Waller's, and where the children were collecting for that purpose, excited general sympathy. As their teacher had not arrived, they were at play in the yard, and seeing the negroes approach, she ran up on a dirt chimney (such as are common to log houses), and remained there unnoticed during the massacre of the eleven that were killed at this place. She remained on her hiding place till just before the arrival of a party, who were in pursuit of the murderers, when she came down and fled to a swamp, where, a mere child as she was, with the horrors of the late scene before her, she lay concealed until the next day, when seeing a party go up to the house, she came up, and on being asked how she escaped, replied with the utmost simplicity, "The Lord helped her." She was taken up behind a gentleman of the party, and returned to the arms of her weeping mother. Miss Whitehead concealed herself between the bed and the mat that supported it, while they murdered her sister in the same room, without discovering her. She was afterwards carried off, and concealed for protection by a slave of the family, who gave evidence against several of them on their trial. Mrs. Nathaniel Francis, while concealed in a closet heard their blows, and the shrieks of the victims of these ruthless savages; they then entered the closet where she was concealed, and went out without discovering her. While in this hiding place, she heard two of her women in a quarrel about the division of her clothes. Mr. John T. Baron, discovering them approaching his house, told his wife to make her escape, and scorning to fly, fell fighting on his own threshold. After firing his rifle, he discharged his gun at them, and then broke it over the villain who first approached him, but he was overpowered and slain. His bravery, however, saved from the hands of these monsters, his lovely and amiable wife, who will long lament a husband as deserving of her love. As directed by him, she attempted to escape through the garden, when she was caught and held by one of her servant girls, but another coming to her rescue, she fled to the woods, and concealed herself. Few indeed, were those who escaped their work of death. But fortunate for society, the hand of retributive justice has overtaken them; and not one that was known to be concerned has escaped.

The Commonwealth,
    vs.   } Charged with making insurrection, and
  Nat Turner. } plotting to take away the lives of divers free white persons, &c. on the 22d of August, 1831.

The court composed of ——, having met for the trial of Nat Turner, the prisoner was brought in and arraigned, and upon his arraignment pleaded *Not guilty;* saying to his counsel, that he did not feel so.

On the part of the Commonwealth, Levi Waller was introduced, who being sworn, deposed as follows: (*agreeably to Nat's own Confession.*) Col. Trezvant* was then introduced, who being sworn, numerated Nat's Confession to him, as follows: (*His Confession as given to Mr. Gray.*) The prisoner introduced no evidence, and the case was submitted without argument to the court, who having found him guilty, Jeremiah Cobb, Esq. Chairman, pronounced the sentence of the court, in the following words: "Nat Turner! Stand up. Have

---

* The committing Magistrate.

you any thing to say why sentence of death should not be pronounced against you?"

Ans. I have not. I have made a full confession to Mr. Gray, and
I have nothing more to say.

"Attend then to the sentence of the Court. You have been arraigned
and tried before this court, and convicted of one of the highest crimes
in our criminal code. You have been convicted of plotting in cold
blood, the indiscriminate destruction of men, of helpless women,
and of infant children. The evidence before us leaves not a shadow
of doubt, but that your hands were often imbrued in the blood of
the innocent; and your own confession tells us that they were stained
with the blood of a master; in your own language, "too indulgent."
Could I stop here, your crime would be sufficiently aggravated. But
the original contriver of a plan, deep and deadly, one that never can
be effected, you managed so far to put it into execution, as to deprive us of many of our most valuable citizens; and this was done
when they were asleep, and defenceless; under circumstances shocking to humanity. And while upon this part of the subject, I cannot
but call your attention to the poor misguided wretches who have
gone before you. They are not few in number—they were your
bosom associates; and the blood of all cries aloud, and calls upon
you, as the author of their misfortune. Yes! You forced them un-
prepared, from Time to Eternity. Borne down by this load of guilt,
your only justification is, that you were led away by fanaticism. If
this be true, from my soul I pity you; and while you have my sympathies, I am, nevertheless called upon to pass the sentence of the
court. The time between this and your execution, will necessarily
be very short; and your only hope must be in another world. The
judgment of the court is, that you be taken hence to the jail from
whence you came, thence to the place of execution, and on Friday
next, between the hours of 10 A.M. and 2 P.M. be hung by the neck
until you are dead! dead! dead! and may the Lord have mercy upon
your soul."

A list of persons murdered in the Insurrection, on the 21st and 22d of August, 1831.

Joseph Travers and wife and three children, Mrs. Elizabeth Turner, Hartwell Prebles, Sarah Newsome, Mrs. P. Reese and son William, Trajan Doyle, Henry Bryant and wife and child, and wife's mother, Mrs. Catherine Whitehead, son Richard and four daughters and grandchild, Salathiel Francis, Nathaniel Francis' overseer and two children, John T. Barrow, George Vaughan, Mrs. Levi Waller and ten children, William Williams, wife and two boys, Mrs. Caswell Worrell and child, Mrs. Rebecca Vaughan, Ann Eliza Vaughan, and son Arthur, Mrs. John K. Williams and child, Mrs. Jacob Williams and three children, and Edwin Drury—amounting to fifty-five.

JOSIAH HENSON
(*1789-1883*)

It is easy to believe that Josiah Henson was indeed the prototype of Uncle Tom, as is generally assumed, not merely because Harriet Beecher Stowe wrote an introduction to his autobiography but also because of the evident traits of religious selflessness, conservative loyalty to the master as well as to liberators, and courage.

He was born of slave parents on a farm in Charles County, Maryland, and as the early chapters given here reveal, the boy witnessed a slave auction and saw his parents beaten. Yet he felt a strong emotion of pride at being elevated to overseer, quickly forgiving the brutalities of the master and the former overseer.

His later career, necessarily omitted here, shows a deep religious conversion which led to his selection in 1828 as a preacher of the Methodist Episcopal Church. So loyal was he that he saved a near-bankrupt master by conducting his slaves to Kentucky and stubbornly resisted the blandishments of freedom when he had an opportunity to escape as he passed through the free soil of Ohio. But by 1830 he was persuaded to run away to Canada with his wife and four children; thereafter he aided other slaves to escape and to earn a living in the North, especially through his own industrial school at Dawn near the Detroit River. He was enabled to visit England several times to secure support for escaped slaves and won international fame, and even received a special honor from Queen Victoria.

Harriet Beecher Stowe heard his story shortly before she wrote *Uncle Tom's Cabin* (1852) and mentioned his career in *A Key to Uncle Tom's Cabin* (1853). Henson's autobiography first appeared in 1849, but an enlarged edition, the one used here, was published in 1858 with Mrs. Stowe's introduction in *Truth Stranger Than Fiction: Father Henson's Story of His Own Life*. Chapters II and III are reproduced here.

After the sale of my father by Newman,* Dr. McPherson would no longer hire out my mother to him. She returned, accordingly, to his estate. He was far kinder to his slaves than the planters generally were, never suffering them to be struck by any one. He was a man of good, kind impulses, liberal, jovial, hearty. No degree of arbitrary power could ever lead him to cruelty. As the first negro-child ever born to him, I was his especial pet. He gave me his own Christian name, Josiah, and with that he also gave me my last name, Henson, after an uncle of his, who was an officer in the Revolutionary war. A bright spot in my childhood was my residence with him—bright, but, alas! fleeting. Events were rapidly maturing which were to change the whole aspect of my life. The kind Doctor was not exempt from that failing which too often besets easy, social natures in a dissipated community. He could not restrain his convivial propensities. Although he maintained a high reputation for goodness of heart and an almost saint-like benevolence, the habit of intemperance steadily gained ground, and finally occasioned his death. Two negroes on the plantation found him one morning lying dead in the middle of a narrow stream, not a foot in depth. He had been away the night previous at a social party, and when returning home had fallen from his horse, probably, and being too intoxicated to stagger through the stream, fell and was drowned. "There's the place where massa got drownded at;" how well I remember having it pointed out to me in those very words.

For two or three years my mother and her young family of six children had resided on this estate; and we had been in the main

---

* [Francis Newman, owner of the Charles County, Maryland, farm where Henson was born, according to Benjamin Brawley, the historian, but this fact is contradicted by Henson's own recollection as given here.—ED.]

very happy. She was a good mother to us, a woman of deep piety, anxious above all things to touch our hearts with a sense of religion. How or where she acquired her knowledge of God, or her acquaintance with the Lord's Prayer, which she so frequently taught us to repeat, I am unable to say. I remember seeing her often on her knees, trying to arrange her thoughts in prayer appropriate to her situation, but which amounted to little more than constant ejaculations, and the repetition of short phrases which were within my infant comprehension, and have remained in my memory to this hour.

Our term of happy union as one family was now, alas! at an end. Mournful as was the Doctor's death to his friends it was a far greater calamity to us. The estate and the slaves must be sold and the proceeds divided among the heirs. We were but property—not a mother, and the children God had given her.

Common as are slave-auctions in the southern states, and naturally as a slave may look forward to the time when he will be put up on the block, still the full misery of the event—of the scenes which precede and succeed it—is never understood till the actual experience comes. The first sad announcement that the sale is to be; the knowledge that all ties of the past are to be sundered; the frantic terror at the idea of being sent "down south;" the almost certainty that one member of a family will be torn from another; the anxious scanning of purchasers' faces; the agony at parting, often forever, with husband, wife, child—these must be seen and felt to be fully understood. Young as I was then, the iron entered into my soul. The remembrance of the breaking up of McPherson's estate is photographed in its minutest features in my mind. The crowd collected round the stand, the huddling group of negroes, the examination of muscle, teeth, the exhibition of agility, the look of the auctioneer, the agony of my mother—I can shut my eyes and see them all.

My brothers and sisters were bid off first, and one by one, while my mother, paralyzed by grief, held me by the hand. Her turn came, and she was bought by Isaac Riley of Montgomery county. Then I was offered to the assembled purchasers. My mother, half distracted with the thought of parting forever from all her children, pushed through the crowd while the bidding for me was going on, to the spot where Riley was standing. She fell at his feet, and clung to his knees, entreating him in tones that a mother only could command, to buy her *baby* as well as herself, and spare to her one, at least, of her little ones. Will it, can it be believed that this man, thus appealed to, was capable not merely of turning a deaf ear to her supplication, but of disengaging himself from her with such violent blows and kicks, as to reduce her to the necessity of creeping out of his reach, and mingling the groan of bodily suffering with the sob of a breaking heart? As she crawled away from the brutal man I heard her sob out, "Oh, Lord Jesus, how long, how long shall I suffer this way!" I must have been then between five and six years old. I seem to see and hear my poor weeping mother now. This was one of my earliest observations of men; an experience which I only shared with thousands of my race, the bitterness of which to any individual who suffers it cannot be diminished by the frequency of its recurrence, while it is dark enough to overshadow the whole after-life with something blacker than a funeral pall.

I was bought by a stranger named Robb, and truly a robber he was to me. He took me to his home, about forty miles distant, and put me into his negro quarters with about forty others, of all ages, colors, and conditions, all strangers to me. Of course nobody cared for me. The slaves were brutalized by this degradation, and had no sympathy for me. I soon fell sick, and lay for some days almost dead on the ground. Sometimes a slave would give me a piece of corn bread or a bit of herring. Finally I became so feeble that I could not move. This, however, was fortunate for me; for in the course of a few weeks Robb met Riley, who had bought my mother, and offered to sell me to him cheap. Riley said he was afraid "the little devil would die," and he did not want to buy a "dead nigger;" but he agreed, finally, to pay a small sum for me in horse-shoeing if I lived, and nothing if I died. Robb was a tavern keeper, and owned a line of stages with the horses, and lived near Montgomery court-house; Riley carried on blacksmithing about five miles from that place. This clenched the bargain, and I was soon sent to my mother. A blessed change it was. I had been lying on a lot of rags thrown on a dirt floor. All day long I had been left alone, crying for water, crying for mother; the slaves, who all left at daylight, when they returned, caring nothing for me. Now, I was once more with my best friend on earth, and under her care; destitute as she was of the proper means of nursing me, I recovered my health, and grew to be an uncommonly vigorous boy and man.

The character of Riley, the master whom I faithfully served for many years, is by no means an uncommon one in any part of the world; the evil is, that a domestic institution should anywhere put it in the power of such a one to tyrannize over his fellow beings, and inflict so much needless misery as is sure to be inflicted by such a man in such a position. Coarse and vulgar in his habits, unprincipled and cruel in his general deportment, and especially addicted to the vice of licentiousness, his slaves had little opportunity for relaxation from wearying labor, were supplied with the scantiest means of sustaining their toil by necessary food, and had no security for personal rights. The natural tendency of slavery is to convert the master into a tyrant, and the slave into the cringing, treacherous, false, and thieving victim of tyranny. Riley and his slaves were no exception to the general rule, but might be cited as apt illustrations of the nature of the relation.

MY BOYHOOD AND YOUTH

My earliest employments were, to carry buckets of water to the men at work, and to hold a horse-plough, used for weeding between the rows of corn. As I grew older and taller, I was entrusted with the care of master's saddle-horse. Then a hoe was put into my hands, and I was soon required to do the day's work of a man; and it was not long before I could do it, at least as well as my associates in misery.

The every-day life of a slave on one of our southern plantations, however frequently it may have been described, is generally little understood at the north; and must be mentioned as a necessary illustration of the character and habits of the slave and the slaveholder, created and perpetuated by their relative position. The principal food of those upon my master's plantation consisted of cornmeal, and salt herrings; to which was added in summer a little buttermilk, and the few vegetables which each might raise for himself and his family, on the little piece of ground which was assigned to him for the purpose, called a truck patch.

In ordinary times we had two regular meals in a day:—breakfast at twelve o'clock, after laboring from daylight, and supper when the work of the remainder of the day was over. In harvest season we had three. Our dress was of tow-cloth; for the children nothing but a shirt; for the older ones a pair of pantaloons or a gown in addition, according to the sex. Besides these, in the winter a round jacket or overcoat, a wool hat once in two or three years, for the males, and a pair of coarse shoes once a year.

We lodged in log huts, and on the bare ground. Wooden floors were an unknown luxury. In a single room were huddled, like cattle, ten or a dozen persons, men, women and children. All ideas of refinement and decency were, of course, out of the question. There were neither bedsteads, nor furniture of any description. Our beds were collections of straw and old rags, thrown down in the corners and boxed in with boards; a single blanket the only covering. Our favorite way of sleeping, however, was on a plank, our heads raised on an old jacket and our feet toasting before the smouldering fire. The wind whistled and the rain and snow blew in through the cracks, and the damp earth soaked in the moisture till the floor was miry as a pig-sty. Such were our houses. In these wretched hovels were we penned at night, and fed by day; here were the children born and the sick—neglected.

Notwithstanding this system of management I grew to be a robust and vigorous lad. At fifteen years of age there were few who could compete with me in work or sport. I was as lively as a young buck, and running over with animal spirits. I could run faster, wrestle better, and jump higher than anybody about me, and at an evening shakedown in our own or a neighbor's kitchen, my feet became absolutely invisible from the rate at which they moved. All this caused my master and my fellow slaves to look upon me as a wonderfully smart fellow, and prophesy the great things I should do when I became a man. My vanity became vastly inflamed, and I fully coincided in their opinion. Julius Caesar never aspired and plotted for the imperial crown more ambitiously than did I to out-hoe, out-reap, out-husk, out-dance, out-everything every competitor; and from all I can learn he never enjoyed his triumph half as much. One word of commendation from the petty despot who ruled over us would set me up for a month.

I have no desire to represent the life of slavery as an experience of nothing but misery. God be praised, that however hedged in by circumstances, the joyful exuberance of youth will bound at times over them all. Ours is a light-hearted race. The sternest and most covetous master cannot frighten or whip the fun out of us; certainly old Riley never did out of me. In those days I had many a merry time, and would have had, had I lived with nothing but moccasins and rattle-snakes in Okafenoke swamp. Slavery did its best to make me wretched; I feel no particular obligation to it; but nature, or the blessed God of youth and joy, was mightier than slavery. Along with memories of miry cabins, frosted feet, weary toil under the blazing sun, curses and blows, there flock in others, of jolly Christmas times, dances before old massa's door for the first drink of egg-nog, extra meat at holiday times, midnight visits to apple orchards, broiling stray chickens, and first-rate tricks to dodge work. The God who makes the pup gambol, and the kitten play, and the bird sing, and the fish leap, was the author in me of many a light-hearted hour. True it was, indeed, that the fun and freedom of Christmas, at which time my master relaxed his front, was generally followed up by a portentous back-action, under which he drove and cursed worse than ever; still the fun and freedom were fixed facts; we had had them and he could not help it.

Besides these pleasant memories I have others of a deeper and richer kind. I early learned to employ my spirit of adventure for the benefit of my fellow-sufferers. The condition of the male slave is bad enough; but that of the female, compelled to perform unfit labor, sick, suffering, and bearing the peculiar burdens of her own sex unpitied and unaided, as well as the toils which belong to the other, is one that must arouse the spirit of sympathy in every heart not dead to all feeling. The miseries which I saw many of the women suffer often oppressed me with a load of sorrow. No *white* knight, rescuing white fair ones from cruel oppression, ever felt the throbbing of a chivalrous heart more intensely than I, a *black* knight, did, in running down a chicken in an out-of-the way place to hide till dark, and then carry to some poor overworked black fair one, to whom it was at once food, luxury, and medicine. No Scotch borderer, levying black mail or sweeping off a drove of cattle, ever felt more assured of the justice of his act than I of mine, in driving a mile or two into the woods a pig or a sheep, and slaughtering it for the good of those whom Riley was starving. I felt good, moral, heroic. The beautiful combination of a high time and a benevolent act—the harmonious interplay of nature and grace—was absolutely entrancing. I felt then the excellency of a sentiment I have since found expressed in a hymn:

> "Religion never was designed
> To make our pleasures less."

Was this wrong? I can only say in reply, that, at this distance of time, my conscience does not reproach me for it. Then I esteemed it among the best of my deeds. It was my training in the luxury of doing good, in the divinity of a sympathetic heart, in the righteousness of indignation against the cruel and oppressive. There and then was my soul made conscious of its heavenly original. This, too, was all the chivalry of which my circumstances and condition in life admitted. I love the sentiment in its splendid environment of castles, and tilts, and gallantry; but having fallen on other times, I love it also in the homely guise of Sambo as Paladin, Dinah as outraged maiden, and old Riley as grim oppressor.

By means of the influence thus acquired, the increased amount of work thus done upon the farm, and by the detection of the knavery of the overseer, who plundered his employer for more selfish ends, and through my watchfulness was caught in the act and dismissed, I was promoted to be superintendent of the farm work, and managed to raise more than double the crops, with more cheerful and willing labor, than was ever seen on the estate before.

Yes, I was now practically overseer. My pride and ambition had made me master of every kind of farm work. But like all ambition its reward was increase of burdens. The crops of wheat, oats, barley, potatoes, corn, tobacco, all had to be cared for by me. I was often compelled to start at midnight with the wagon for the distant market, to drive on through mud and rain till morning, sell the produce, reach home hungry and tired, and nine times out of ten reap my sole reward in curses for not getting higher prices. My master was a fearful blasphemer. Clearly as he saw my profitableness to him, he was too much of a brute, and too great a fool through his brutality, to reward me with kindness or even decent treatment. Previous to my attaining this important station, however, an incident occurred which produced so powerful an influence on my intellectual development, my prospect of improvement in character, as well as condition, my chance of religious culture, and in short, on my whole nature, body and soul, that it deserves especial notice and commemoration. This, however, requires another chapter.

MAIMED FOR LIFE

The difference between the manner in which it was designed that all men should regard one another as children of the same. Father, and the manner in which men actually do treat each other, as if they were placed here for mutual annoyance and destruction, is well exemplified by an incident that happened to me within a year or two from this period; that is, when I was nineteen or twenty years old. My master's habits were such as were common enough among the dissipated planters of the neighborhood; and one of their frequent practices was to assemble on Saturday or Sunday, which were their holidays, and gamble, run horses, or fight game-cocks, discuss politics, and drink whiskey and brandy and water all day long. Perfectly aware that they would not be able to find their own way home at night, each one ordered his body-servant to come after him and help him home. I was chosen for this confidential duty by my master; and many is the time I have held him on his horse, when he could not hold himself in the saddle, and walked by his side in darkness and mud from the tavern to his house. Of course, quarrels and brawls of the most violent description were frequent consequences of these meetings; and whenever they became especially dangerous, and glasses were thrown, dirks drawn, and pistols fired, it was the duty of the slaves to rush in, and each one drag his master from the fight, and carry him home. To tell the truth, this was a part of my business for which I felt no reluctance. I was young, remarkably athletic and self-relying, and in such affrays I carried it with a high hand, and would elbow my way among the whites,—whom it would have been almost death for me to strike,—seize my master and drag him out, mount him on his horse, or crowd him into his buggy, with the ease with which I would handle a bag of corn. I knew that I was doing for him what he could not do for himself, and showing my superiority to others, and acquiring their respect in some degree, at the same time.

On one of these occasions my master got into a quarrel with his brother's overseer, Bryce Litton. All present sided with Litton against him, and soon there was a general row. I was sitting, at the time, out on the front steps of the tavern, and, hearing the scuffle, rushed in to look after my charge. My master, a stout man and a terrible bruiser, could generally hold his own in an ordinary general fight, and clear a handsome space around him; but now he was cornered, and a dozen were striking at him with fists, crockery, chairs, and anything that came handy. The moment he saw me he hallooed, "That's it, Sie! pitch in! show me fair play." It was a rough business, and I went in roughly, shoving, tripping, and doing my best for the rescue. With infinite trouble, and many a bruise on my own head and shoulders, I at length got him out of the room. He was crazy with drink and rage, and struggled hard with me to get back and renew the fight. But I managed to force him into his wagon, jump in, and drive off.

By ill-luck, in the height of the scuffle, Bryce Litton got a severe fall. Whether the whisky he had drank, or a chance shove from me, was the cause, I am unable to say. He, however, attributed it to me, and treasured up his vengeance for the first favorable opportunity. The opportunity soon came.

About a week afterwards I was sent by my master to a place a few miles distant, on horseback, with some letters. I took a short cut through a lane, separated by gates from the high road, and bounded by a fence on each side. This lane passed through some of the farm owned by my master's brother, and his overseer was in the adjoining field, with three negroes, when I went by. On my return, half an hour afterwards, the overseer was sitting on the fence; but I could see nothing of the black fellows. I rode on, utterly unsuspicious of any trouble; but as I approached he jumped off the fence, and at the same moment two of the negroes sprang up from under the bushes where they had been concealed, and stood with him immediately in front of me, while the third sprang over the fence just behind me. I was thus enclosed between what I could no longer doubt were hostile forces. The overseer seized my horse's bridle, and ordered me to alight, in the usual elegant phraseology addressed by such men to slaves. I asked what I was to alight for. "To take the cursedest flogging you ever had in your life, you d—d black scoundrel." "But what am I to be flogged for, Mr. L.?" I asked. "Not a word," said he, "but 'light at once, and take off your jacket." I saw there was nothing else to be done, and slipped off the horse on the opposite side from him. "Now take off your shirt," cried he; and as I demurred at this, he lifted a stick he had in his hand to strike me, but so suddenly and violently that he frightened the horse, which broke away from him and ran home. I was thus left without means of escape, to sustain the attacks of four men, as well as I might. In avoiding Mr. L.'s blow, I had accidentally got into a corner of the fence, where I could not be approached except in front. The overseer called upon the negroes to seize me; but they, knowing something of my physical power, were rather slow to obey. At length they did their best, and as they brought themselves within my reach, I knocked them down successively; and one of them trying to trip up my feet when he was down, I gave him a kick with my heavy shoe, which knocked out several teeth, and sent him howling away.

Meanwhile Bryce Litton played away on my head with a stick, not heavy enough, indeed, to knock me down, but drawing blood freely; shouting all the while, "Won't you give up! won't you give up! you black son of a bitch!" Exasperated at my defence, he suddenly seized a heavy fence-rail, and rushed at me to bring matters to a sudden close. The ponderous blow fell; I lifted my arm to ward it off; the bone cracked like a pipe-stem, and I fell headlong to the ground. Repeated blows then rained on my back, till both shoulder-blades were broken, and the blood gushed copiously from my mouth. In vain the negroes interposed. "Didn't you see the damned nigger strike me?" Of course they must say "yes," although the lying coward had avoided close quarters, and fought with his stick alone. At length, his vengeance satisfied, he desisted, telling me to learn what it was to strike a white man.

Meanwhile an alarm had been raised at the house by the return of the horse without his rider, and my master started off with a small party to learn what the trouble was. When he first saw me he was swearing with rage. "You've been fighting, you damned nigger!" I told him Bryce Litton had been beating me, because I shoved him the other night at the tavern, when they had a fuss. Seeing how much I was injured, he became still more fearfully mad; and after having me carried home, mounted his horse and rode over to Montgomery Court House, to enter a complaint. Little good came of it. Litton swore that when he spoke to me in the lane, I "sassed" him, jumped off my horse and made at him, and would have killed him but for the help of his negroes. Of course no negro's testimony could be admitted against a white man, and he was acquitted. My master was obliged to pay all the costs of court; and although he had the satisfaction of calling Litton a liar and scoundrel, and giving him a tremendous bruising, still even this partial compensation was rendered less gratifying by what followed, which was a suit for damages and a heavy fine.

My sufferings after this cruel treatment were intense. Besides my broken arm and the wounds on my head, I could feel and hear the pieces of my shoulder-blades grate against each other with every breath. No physician or surgeon was called to dress my wounds; and I never knew one to be called on Riley's estate on any occasion whatever. "A nigger will get well anyway," was a fixed principle of faith, and facts seemed to justify it. The robust, physical health produced by a life of out-door labor, made our wounds heal up with as little inflammation as they do in the case of cattle. I was attended by my master's sister, Miss Patty, as we called her, the Esculapius of the plantation. She was a powerful, big-boned woman, who flinched at no responsibility, from wrenching out teeth to setting bones. I have seen her go into the house and get a rifle to shoot a furious ox that the negroes were in vain trying to butcher. She splintered my arm and bound up my back as well as she knew how. Alas! it was but cobbler's work. From that day to this I have been unable to raise my hands as high as my head. It was five months before I could work at all, and the first time I tried to plough, a hard knock of the colter against a stone shattered my shoulder-blades again, and gave me even greater agony than at first. And so I have gone through life maimed and mutilated. Practice in time enabled me to perform many of the farm labors with considerable efficiency; but the free, vigorous play of muscle and arm was gone forever.

My situation as overseer I retained, together with the especial favor of my master, who was not displeased either with saving the expense of a large salary for a white superintendent, or with the superior crops I was able to raise for him. I will not deny that I used his property more freely than he would have done himself, in supplying his people with better food; but if I cheated him in this way, in small matters, it was unequivocally for his own benefit in more important ones; and I accounted, with the strictest honesty, for every dollar I received in the sale of the property entrusted to me. Gradually the disposal of everything raised on the farm,—the wheat, oats, hay, fruit, butter, and whatever else there might be,—was confided to me, as it was quite evident that I could and did sell for better prices than any one else he could employ; and he was quite incompetent to attend to the business himself. For many years I was his factotum, and supplied him with all his means for all his purposes, whether they were good or bad. I had no reason to think highly of his moral character; but it was my duty to be faithful to him in the position in which he placed me; and I can boldly declare, before God and man, that I was so. I forgave him the causeless blows and injuries he had inflicted on me in childhood and youth, and was proud of the favor he now showed me, and of the character and reputation I had earned by strenuous and persevering efforts.

SOLOMON NORTHUP
(1818-18—?)

This remarkable story of a free Negro kidnapped into slavery is vouched
for by the affidavits of witnesses and sworn depositions by Louisiana and
New York officials. Solomon Northup was a talented mulatto businessman
and laborer of Saratoga Springs, New York, the son of a freeman and a
nearly white mother. He had read widely, played the violin for social
groups, shown unusual initiative in transporting large rafts of lumber from
Lake Champlain to Troy, and earned money as a farm hand and construc-
tion worker. In 1841, when he was kidnapped, he was married to an intelligent woman who earned high wages as a cook, had three children, and
lived in a comfortable home.

Apparently two strangers drugged him in Washington after promising
him a part in an entertainment group. Even his "free papers" vouching
for his free status did not save him from being transported to New Orleans
and enslaved on a Louisiana cotton plantation. Eventually he was freed
through the efforts of his wife and the direct intercession of the Governor
of New York.

This is taken from Solomon Northup, *Twelve Years a Slave* (Auburn,
Buffalo, 1854), chapters 12 and 15.

A LOUISIANA COTTON PLANTATION

Edwin Epps, of whom much will be said during the remainder of this history, is a large, portly, heavy-bodied man with light hair, high cheek bones, and a Roman nose of extraordinary dimensions. He has blue eyes, a fair complexion, and is, as I should say, full six feet high. He has the sharp, inquisitive expression of a jockey. His manners are repulsive and coarse, and his language gives speedy and unequivocal evidence that he has never enjoyed the advantages of an education. He has the faculty of saying most provoking things, in that respect even excelling old Peter Tanner. At the time I came into his possession, Edwin Epps was fond of the bottle, his "sprees" sometimes extending over the space of two whole weeks. Latterly, however, he had reformed his habits, and when I left him, was as strict a specimen of temperance as could be found on Bayou Boeuf. When "in his cups," Master Epps was a roystering, blustering, noisy fellow, whose chief delight was in dancing with his "niggers," or lashing them about the yard with his long whip, just for the pleasure of hearing them screech and scream, as the great welts were planted on their backs. When sober, he was silent, reserved and cunning, not beating us indiscriminately, as in his drunken moments, but sending the end of his rawhide to some tender spot of a lagging slave, with a sly dexterity peculiar to himself.

He had been a driver and overseer in his younger years, but at this time was in possession of a plantation on Bayou Huff Power, two and a half miles from Holmesville, eighteen from Marksville, and twelve from Cheneyville. It belonged to Joseph B. Roberts, his wife's uncle, and was leased by Epps. His principal business was raising cotton, and inasmuch as some may read this book who have never seen a cotton field, a description of the manner of its culture may not be out of place.

The ground is prepared by throwing up beds or ridges, with the plough—back-furrowing, it is called. Oxen and mules, the latter almost exclusively, are used in ploughing. The women as frequently as the men perform this labor, feeding, currying, and taking care of their teams, and in all respects doing the field and stable work, precisely as do the ploughboys of the North.

The beds, or ridges, are six feet wide, that is, from water furrow to water furrow. A plough drawn by one mule is then run along the top of the ridge or center of the bed, making the drill, into which a girl usually drops the seed, which she carries in a bag hung round her neck. Behind her comes a mule and harrow, covering up the seed, so that two mules, three slaves, a plough and harrow, are employed in planting a row of cotton. This is done in the months of March and April. Corn is planted in February. When there are no cold rains, the cotton usually makes its appearance in a week. In the course of eight or ten days afterwards the first hoeing is commenced. This is performed in part, also, by the aid of the plough and mule. The plough passes as near as possible to the cotton on both sides, throwing the furrow from it. Slaves follow with their hoes, cutting up the grass and cotton, leaving hills two feet and a half apart. This is called scraping cotton. In two weeks more commences the second hoeing. This time the furrow is thrown towards the cotton. Only one stalk, the largest, is now left standing in each hill. In another fortnight it is hoed the third time, throwing the furrow towards the cotton in the same manner as before, and killing all the grass between the rows. About the first of July, when it is a foot high or thereabouts, it is hoed the fourth and last time. Now the whole space between the rows is ploughed, leaving a deep water furrow in the center. During all these hoeings the overseer or driver follows the slaves on horseback with a whip, such as has been described. The fastest hoer takes the lead row. He is usually about a rod in advance of his companions. If one of them passes him, he is whipped. If one falls behind or is a moment idle, he is whipped. In fact, the lash is flying from morning until night, the whole day long. The hoeing season thus continues from April until July, a field having no sooner been finished once, than it is commenced again.

In the latter part of August begins the cotton picking season. At this time each slave is presented with a sack. A strap is fastened to it, which goes over the neck, holding the mouth of the sack breast high, while the bottom reaches nearly to the ground. Each one is also presented with a large basket that will hold about two barrels. This is to put the cotton in when the sack is filled. The baskets are carried to the field and placed at the beginning of the rows.

When a new hand, one unaccustomed to the business, is sent for the first time into the field, he is whipped up smartly, and made for that day to pick as fast as he can possibly. At night it is weighed, so that his capability in cotton picking is known. He must bring in the same weight each night following. If it falls short, it is considered evidence that he has been laggard, and a greater or less number of lashes is the penalty.

An ordinary day's work is two hundred pounds. A slave who is accustomed to picking, is punished, if he or she brings in a less quantity than that. There is a great difference among them as regards this kind of labor. Some of them seem to have a natural knack, or quickness, which enables them to pick with great celerity, and with both hands, while others, with whatever practice or industry, are utterly unable to come up to the ordinary standard. Such hands are taken from the cotton field and employed in other business. Patsey, of whom I shall have more to say, was known as the most remarkable cotton picker on Bayou Boeuf. She picked with both hands and with such surprising rapidity, that five hundred pounds a day was not unusual for her.

Each one is tasked, therefore, according to his picking abilities, none, however, to come short of two hundred weight. I, being unskillful always in that business, would have satisfied my master by bringing in the latter quantity, while on the other hand, Patsey would surely have been beaten if she failed to produce twice as much.

The cotton grows from five to seven feet high, each stalk having a great many branches, shooting out in all directions, and lapping each other above the water furrow.

There are few sights more pleasant to the eye, than a wide cotton field when it is in the bloom. It presents an appearance of purity, like an immaculate expanse of light, new-fallen snow.

Sometimes the slave picks down one side of a row, and back upon the other, but more usually, there is one on either side, gathering all that has blossomed, leaving the unopened bolls for a succeeding picking. When the sack is filled, it is emptied into the basket and trodden down. It is necessary to be extremely careful the first time going through the field, in order not to break the branches off the stalks. The cotton will not bloom upon a broken branch. Epps never failed to inflict the severest chastisement on the unlucky servant who, either carelessly or unavoidably, was guilty in the least degree in this respect.

The hands are required to be in the cotton field as soon as it is light in the morning, and, with the exception of ten or fifteen minutes, which is given them at noon to swallow their allowance of cold bacon, they are not permitted to be a moment idle until it is too dark to see, and when the moon is full, they often times labor till the middle of the night. They do not dare to stop even at dinner time, nor return to the quarters, however late it be, until the order to halt is given by the driver.

The day's work over in the field, the baskets are "toted," or in other words, carried to the gin-house, where the cotton is weighed. No matter how fatigued and weary he may be—no matter how much he longs for sleep and rest—a slave never approaches the gin-house with his basket of cotton but with fear. If it falls short in weight—if he has not performed the full task appointed him, he knows that he must suffer. And if he has exceeded it by ten or twenty pounds, in all probability his master will measure the next day's task accordingly. So whether he has too little or too much, his approach to the gin-house is always with fear and trembling. Most frequently they have too little, and therefore it is they are not anxious to leave the field. After weighing, follow the whippings; and then the baskets are carried to the cotton house, and their contents stored away like hay, all hands being sent in to tramp it down. If the cotton is not dry, instead of taking it to the gin-house at once, it is laid upon platforms, two feet high, and some three times as wide, covered with boards or plank, with narrow walks running between them.

This done, the labor of the day is not yet ended, by any means. Each one must then attend to his respective chores. One feeds the mules, another the swine—another cuts the wood, and so forth; besides, the packing is all done by candle light. Finally, at a late hour, they reach the quarters, sleepy and overcome with the long day's toil. Then a fire must be kindled in the cabin, the corn ground in the small hand-mill, and supper, and dinner for the next day in the field, prepared. All that is allowed them is corn and bacon, which is given out at the corncrib and smoke-house every Sunday morning. Each one receives, as his weekly allowance, three and a half pounds of bacon, and corn enough to make a peck of meal. That is all—no tea, coffee, sugar, and with the exception of a very scanty sprinkling now and then, no salt. I can say, from a ten years' residence with Master Epps, that no slave of his is ever likely to suffer from the gout, superinduced by excessive high living. Master Epps' hogs were fed on *shelled* corn—it was thrown out to his "niggers" in the ear. The former, he thought, would fatten faster by shelling, and soaking it in the water—the latter, perhaps, if treated in the same manner, might grow too fat to labor. Master Epps was a shrewd calculator, and knew how to manage his own animals, drunk or sober.

The corn mill stands in the yard beneath a shelter. It is like a common coffee mill, the hopper holding about six quarts. There was one privilege which Master Epps granted freely to every slave he had. They might grind their corn nightly, in such small quantities as their daily wants required, or they might grind the whole week's allowance at one time, on Sundays, just as they preferred. A very generous man was Master Epps!

I kept my corn in a small wooden box, the meal in a gourd; and, by the way, the gourd is one of the most convenient and necessary utensils on a plantation. Besides supplying the place of all kinds of crockery in a slave cabin, it is used for carrying water to the fields. Another, also, contains the dinner. It dispenses with the necessity of pails, dippers, basins, and such tin and wooden superfluities altogether.

When the corn is ground, and fire is made, the bacon is taken down from the nail on which it hangs, a slice cut off and thrown upon the coals to broil. The majority of slaves have no knife, much less a fork. They cut their bacon with the axe at the woodpile. The corn meal is mixed with a little water, placed in the fire, and baked. When it is "done brown," the ashes are scraped off, and being placed upon a chip, which answers for a table, the tenant of the slave hut is ready to sit down upon the ground to supper. By this time it is usually midnight. The same fear of punishment with which they approach the gin-house, possesses them again on lying down to get a snatch of rest. It is the fear of oversleeping in the morning. Such an offence would certainly be attended with not less than twenty lashes. With a prayer that he may be on his feet and wide awake at the first sound of the horn, he sinks to his slumbers nightly.

The softest couches in the world are not to be found in the log mansion of the slave. The one whereon I reclined year after year, was a plank twelve inches wide and ten feet long. My pillow was a stick of wood. The bedding was a coarse blanket, and not a rag or shred beside. Moss might be used, were it not that it directly breeds a swarm of fleas.

The cabin is constructed of logs, without floor or window. The latter is altogether unnecessary, the crevices between the logs admitting sufficient light. In stormy weather the rain drives through them, rendering it comfortless and extremely disagreeable. The rude door hangs on great wooden hinges. In one end is constructed an awkward fire-place.

An hour before day light the horn is blown. Then the slaves

arouse, prepare their breakfast, fill a gourd with water, in another deposit their dinner of cold bacon and corn cake, and hurry to the field again. It is an offence invariably followed by a flogging, to be found at the quarters after daybreak. Then the fears and labors of another day begin; and until its close there is no such thing as rest. He fears he will be caught lagging through the day; he fears to approach the gin-house with his basket-load of cotton at night; he fears, when he lies down, that he will oversleep himself in the morning. Such is a true, faithful, unexaggerated picture and description of the slave's daily life, during the time of cotton-picking, on the shores of Bayou Boeuf.

In the month of January, generally, the fourth and last picking is completed. Then commences the harvesting of corn. This is considered a secondary crop, and receives far less attention than the cotton. It is planted, as already mentioned, in February. Corn is grown in that region for the purpose of fattening hogs and feeding slaves; very little, if any, being sent to market. It is the white variety, the ear of great size, and the stalk growing to the height of eight, and often times ten feet. In August the leaves are stripped off, dried in the sun, bound in small bundles, and stored away as provender for the mules and oxen. After this the slaves go through the field, turning down the ear, for the purpose of keeping the rains from penetrating to the grain. It is left in this condition until after cotton-picking is over, whether earlier or later. Then the ears are separated from the stalks and deposited in the corncrib with the husks on; otherwise, stripped of the husks, the weevil would destroy it. The stalks are left standing in the field.

The Carolina, or sweet potato, is also grown in that region to some extent. They are not fed, however, to hogs or cattle, and are considered but of small importance. They are preserved by placing them upon the surface of the ground, with a slight covering of earth or cornstalks. There is not a cellar on Bayou Boeuf. The ground is so low it would fill with water. Potatoes are worth from two to three "bits," or shillings a barrel; corn, except when there is an unusual scarcity, can be purchased at the same rate.

As soon as the cotton and corn crops are secured, the stalks are pulled up, thrown into piles and burned. The ploughs are started at the same time, throwing up the beds again, preparatory to another planting. The soil, in the parishes of Rapides and Avoyelles, and throughout the whole country, so far as my observation extended, is of exceeding richness and fertility. It is a kind of marl, of a brown or reddish color. It does not require those invigorating composts necessary to more barren lands, and on the same field the same crop is grown for many successive years.

Ploughing, planting, picking cotton, gathering the corn, and pulling and burning stalks, occupies the whole of the four seasons of the year. Drawing and cutting wood, pressing cotton, fattening and killing hogs, are but incidental labors.

In the month of September or October, the hogs are run out of the swamps by dogs, and confined in pens. On a cold morning, generally about New Year's day, they are slaughtered. Each carcass is cut into six parts, and piled one above the other in salt, upon large tables in the smoke-house. In this condition it remains a fortnight, when it is hung up, and a fire built, and continued more than half the time during the remainder of the year. This thorough smoking is necessary to prevent the bacon from becoming infested with worms. In so warm a climate it is difficult to preserve it, and very many times myself and my companions have received our weekly allowance of three pounds and a half, when it was full of these disgusting vermin.

Although the swamps are overrun with cattle, they are never made the source of profit, to any considerable extent. The planter cuts his mark upon the ear, or brands his initials upon the side, and turns them into the swamps, to roam unrestricted within their almost limitless confines. They are the Spanish breed, small and spike-horned. I have known of droves being taken from Bayou Boeuf, but it is of very rare occurrence. The value of the best cows is about five dollars each. Two quarts at one milking, would be considered an unusual large quantity. They furnish little tallow, and that of a soft, inferior quality. Notwithstanding the great number of cows that throng the swamps, the planters are indebted to the North for their cheese and butter, which is purchased in the New-Orleans market. Salted beef is not an article of food either in the great house, or in the cabin.

Master Epps was accustomed to attend shooting matches for the purpose of obtaining what fresh beef he required. These sports occurred weekly at the neighboring village of Holmesville. Fat beeves are driven thither and shot at, a stipulated price being demanded for the privilege. The lucky marksman divides the flesh among his fellows, and in this manner the attending planters are supplied.

The great number of tame and untamed cattle which swarm the woods and swamps of Bayou Boeuf, most probably suggested that appellation to the French, inasmuch as the term, translated, signifies the creek or river of the wild ox.

Garden products, such as cabbages, turnips and the like, are cultivated for the use of the master and his family. They have greens and vegetables at all times and seasons of the year. "The grass withereth and the flower fadeth" before the desolating winds of autumn in the chill northern latitudes, but perpetual verdure overspreads the hot lowlands, and flowers bloom in the heart of winter, in the region of Bayou Boeuf.

There are no meadows appropriated to the cultivation of the grasses. The leaves of the corn supply a sufficiency of food for the laboring cattle, while the rest provide for themselves all the year in the ever-growing pasture.

A LOUISIANA SUGAR PLANTATION

In consequence of my inability in cotton-picking, Epps was in the habit of hiring me out on sugar plantations during the season of cane-cutting and sugar-making. He received for my services a dollar a day, with the money supplying my place on his cotton plantation. Cutting cane was an employment that suited me, and for three successive years I held the lead row at Hawkins', leading a gang of from fifty to an hundred hands.

In a previous chapter the mode of cultivating cotton is described. This may be the proper place to speak of the manner of cultivating cane.

The ground is prepared in beds, the same as it is prepared for the reception of the cotton seed, except it is ploughed deeper. Drills are made in the same manner. Planting commences in January, and continues until April. It is necessary to plant a sugar field only once in three years. Three crops are taken before the seed or plant is exhausted.

Three gangs are employed in the operation. One draws the cane from the rick, or stack, cutting the top and flags from the stalk, leaving only that part which is sound and healthy. Each joint of the cane has an eye, like the eye of a potato, which sends forth a sprout when buried in the soil. Another gang lays the cane in the drill, placing two stalks side by side in such manner that joints will occur once in four or six inches. The third gang follows with hoes, drawing earth upon the stalks, and covering them to the depth of three inches.

In four weeks, at the farthest, the sprouts appear above the ground, and from this time forward grow with great rapidity. A sugar field is hoed three times, the same as cotton, save that a greater quantity of earth is drawn to the roots. By the first of August hoeing is usually over. About the middle of September, whatever is required for seed is cut and stacked in ricks, as they are termed. In October it is ready for the mill or sugar-house, and then the general cutting begins. The blade of a cane-knife is fifteen inches long, three inches wide in the middle, and tapering towards the point and handle. The blade is thin, and in order to be at all serviceable must be kept very sharp. Every third hand takes the lead of two others, one of whom is on each side of him. The lead hand, in the first place, with a blow of his knife shears the flags from the stalk. He next cuts off the top down as far as it is green. He must be careful to sever all the green from the ripe part, inasmuch as the juice of the former sours the molasses, and renders it unsalable. Then he severs the stalk at the root, and lays it directly behind him. His right and left hand companions lay their stalks, when cut in the same manner, upon his. To every three hands there is a cart, which follows, and the stalks are thrown into it by the younger slaves, when it is drawn to the sugar-house and ground.

If the planter apprehends a frost, the cane is winrowed. Winrowing is the cutting the stalks at an early period and throwing them lengthwise in the water furrow in such a manner that the tops will cover the butts of the stalks. They will remain in this condition three weeks or a month without souring, and secure from frost. When the proper time arrives, they are taken up, trimmed and carted to the sugar-house.

In the month of January the slaves enter the field again to prepare for another crop. The ground is now strewn with the tops and flags cut from the past year's cane. On a dry day fire is set to this combustible refuse, which sweeps over the field, leaving it bare and clean, and ready for the hoes. The earth is loosened about the roots of the old stubble, and in process of time another crop springs up from the last year's seed. It is the same the year following; but the third year the seed has exhausted its strength, and the field must be ploughed and planted again. The second year the cane is sweeter and yields more than the first, and the third year more than the second.

During the three seasons I labored on Hawkins' plantation, I was employed a considerable portion of the time in the sugar-house. He is celebrated as the producer of the finest variety of white sugar. The following is a general description of his sugar-house and the process of manufacture:

The mill is an immense brick building, standing on the shore of the bayou. Running out from the building is an open shed, at least an hundred feet in length and forty or fifty feet in width. The boiler in which the steam is generated is situated outside the main building; the machinery and engine rest on a brick pier, fifteen feet above the floor, within the body of the building. The machinery turns two great iron rollers, between two and three feet in diameter and six or eight feet in length. They are elevated above the brick pier, and roll in towards each other. An endless carrier, made of chain and wood, like leathern belts used in small mills, extends from the iron rollers out of the main building and through the entire length of the open shed. The carts in which the cane is brought from the field as fast as it is cut, are unloaded at the sides of the shed. All along the endless carrier are ranged slave children, whose business it is to place the cane upon it, when it is conveyed through the shed into the main building, where it falls between the rollers, is crushed, and drops upon another carrier that conveys it out of the main building in an opposite direction, depositing it in the top of a chimney upon a fire beneath, which consumes it. It is necessary to burn it in this manner, because otherwise it would soon fill the building, and more especially because it would soon sour and engender disease. The juice of the cane falls into a conductor underneath the iron rollers, and is carried into a reservoir. Pipes convey it from thence into five filterers, holding several hogsheads each. These filterers are filled with bone-black, a substance resembling pulverized charcoal. It is made of bones calcinated in close vessels, and is

used for the purpose of decolorizing, by filtration, the cane juice before boiling. Through these five filterers it passes in succession, and
then runs into a large reservoir underneath the ground floor, from
whence it is carried up, by means of a steam pump, into a clarifier
made of sheet iron, where it is heated by steam until it boils. From
the first clarifier it is carried in pipes to a second and a third, and
thence into close iron pans, through which tubes pass, filled with
steam. While in a boiling state it flows through three pans in succession, and is then carried in other pipes down to the coolers on the
ground floor. Coolers are wooden boxes with sieve bottoms made of
the finest wire. As soon as the syrup passes into the coolers, and is
met by the air, it grains, and the molasses at once escapes through
the sieves into a cistern below. It is then white or loaf sugar of the
finest kind—clear, clean, and as white as snow. When cool, it is
taken out, packed in hogsheads, and is ready for market. The molasses is then carried from the cistern into the upper story again,
and by another process converted into brown sugar.

There are larger mills, and those constructed differently from the
one thus imperfectly described, but none, perhaps, more celebrated
than this anywhere on Bayou Boeuf. Lambert, of New Orleans, is a
partner of Hawkins. He is a man of vast wealth, holding, as I have
been told, an interest in over forty different sugar plantations in
Louisiana.

* * * * * * * *

The only respite from constant labor the slave has through the
whole year, is during the Christmas holidays. Epps allowed us three—
others allow four, five and six days, according to the measure of their
generosity. It is the only time to which they look forward with any
interest or pleasure. They are glad when night comes, not only because it brings them a few hours repose, but because it brings them
one day nearer Christmas. It is hailed with equal delight by the old
and the young; even Uncle Abram ceases to glorify Andrew Jackson,
and Patsey forgets her many sorrows, amid the general hilarity of

the holidays. It is the time of feasting, and frolicking, and fiddling—the carnival season with the children of bondage. They are the only days when they are allowed a little restricted liberty, and heartily indeed do they enjoy it.

It is the custom for one planter to give a "Christmas supper," inviting the slaves from neighboring plantations to join his own on the occasion; for instance, one year it is given by Epps, the next by Marshall, the next by Hawkins, and so on. Usually from three to five hundred are assembled, coming together on foot, in carts, on horseback, on mules, riding double and triple, sometimes a boy and girl, at others a girl and two boys, and at others again a boy, a girl and an old woman. Uncle Abram astride a mule, with Aunt Phebe and Patsey behind him, trotting towards a Christmas supper, would be no uncommon sight on Bayou Boeuf.

Then, too, "of all days i' the year," they array themselves in their best attire. The cotton coat has been washed clean, the stump of a tallow candle has been applied to the shoes, and if so fortunate as to possess a rimless or a crownless hat, it is placed jauntily on the head. They are welcomed with equal cordiality, however, if they come bare-headed and bare-footed to the feast. As a general thing, the women wear handkerchiefs tied about their heads, but if chance has thrown in their way a fiery red ribbon, or a cast-off bonnet of their mistress' grandmother, it is sure to be worn on such occasions. Red —the deep blood red—is decidedly the favorite color among the enslaved damsels of my acquaintance. If a red ribbon does not encircle the neck, you will be certain to find all the hair of their woolly heads tied up with red strings of one sort or another.

The table is spread in the open air, and loaded with varieties of meat and piles of vegetables. Bacon and corn meal at such times are dispensed with. Sometimes the cooking is performed in the kitchen on the plantation, at others in the shade of wide branching trees. In the latter case, a ditch is dug in the ground, and wood laid in and burned until it is filled with glowing coals, over which chickens, ducks, turkeys, pigs, and not unfrequently the entire body of a wild ox, are roasted. They are furnished also with flour, of which biscuits are made, and often with peach and other preserves, with tarts, and every manner and description of pies, except the mince, that being an article of pastry as yet unknown among them. Only the slave who has lived all the years on his scanty allowance of meal and bacon, can appreciate such suppers. White people in great numbers assemble to witness the gastronomical enjoyments.

They seat themselves at the rustic table—the males on one side, the females on the other. The two between whom there may have been an exchange of tenderness, invariably manage to sit opposite; for the omnipresent Cupid disdains not to hurl his arrows into the simple hearts of slaves. Unalloyed and exulting happiness lights up the dark faces of them all. The ivory teeth, contrasting with their black complexions, exhibit two long, white streaks the whole extent of the table. All round the bountiful board a multitude of eyes roll in ecstacy. Giggling and laughter and the clattering of cutlery and crockery succeed. Cuffee's elbow hunches his neighbor's side, impelled by an involuntary impulse of delight; Nelly shakes her finger at Sambo and laughs, she knows not why, and so the fun and merriment flows on.

When the viands have disappeared, and the hungry maws of the children of toil are satisfied, then, next in the order of amusement, is the Christmas dance. My business on these gala days always was to play on the violin. The African race is a music-loving one, proverbially; and many there were among my fellow-bondsmen whose organs of tune were strikingly developed, and who could thumb the banjo with dexterity; but at the expense of appearing egotistical, I must, nevertheless, declare, that I was considered the Ole Bull of Bayou Boeuf. My master often received letters, sometimes from a distance of ten miles, requesting him to send me to play at a ball or festival of the whites. He received his compensation, and usually I also returned with many picayunes jingling in my pockets—the extra contributions of those to whose delight I had administered. In this manner I became more acquainted than I otherwise would, up and down the bayou. The young men and maidens of Holmesville always knew there was to be a jollification somewhere, whenever Platt Epps was seen passing through the town with his fiddle in his hand. "Where are you going now, Platt?" and "What is coming off tonight, Platt?" would be interrogatories issuing from every door and window, and many a time when there was no special hurry, yielding to pressing importunities, Platt would draw his bow, and sitting astride his mule, perhaps, discourse musically to a crowd of delighted children, gathered around him in the street.

Alas! had it not been for my beloved violin, I scarcely can conceive how I could have endured the long years of bondage. It introduced me to great houses—relieved me of many days' labor in the field—supplied me with conveniences for my cabin—with pipes and tobacco, and extra pairs of shoes, and oftentimes led me away from the presence of a hard master, to witness scenes of jollity and mirth. It was my companion—the friend of my bosom—triumphing loudly when I was joyful, and uttering its soft, melodious consolations when I was sad. Often, at midnight, when sleep had fled affrighted from the cabin, and my soul was disturbed and troubled with the contemplation of my fate, it would sing me a song of peace. On holy Sabbath days, when an hour or two of leisure was allowed, it would accompany me to some quiet place on the bayou bank, and, lifting up its voice, discourse kindly and pleasantly indeed. It heralded my name round the country—made me friends, who, otherwise would not have noticed me—gave me an honored seat at the yearly feasts, and secured the loudest and heartiest welcome of them all at the Christmas dance. The Christmas dance! Oh, ye pleasure-seeking sons and daughters of idleness, who move with measured step, listless and snail-like, through the slow-winding cotillion, if ye wish to look upon the celerity, if not the "poetry of motion"—upon genuine happiness, rampant and unrestrained—go down to Louisiana, and see the slaves dancing in the starlight of a Christmas night.

On that particular Christmas I have now in my mind, a description whereof will serve as a description of the day generally, Miss

Lively and Mr. Sam, the first belonging to Stewart, the latter to Roberts, started the ball. It was well known that Sam cherished an ardent passion for Lively, as also did one of Marshall's and another of Carey's boys; for Lively was *lively* indeed, and a heart-breaking coquette withal. It was a victory for Sam Roberts, when, rising from the repast, she gave him her hand for the first "figure" in preference to either of his rivals. They were somewhat crest-fallen, and, shaking their heads angrily, rather intimated they would like to pitch into Mr. Sam and hurt him badly. But not an emotion of wrath ruffled the placid bosom of Samuel as his legs flew like drum-sticks down the outside and up the middle, by the side of his bewitching partner. The whole company cheered them vociferously, and, excited with the applause, they continued "tearing down" after all the others had become exhausted and halted a moment to recover breath. But Sam's superhuman exertions overcame him finally, leaving Lively alone, yet whirling like a top. Thereupon one of Sam's rivals, Pete Marshall, dashed in, and, with might and main, leaped and shuffled and threw himself into every conceivable shape, as if determined to show Miss Lively and all the world that Sam Roberts was of no account.

Pete's affection, however, was greater than his discretion. Such violent exercise took the breath out of him directly, and he dropped like an empty bag. Then was the time for Harry Carey to try his hand; but Lively also soon out-winded him, amidst hurrahs and shouts, fully sustaining her well-earned reputation of being the "fastest gal" on the bayou.

One "set" off, another takes its place, he or she remaining longest on the floor receiving the most uproarious commendation, and so the dancing continues until broad daylight. It does not cease with the sound of the fiddle, but in that case they set up a music peculiar to themselves. This is called "patting," accompanied with one of those unmeaning songs, composed rather for its adaptation to a certain tune or measure, than for the purpose of expressing any distinct idea. The patting is performed by striking the hands on the knees, then striking the hands together, then striking the right shoulder with one hand, the left with the other—all the while keeping time with the feet, and singing, perhaps, this song:

> "Harper's creek and roarin' ribber,
> Thar, my dear, we'll live forebber;
> Den we'll go to de Ingin nation,
> All I want in dis creation,
> Is pretty little wife and big plantation.
> *Chorus.*   Up dat oak and down dat ribber,
> Two overseers and one little nigger"

Or, if these words are not adapted to the tune called for, it may be that "Old Hog Eye" *is*—a rather solemn and startling specimen of versification, not, however, to be appreciated unless heard at the South. It runneth as follows:

> "Who's been here since I've been gone?
> Pretty little gal wid a josey on.
> > Hog Eye!
> > Old Hog Eye,
> > And Hosey too!
> Never see de like since I was born,
> Here come a little gal wid a josey on.
> > Hog Eye!
> > Old Hog Eye!
> > And Hosey too!"

Or, may be the following, perhaps, equally nonsensical, but full of melody, nevertheless, as it flows from the negro's mouth:

> "Ebo Dick and Jurdan's Jo,
> Them two niggers stole my yo'.
> > *Chorus.*   Hop Jim along,
> > Walk Jim along,
> > Talk Jim along," &c.
> Old black Dan, as black as tar,
> He dam glad he was not dar.
> > Hop Jim along," &c.

During the remaining holidays succeeding Christmas, they are provided with passes, and permitted to go where they please within a limited distance, or they may remain and labor on the plantation, in which case they are paid for it. It is very rarely, however, that the latter alternative is accepted. They may be seen at these times hurrying in all directions, as happy looking mortals as can be found on the face of the earth. They are different beings from what they are in the field; the temporary relaxation, the brief deliverance from fear, and from the lash, producing an entire metamorphosis in their appearance and demeanor. In visiting, riding, renewing old friendships, or, perchance, reviving some old attachment, or pursuing whatever pleasure may suggest itself, the time is occupied. Such is "southern life as it is," *three days in the year,* as I found it—the other three hundred and sixty-two being days of weariness, and fear, and suffering, and unremitting labor.

Marriage is frequently contracted during the holidays, if such an institution may be said to exist among them. The only ceremony required before entering into that "holy estate," is to obtain the consent of the respective owners. It is usually encouraged by the masters of female slaves. Either party can have as many husbands or wives as the owner will permit, and either is at liberty to discard the other at pleasure. The law in relation to divorce, or to bigamy, and so forth, is not applicable to property, of course. If the wife does not belong on the same plantation with the husband, the latter is permitted to visit her on Saturday nights, if the distance is not too far. Uncle Abram's wife lived seven miles from Epps', on Bayou Huff Power. He had permission to visit her once a fortnight, but he was growing old, as has been said, and truth to say, had latterly well nigh forgotten her. Uncle Abram had no time to spare from his meditations on General Jackson—connubial dalliance being well enough for the young and thoughtless, but unbecoming a grave and solemn philosopher like himself.

FREDERICK DOUGLASS
(*1817-1895*)

Quite unlike Josiah Henson, who resembled Uncle Tom, Frederick Douglass symbolizes the militant outlook of modern Negro leaders. A tall, vigorous mulatto, he had been born in Talbot County, Maryland, of a slave mother and an unknown white father. As his book shows, he was a sensitive man who greatly resented the frequent abuses of his condition. Yet he managed to learn how to read and write and to conspire successfully for freedom. He escaped in 1838, married a free colored woman in New York City, and moved to an abolitionist atmosphere at New Bedford, Massachusetts.

Then began his remarkable career as a devoted follower of Garrison and an influential orator and agent of the Massachusetts Anti-Slavery Society. Like James Forten, the gifted grandfather of Charlotte Forten, he fought segregation as well as slavery. In 1845 he published the *Narrative of the Life of Frederick Douglass*, which was subsequently greatly enlarged. After visiting England and Ireland, where he was lionized, he returned in 1847 with enough funds to publish his newspaper, *North Star*, which not only demanded immediate emancipation but also woman suffrage and other liberal causes. As a friend of John Brown, he narrowly escaped arrest for conspiracy and when the Civil War came, he helped to arouse the Union forces to the fact that abolition was the real issue. Lincoln counselled with him on race questions and postwar presidents rewarded him with various honors such as the ministership to Haiti. It is symbolically significant that he died in 1895, the year that Booker T. Washington delivered his Atlanta Compromise speech, urging patient conservative accommodation instead of Douglass' ideal of constant agitation for early social equality.

These selections are taken from the 1883 edition of Douglass' *Autobiography* and represent all of chapters 4, 5, and 6.

It was generally supposed that slavery in the State of Maryland
existed in its mildest form, and that it was totally divested of those
harsh and terrible peculiarities which characterized the slave system
in the Southern and South Western States of the American Union.
The ground of this opinion was the contiguity of the free States, and
the influence of their moral, religious, and humane sentiments. Public opinion was, indeed, a measurable restraint upon the cruelty and
barbarity of masters, overseers, and slave-drivers, whenever and
wherever it could reach them; but there were certain secluded and
out of the way places, even in the State of Maryland, fifty years
ago, seldom visited by a single ray of healthy public sentiment,
where slavery, rapt in its own congenial darkness, could and did
develop all its malign and shocking characteristics, where it could be
indecent without shame, cruel without shuddering, and murderous
without apprehension or fear of exposure, or punishment. Just such a
secluded, dark, and out of the way place, was the home plantation of
Colonel Edward Lloyd, in Talbot county, eastern shore of Maryland.
It was far away from all the great thoroughfares of travel and commerce, and proximate to no town or village. There was neither school-
house nor town-house in its neighborhood. The school-house was unnecessary, for there were no children to go to school. The children
and grand-children of Col. Lloyd were taught in the house by a
private tutor (a Mr. Page from Greenfield, Massachusetts, a tall,
gaunt, sapling of a man, remarkably dignified, thoughtful, and reti-
cent, and who did not speak a dozen words to a slave in a whole
year). The overseer's children went off somewhere in the State to
school, and therefore could bring no foreign or dangerous influence
from abroad to embarrass the natural operation of the slave system

of the place. Not even the commonest mechanics, from whom there might have been an occasional outburst of honest and telling indignation at cruelty and wrong on other plantations, were white men here. Its whole public was made up of and divided into three classes, slaveholders, slaves, and overseers. Its blacksmiths, wheelwrights, shoemakers, weavers, and coopers, were slaves. Not even commerce, selfish and indifferent to moral considerations as it usually is, was permitted within its secluded precincts. Whether with a view of guarding against the escape of its secrets, I know not, but it is a fact, that every leaf and grain of the products of this plantation and those of the neighboring farms, belonging to Col. Lloyd, were transported to Baltimore in his own vessels, every man and boy on board of which, except the captain, were owned by him as his property. In return, everything brought to the plantation came through the same channel. To make this isolation more apparent it may be stated that the adjoining estates to Col. Lloyd's were owned and occupied by friends of his, who were as deeply interested as himself in maintaining the slave system in all its rigor. These were the Tilgmans, the Goldboroughs, the Lockermans, the Pacas, the Skinners, Gibsons, and others of lesser affluence and standing.

The fact is, public opinion in such a quarter, the reader must see, was not likely to be very efficient in protecting the slave from cruelty. To be a restraint upon abuses of this nature, opinion must emanate from humane and virtuous communities, and to no such opinion or influence was Col. Lloyd's plantation exposed. It was a little nation by itself, having its own language, its own rules, regulations, and customs. The troubles and controversies arising here were not settled by the civil power of the State. The overseer was the important dignitary. He was generally accuser, judge, jury, advocate, and executioner. The criminal was always dumb—and no slave was allowed to testify, other than against his brother slave.

There were, of course, no conflicting rights of property, for all the people were the property of one man, and they could themselves own no property. Religion and politics were largely excluded. One class of the population was too high to be reached by the common preacher, and the other class was too low in condition and ignorance to be much cared for by religious teachers, and yet some religious ideas did enter this dark corner.

This, however, is not the only view which the place presented. Though civilization was in many respects shut out, nature could not be. Though separated from the rest of the world, though public opinion, as I have said, could seldom penetrate its dark domain, though the whole place was stamped with its own peculiar iron-like individuality, and though crimes, high-handed and atrocious, could be committed there with strange and shocking impunity, it was to outward seeming a most strikingly interesting place, full of life, activity, and spirit, and presented a very favorable contrast to the indolent monotony and languor of Tuckahoe. It resembled in some respects descriptions I have since read of the old baronial domains of Europe. Keen as was my regret, and great as was my sorrow, at leaving my old home, I was not long in adapting myself to this my new one. A man's troubles are always half disposed of when he finds endurance the only alternative. I found myself here; there was no getting away; and naught remained for me but to make the best of it. Here were plenty of children to play with, and plenty of pleasant resorts for boys of my age and older. The little tendrils of affection so rudely broken from the darling objects in and around my grandmother's home, gradually began to extend and twine themselves around the new surroundings. Here for the first time I saw a large wind-mill, with its wide-sweeping white wings, a commanding object to a child's eye. This was situated on what was called Long Point—a tract of land dividing Miles river from the Wye. I spent many hours here watching the wings of this wondrous mill. In the river, or what was called the "Swash," at a short distance from the shore, quietly lying at anchor, with her small row boat dancing at her stern, was a large sloop, the Sally Lloyd, called by that name in honor of the favorite daughter of the Colonel. These two objects, the sloop and mill, as I remember, awakened thoughts, ideas, and

wondering. Then here were a great many houses, human habitations
full of the mysteries of life at every stage of it. There was the little
red house up the road, occupied by Mr. Sevier, the overseer; a little
nearer to my old master's stood a long, low, rough building literally
alive with slaves of all ages, sexes, conditions, sizes, and colors. This
was called the long quarter. Perched upon a hill east of our house,
was a tall dilapidated old brick building, the architectural dimensions of which proclaimed its creation for a different purpose, now
occupied by slaves, in a similar manner to the long quarters. Besides
these, there were numerous other slave houses and huts, scattered
around in the neighborhood, every nook and corner of which, were
completely occupied.

Old master's house, a long brick building, plain but substantial,
was centrally located, and was an independent establishment. Besides these houses there were barns, stables, store houses, tobacco-
houses, blacksmith shops, wheelwright shops, cooper shops; but
above all there stood the grandest building my young eyes had ever
beheld, called by everyone on the plantation the *great* house. This
was occupied by Col. Lloyd and his family. It was surrounded by
numerous and variously shaped out-buildings. There were kitchens,
wash-houses, dairies, summer-houses, green-houses, hen-houses, tur-
key-houses, pigeon-houses, and arbors of many sizes and devices, all
neatly painted or whitewashed—interspersed with grand old trees,
ornamental and primitive, which afforded delightful shade in summer and imparted to the scene a high degree of stately beauty. The
great house itself was a large white wooden building with wings on
three sides of it. In front a broad portico extended the entire length
of the building, supported by a long range of columns, which gave to
the Colonel's home an air of great dignity and grandeur. It was a
treat to my young and gradually opening mind to behold this elaborate exhibition of wealth, power, and beauty.

The carriage entrance to the house was by a large gate, more than
a quarter of a mile distant. The intermediate space was a beautiful
lawn, very neatly kept and cared for. It was dotted thickly over with

trees and flowers. The road or lane from the gate to the great house was richly paved with white pebbles from the beach, and in its course formed a complete circle around the lawn. Outside this select enclosure were parks, as about the residences of the English nobility, where rabbits, deer, and other wild game might be seen peering and playing about, with "none to molest them or make them afraid." The tops of the stately poplars were often covered with red-winged blackbirds, making all nature vocal with the joyous life and beauty of their wild, warbling notes. These all belonged to me as well as to Col. Edward Lloyd, and, whether they did or not, I greatly enjoyed them. Not far from the great house were the stately mansions of the dead Lloyds—a place of somber aspect. Vast tombs, embowered beneath the weeping willow and the fir tree, told of the generations of the family, as well as their wealth. Superstition was rife among the slaves about this family burying-ground. Strange sights had been seen there by some of the older slaves, and I was often compelled to hear stories of shrouded ghosts, riding on great black horses, and of balls of fire which had been seen to fly there at midnight, and of startling and dreadful sounds that had been repeatedly heard. Slaves knew enough of the Orthodox theology at the time, to consign all bad slaveholders to hell, and they often fancied such persons wishing themselves back again to wield the lash. Tales of sights and sounds strange and terrible, connected with the huge black tombs, were a great security to the grounds about them, for few of the slaves had the courage to approach them during the day time. It was a dark, gloomy and forbidding place, and it was difficult to feel that the spirits of the sleeping dust there deposited reigned with the blest in the realms of eternal peace.

Here was transacted the business to twenty or thirty different farms, which, with the slaves upon them, numbering, in all, not less than a thousand, all belonged to Col. Lloyd. Each farm was under the management of an overseer, whose word was law.

Mr. Lloyd at this time was very rich. His slaves alone, numbering as I have said not less than a thousand, were an immense fortune, and though scarcely a month passed without the sale of one or more lots to the Georgia traders, there was no apparent diminution in the number of his human stock. The selling of any to the State of Georgia was a sore and mournful event to those left behind, as well as to the victims themselves.

The reader has already been informed of the handicrafts carried on here by the slaves. "Uncle" Toney was the blacksmith, "Uncle" Harry the cartwright, and "Uncle" Abel was the shoemaker, and these had assistants in their several departments. These mechanics were called "Uncles" by all the younger slaves, not because they really sustained that relationship to any, but according to plantation etiquette as a mark of respect, due from the younger to the older slaves. Strange and even ridiculous as it may seem, among a people so uncultivated and with so many stern trials to look in the face, there is not to be found among any people a more rigid enforcement of the law of respect to elders than is maintained among them. I set this down as partly constitutional with the colored race and partly conventional. There is no better material in the world for making a gentleman than is furnished in the African.

Among other slave notabilities, I found here one called by everybody, white and colored, "Uncle" Isaac Copper. It was seldom that a slave, however venerable, was honored with a surname in Maryland, and so completely has the south shaped the manners of the north in this respect that their right to such honor is tardily admitted even now. It goes sadly against the grain to address and treat a negro as one would address and treat a white man. But once in a while, even in a slave state, a negro had a surname fastened to him by common consent. This was the case with "Uncle" Isaac Copper. When the "Uncle" was dropped, he was called Doctor Copper. He was both our Doctor of Medicine and our Doctor of Divinity. Where he took his degree I am unable to say, but he was too well established in his profession to permit question as to his native skill, or attainments. One qualification he certainly had. He was a confirmed cripple, wholly unable to work, and was worth nothing for sale in the market.

Though lame, he was no sluggard. He made his crutches do him good service, and was always on the alert looking up the sick, and such as were supposed to need his aid and counsel. His remedial prescriptions embraced four articles. For diseases of the body, epsom salts and castor oil; for those of the soul, the "Lord's prayer," and a few stout hickory switches.

I was early sent to Doctor Isaac Copper, with twenty or thirty other children, to learn the Lord's prayer. The old man was seated on a huge three-legged oaken stool, armed with several large hickory switches, and from the point where he sat, lame as he was, he could reach every boy in the room. After standing a while to learn what was expected of us, he commanded us to kneel down. This done, he told us to say everything he said. "Our Father"—this we repeated after him with promptness and uniformity—"who art in Heaven," was less promptly and uniformly repeated, and the old gentleman paused in the prayer to give us a short lecture, and to use his switches on our backs.

Everybody in the South seemed to want the privilege of whipping somebody else. Uncle Isaac, though a good old man, shared the common passion of his time and country. I cannot say I was much edified by attendance upon his ministry. There was even at that time something a little inconsistent and laughable, in my mind, in the blending of prayer with punishment.

I was not long in my new home before I found that the dread I had conceived of Captain Anthony was in a measure groundless. Instead of leaping out from some hiding place and destroying me, he hardly seemed to notice my presence. He probably thought as little of my arrival there, as of an additional pig to his stock. He was the chief agent of his employer. The overseers of all the farms composing the Lloyd estate, were in some sort under him. The Colonel himself seldom addressed an overseer, or allowed himself to be addressed by one. To Captain Anthony, therefore, was committed the headship of all the farms. He carried the keys of all the store-houses, weighed and measured the allowances of each slave, at the end of each month; superintended the storing of all goods brought to the store-house; dealt out the raw material to the different handicrafts-men, shipped the grain, tobacco, and all other saleable produce of the numerous farms to Baltimore, and had a general oversight of all the workshops of the place. In addition to all this he was frequently called abroad to Easton and elsewhere in the discharge of his numerous duties as chief agent of the estate.

The family of Captain Anthony consisted of two sons—Andrew and Richard, his daughter Lucretia and her newly married husband, Captain Thomas Auld. In the kitchen were Aunt Katy, Aunt Esther, and ten or a dozen children, most of them older than myself. Capt. Anthony was not considered a rich slave-holder, though he was pretty well off in the world. He owned about thirty slaves and three farms in the Tuckahoe district. The more valuable part of his property was in slaves, of whom he sold one every year, which brought him in seven or eight hundred dollars, besides his yearly salary and other revenue from his lands.

I have been often asked during the earlier part of my free life at the north, how I happened to have so little of the slave accent in my speech. The mystery is in some measure explained by my association with Daniel Lloyd, the youngest son of Col. Edward Lloyd. The law of compensation holds here as well as elsewhere. While this lad could not associate with ignorance without sharing its shade, he could not give his black playmates his company without giving them his superior intelligence as well. Without knowing this, or caring about it at the time, I, for some cause or other, was attracted to him and was much his companion.

I had little to do with the older brothers of Daniel—Edward and Murray. They were grown up and were fine looking men. Edward was especially esteemed by the slave children and by me among the rest, not that he ever said anything to us or for us which could be called particularly kind. It was enough for us that he never looked or acted scornfully toward us. The idea of rank and station was rigidly maintained on this estate. The family of Captain Anthony never visited the great house, and the Lloyds never came to our house. Equal non-intercourse was observed between Captain Anthony's family and the family of Mr. Sevier, the overseer.

Such, kind readers, was the community and such the place in which my earliest and most lasting impressions of the workings of slavery were received—of which impressions you will learn more in the after coming chapters of this book.

A SLAVEHOLDER'S CHARACTER

Although my old master, Captain Anthony, gave me, at the first of my coming to him from my grandmother's, very little attention, and although that little was of a remarkably mild and gentle description, a few months only were sufficient to convince me that mildness and gentleness were not the prevailing or governing traits of his character. These excellent qualities were displayed only occasionally. He could, when it suited him, appear to be literally insensible to the claims of humanity. He could not only be deaf to the appeals of the helpless against the aggressor, but he could himself commit outrages deep, dark, and nameless. Yet he was not by nature worse than other men. Had he been brought up in a free state, surrounded by the full restraints of civilized society—restraints which are necessary to the freedom of all its members, alike and equally, Capt. Anthony might have been as humane a man as are members of such society generally. A man's character always takes its hue, more or less, from the form and color of things about him. The slaveholder, as well as the slave, was the victim of the slave system. Under the whole heavens there could be no relation more unfavorable to the development of honorable character than that sustained by the slaveholder to the slave. Reason is imprisoned here and passions run wild. Could the reader have seen Captain Anthony gently leading me by the hand, as he sometimes did, patting me on the head, speaking to me in soft, caressing tones and calling me his little Indian boy, he would have deemed him a kind-hearted old man, and really almost fatherly to the slave boy. But the pleasant moods of a slaveholder are transient and fitful. They neither come often nor remain long. The temper of the old man was subject to special trials, but since these trials were never borne patiently, they added little to his natural stock of patience. Aside from his troubles with his slaves and those of Mr. Lloyd's, he made the impression upon me of being an unhappy man. Even to my child's eye he wore a troubled and at times a haggard aspect. His strange movements excited my curiosity and awakened my compassion. He seldom walked alone without muttering to himself, and he occasionally stormed about as if defying an army of invisible foes. Most of his leisure was spent in walking around, cursing and gesticulating as if possessed by a demon. He was evidently a wretched man, at war with his own soul and all the world around him. To be overheard by the children disturbed him very little. He made no more of our presence than that of the ducks and geese he met on the green. But when his gestures were most violent, ending with a threatening shake of the head and a sharp snap of his middle finger and thumb, I deemed it wise to keep at a safe distance from him.

One of the first circumstances that opened my eyes to the cruelties and wickedness of slavery and its hardening influences upon my old master, was his refusal to interpose his authority to protect and shield a young woman, a cousin of mine, who had been most cruelly abused and beaten by his overseer in Tuckahoe. This overseer, a Mr. Plummer, was like most of his class, little less than a human brute; and in addition to his general profligacy and repulsive coarseness, he was a miserable drunkard, a man not fit to have the management of a drove of mules. In one of his moments of drunken madness he committed the outrage which brought the young woman in question down to my old master's for protection. The poor girl, on her arrival at our house, presented a most pitiable appearance. She had left in haste and without preparation, and probably without the knowledge of Mr. Plummer. She had traveled twelve miles, bare-footed, bare-necked, and bare-headed. Her neck and shoulders were covered with scars newly made, and not content with marring her neck and shoulders with the cowhide, the cowardly wretch had dealt her a blow on the head with a hickory club, which cut a horrible gash and left her face literally covered with blood. In this condition the poor young woman came down to implore protection at the hands of my old master. I expected to see him boil over with rage at the revolting deed, and to hear him fill the air with curses upon the brutal Plummer; but I was disappointed. He sternly told her in an angry tone, "She deserved every bit of it, and if she did not go home instantly he would himself take the remaining skin from her neck and back." Thus the poor girl was compelled to return without re-dress, and perhaps to receive an additional flogging for daring to ap-peal to authority higher than that of the overseer.

I did not at that time understand the philosophy of this treatment of my cousin. I think I now understand it. This treatment was a part of the system, rather than a part of the man. To have en-couraged appeals of this kind would have occasioned much loss of time, and leave the overseer powerless to enforce obedience. Never-theless, when a slave had nerve enough to go straight to his master, with a well-founded complaint against an overseer, though he might be repelled and have even that of which he complained at the time repeated, and though he might be beaten by his master as well as by the overseer, for his temerity, in the end, the policy of complaining was generally vindicated by the relaxed rigor of the overseer's treat-ment. The latter became more careful and less disposed to use the lash upon such slaves thereafter.

The overseer very naturally disliked to have the ear of the master disturbed by complaints, and either for this reason or because of ad-vice privately given him by his employer, he generally modified the rigor of his rule after complaints of this kind had been made against him. For some cause or other the slaves, no matter how often they were repulsed by their masters, were ever disposed to regard them with less abhorrence than the overseer. And yet these masters would often go beyond their overseers in wanton cruelty. They wielded the lash without any sense of responsibility. They could cripple or kill without fear of consequences. I have seen my old master in a tempest of wrath, full of pride, hatred, jealousy, and revenge, where he seemed a very fiend.

The circumstances which I am about to narrate, and which gave rise to this fearful tempest of passion, were not singular, but very common in our slave-holding community.

The reader will have noticed that among the names of slaves, Esther is mentioned. This was a young woman who possessed that which was ever a curse to the slave girl—namely, personal beauty. She was tall, light-colored, well formed, and made a fine appearance. Esther was courted by "Ned Roberts," the son of a favorite slave of Col. Lloyd, who was as fine-looking a young man as Esther was a woman. Some slave-holders would have been glad to have promoted the marriage of two such persons, but for some reason, Captain Anthony disapproved of their courtship. He strictly ordered her to quit the company of young Roberts, telling her that he would punish her severely if he ever found her again in his company. But it was impossible to keep this couple apart. Meet they would, and meet they did. Had Mr. Anthony been himself a man of honor, his motives in this matter might have appeared more favorably. As it was, they appeared as abhorrent as they were contemptible. It was one of the damning characteristics of slavery, that it robbed its victims of every earthly incentive to a holy life. The fear of God and the hope of heaven were sufficient to sustain many slave women amidst the snares and dangers of their strange lot; but they were ever at the mercy of the power, passion, and caprice of their owners. Slavery provided no means for the honorable perpetuation of the race. Yet despite of this destitution there were many men and women among the slaves who were true and faithful to each other through life.

But to the case in hand. Abhorred and circumvented as he was, Captain Anthony, having the power, was determined on revenge. I happened to see its shocking execution, and shall never forget the scene. It was early in the morning, when all was still, and before any of the family in the house or kitchen had risen. I was, in fact, awakened by the heart-rending shrieks and piteous cries of poor Esther. My sleeping-place was on the dirt floor of a little rough closet which opened into the kitchen, and through the cracks in its unplaned boards I could distinctly see and hear what was going on, without being seen. Esther's wrists were firmly tied, and the twisted rope was fastened to a strong iron staple in a heavy wooden beam above, near the fire-place. Here she stood on a bench, her arms tightly drawn above her head. Her back and shoulders were perfectly bare. Behind her stood old master, with cowhide in hand, pursuing his barbarous work with all manner of harsh, coarse, and tantalizing epithets. He was cruelly deliberate, and protracted the torture as one who was delighted with the agony of his victim. Again and again he drew the hateful scourge through his hand, adjusting it with a view of dealing the most pain-giving blow his strength and skill could inflict. Poor Esther had never before been severely whipped. Her shoulders were plump and tender. Each blow, vigorously laid on, brought screams from her as well as blood. "Have mercy! Oh, mercy!" she cried. "I won't do so no more." But her piercing cries seemed only to increase his fury. The whole scene, with all its attendants, was revolting and shocking to the last degree, and when the motives for the brutal castigation are known, language has no power to convey a just sense of its dreadful criminality. After laying on I dare not say how many stripes, old master untied his suffering victim. When let down she could scarcely stand. From my heart I pitied her, and child as I was, and new to such scenes, the shock was tremendous. I was terrified, hushed, stunned, and bewildered. The scene here described was often repeated, for Edward and Esther continued to meet, notwithstanding all efforts to prevent their meeting.

A CHILD'S REASONING

The incidents related in the foregoing chapter led me thus early to inquire into the origin and nature of slavery. Why am I a slave? Why are some people slaves and others masters? These were perplexing questions and very troublesome to my childhood. I was told by some one very early that *"God up in the sky"* had made all things, and had made black people to be slaves and white people to be masters. I was told too that God was good and that he knew what was best for everybody. This was, however, less satisfactory than the first statement. It came point blank against all my notions of goodness. The case of Aunt Esther was in my mind. Besides, I could not tell how anybody could know that God made black people to be slaves. Then I found, too, that there were puzzling exceptions to this theory of slavery, in the fact that all black people were not slaves, and all white people were not masters. An incident occurred about this time that made a deep impression on my mind. One of the men slaves of Captain Anthony and my Aunt Jennie ran away. A great noise was made about it. Old master was furious. He said he would follow them and catch them and bring them back, but he never did it, and somebody told me that Uncle Noah and Aunt Jennie had gone to the free states and were free. Besides this occurrence, which brought much light to my mind on the subject, there were several slaves on Mr. Lloyd's place who remembered being brought from Africa. There were others that told me that their fathers and mothers were stolen from Africa.

This to me was important knowledge, but not such as to make me feel very easy in my slave condition. The success of Aunt Jennie and Uncle Noah in getting away from slavery was, I think, the first fact that made me seriously think of escape for myself. I could not have been more than seven or eight years old at the time of this occurrence, but young as I was I was already a fugitive from slavery in spirit and purpose.

Up to the time of the brutal treatment of my Aunt Esther, already narrated, and the shocking plight in which I had seen my cousin from Tuckahoe, my attention had not been especially directed to the grosser and more revolting features of slavery. I had, of course, heard of whippings and savage mutilations of slaves by brutal overseers, but happily for me I had always been out of the way of such occurrences. My play time was spent outside of the corn and tobacco fields, where the overseers and slaves were brought together and in conflict. But after the case of my Aunt Esther I saw others of the same disgusting and shocking nature. The one of these which agitated and distressed me most was the whipping of a woman, not belonging to my old master, but to Col. Lloyd. The charge against her was very common and very indefinite, namely, *"impudence."* This crime could be committed by a slave in a hundred different ways, and depended much upon the temper and caprice of the overseer as to whether it was committed at all. He could create the offense whenever it pleased him. A look, a word, a gesture, accidental or intentional, never failed to be taken as impudence when he was in the right mood for such an offense. In this case there were all the necessary conditions for the commission of the crime charged. The offender was nearly white, to begin with; she was the wife of a favorite hand on board of Mr. Lloyd's sloop and was besides the mother of five sprightly children. Vigorous and spirited woman that she was, a wife and a mother, with a predominating share of the blood of the master running in her veins. Nellie (for that was her name) had all the qualities essential to impudence to a slave overseer. My attention was called to the scene of the castigation by the loud screams and curses that proceeded from the direction of it. When I came near the parties engaged in the struggle, the overseer had hold of Nelly, endeavoring with his whole strength to drag her to a tree against her resistance. Both his and her faces were bleeding, for the woman was doing her best. Three of her children were present, and though quite small, (from seven to ten years old I should think,) they gallantly took the side of their mother against the overseer, and pelted him well with stones and epithets. Amid the screams of the children *"Let my mammy go! Let my mammy go!"* the hoarse voice of the maddened overseer was heard in terrible oaths that he would teach her how to give a white man *"impudence."* The blood on his face and on hers attested her skill in the use of her nails, and his dogged determination to conquer. His purpose was to tie her up to a tree and give her, in slave-holding parlance, a "genteel flogging," and he evidently had not expected the stern and protracted resistance he was meeting, or the strength and skill needed to its execution. There were times when she seemed likely to get the better of the brute, but he finally overpowered her, and succeeded in getting her arms firmly tied to the tree towards which he had been dragging her. The victim was now at the mercy of his merciless lash. What followed I need not here describe. The cries of the now helpless woman, while undergoing the terrible infliction, were mingled with the hoarse curses of the overseer and the wild cries of her distracted children. When the poor woman was untied, her back was covered with blood. She was whipped, terribly whipped, but she was not subdued, and continued to denounce the overseer, and pour upon him every vile epithet she could think of. Such floggings are seldom repeated by overseers on the same persons. They prefer to whip those who were the most easily whipped. The doctrine that submission to violence is the best cure for violence did not hold good as between slaves and overseers. He was whipped oftener who was whipped easiest. That slave who had the courage to stand up for himself against the overseer, although he might have many hard stripes at first, became while legally a slave virtually a freeman. "You can shoot me," said a slave to Rigby Hopkins, "but you can't whip me," and the result was he was neither whipped nor shot. I do not know that Mr. Sevier ever attempted to whip Nelly again. He probably did, for not long after he was taken sick and died. It was commonly said that his death-bed was a wretched one, and that, the ruling passion being strong in death, he died flourishing the slave whip and with horrid oaths upon his lips. This deathbed scene may only be the imagining of the slaves. One thing is certain, that when he was in health his profanity was enough to chill the blood of an ordinary man. Nature, or habit, had given to his face an expression of uncommon savageness. Tobacco and rage had ground his teeth short, and nearly every sentence that he uttered was commenced or completed with an oath. Hated for his cruelty, despised for his cowardice, he went to his grave lamented by nobody on the place outside of his own house, if, indeed, he was even lamented there.

In Mr. James Hopkins, the succeeding overseer, we had a different and a better man, as good perhaps as any man could be in the position of a slave overseer. Though he sometimes wielded the lash, it was evident that he took no pleasure in it and did it with much reluctance. He stayed but a short time here, and his removal from the position was much regretted by the slaves generally. Of the successor of Mr. Hopkins I shall have something to say at another time and in another place.

For the present we will attend to a further description of the business-like aspect of Col. Lloyd's *"Great House"* farm. There was always much bustle and noise here on the two days at the end of each month, for then the slaves belonging to the different branches of this great estate assembled here by their representatives to obtain their monthly allowances of corn-meal and pork. These were gala days for the slaves of the outlying farms, and there was much rivalry among them as to who should be elected to go up to the Great House farm for the *"Allowances,"* and indeed to attend to any other business at this great place, to them the capitol of a little nation. Its beauty and grandeur, its immense wealth, its numerous population, and the fact that uncles Harry, Peter, and Jake, the sailors on board the sloop, usually kept on sale trinkets which they bought in Baltimore to sell to their less fortunate fellow-servants, made a visit to the Great House farm a high privilege, and eagerly sought. It was valued, too, as a mark of distinction and confidence; but probably the chief motive among the competitors for the office was the opportunity it afforded to shake off the monotony of the field and to get beyond the overseer's eye and lash. Once on the road with an oxteam, and seated on the tongue of the cart, with no overseer to look after him, he felt himself comparatively free.

Slaves were expected to sing as well as to work. A silent slave was not liked, either by masters or by overseers. *"Make a noise there! make a noise there!"* and "bear a hand," were words usually addressed to slaves when they were silent. This, and the natural disposition of the negro to make a noise in the world, may account for the almost constant singing among them when at their work. There was generally more or less singing among the teamsters at all times. It was a means of telling the overseer, in the distance, where they were, and what they were about. But on the allowance days those commissioned to the Great House farm were peculiarly vocal. While on the way they would make the grand old woods for miles around reverberate with their wild and plaintive notes. They were indeed both merry and sad. Child as I was, these wild songs greatly depressed my spirits. Nowhere outside of dear old Ireland, in the days of want and famine have I heard sound so mournful.

In all these slave songs there was ever some expression of praise of the Great House farm—something that would please the pride of the Lloyds.

> I am going away to the Great House farm,
> O, yea! O, yea! O, yea!
> My old master is a good old master,
> O, yea! O, yea! O yea!

These words would be sung over and over again, with others, improvised as they went along—jargon, perhaps, to the reader, but full of meaning to the singers. I have sometimes thought that the mere hearing of these songs would have done more to impress the good people of the north with the soul-crushing character of slavery than whole volumes exposing the physical cruelties of the slave system;

for the heart has no language like song. Many years ago, when rec-
ollecting my experience in this respect, I wrote of these slave songs
in the following strain:

"I did not, when a slave, fully understand the deep meaning of
those rude and apparently incoherent songs. I was, myself, within
the circle, so that I could then neither hear nor see as those without
might see and hear. They breathed the prayer and complaint of souls
overflowing with the bitterest anguish. They depressed my spirits
and filled my heart with ineffable sadness."

The remark in the olden time was not unfrequently made, that
slaves were the most contented and happy laborers in the world,
and their dancing and singing were referred to in proof of this alleged fact; but it was a great mistake to suppose them happy because they sometimes made those joyful noises. The songs of the
slaves represented their sorrows, rather than their joys. Like tears,
they were a relief to aching hearts. It is not inconsistent with the
constitution of the human mind, that avails itself of one and the
same method for expressing opposite emotions. Sorrow and desolation
have their songs, as well as joy and peace.

It was the boast of slaveholders that their slaves enjoyed more of
the physical comforts of life than the peasantry of any country in
the world. My experience contradicts this. The men and the women
slaves on Col. Lloyd's farm received as their monthly allowance of
food, eight pounds of pickled pork, or its equivalent in fish. The pork
was often tainted, and the fish were of the poorest quality. With
their pork or fish, they had given them one bushel of Indian meal,
unbolted, of which quite fifteen per cent was more fit for pigs than
for men. With this one pint of salt was given, and this was the entire
monthly allowance of a full-grown slave, working constantly in the
open field from morning till night every day in the month except
Sunday. There is no kind of work which really requires a better supply of food to prevent physical exhaustion than the field work of a
slave. The yearly allowance of clothing was not more ample than the

supply of food. It consisted of two tow-linen shirts, one pair of trowsers of the same coarse material, for summer, and a woolen pair of trowsers and a woolen jacket for winter, with one pair of yarn stockings and a pair of shoes of the coarsest description. Children under ten years old had neither shoes, stockings, jackets, nor trowsers. They had two coarse tow-linen shirts per year, and when these were worn out they went naked till the next allowance day—and this was the condition of the little girls as well as the boys. As to beds, they had none. One coarse blanket was given them, and this only to the men and women. The children stuck themselves in holes and corners about the quarters, often in the corners of huge chimneys, with their feet in the ashes to keep them warm. The want of beds, however, was not considered a great privation by the field hands. Time to sleep was of far greater importance. For when the day's work was done most of these had their washing, mending, and cooking to do, and having few or no facilities for doing such things, very many of their needed sleeping hours were consumed in necessary preparations for the labors of the coming day. The sleeping apartments, if they could have been properly called such, had little regard to comfort or decency. Old and young, male and female, married and single, dropped down upon the common clay floor, each covering up with his or her blanket, their only protection from cold or exposure. The night, however, was shortened at both ends. The slaves worked often as long as they could see, and were late in cooking and mending for the coming day, and at the first gray streak of the morning they were summoned to the field by the overseer's horn. They were whipped for over-sleeping more than for any other fault. Neither age nor sex found any favor. The overseer stood at the quarter door, armed with stick and whip, ready to deal heavy blows upon any who might be a little behind time. When the horn was blown there was a rush for the door, for the hindermost one was sure to get a blow from the overseer. Young mothers who worked in the field were allowed an hour about ten o'clock in the morning to go home to nurse their children. This was when they were not required to take them to the field with them, and leave them upon "turning row," or in the corner of the fences.

As a general rule the slaves did not come to their quarters to take their meals, but took their ash-cake (called thus because baked in the ashes) and piece of pork, or their salt herrings, where they were at work.

But let us now leave the rough usage of the field, where vulgar coarseness and brutal cruelty flourished as rank as weeds in the tropics, where a vile wretch, in the shape of a man, rides, walks, and struts about, with whip in hand, dealing heavy blows and leaving deep gashes on the flesh of men and women, and turn our attention to the less repulsive slave life as it existed in the home of my childhood. Some idea of the splendor of that place sixty years ago has already been given. The contrast between the condition of the slaves and that of their masters was marvelously sharp and striking. There were pride, pomp, and luxury on the one hand, servility, dejection, and misery on the other.

LUXURIES AT THE GREAT HOUSE

The close-fisted stinginess that fed the poor slave on coarse corn-meal and tainted meat, that clothed him in crashy tow-linen and hurried him on to toil through the field in all weathers, with wind and rain beating through his tattered garments, that scarcely gave even the young slave-mother time to nurse her infant in the fence-corner, wholly vanished on approaching the sacred precincts of the "Great House" itself. There the scriptural phrase descriptive of the wealthy found exact illustration. The highly-favored inmates of this mansion were literally arrayed in "purple and fine linen, and fared sumptuously every day." The table of this house groaned under the blood-bought luxuries gathered with painstaking care at home and abroad. Fields, forests, rivers, and seas were made tributary. Immense wealth and its lavish expenditures filled the Great House with all that could please the eye or tempt the taste. Fish, flesh, and fowl were here in profusion. Chickens of all breeds; ducks of all kinds, wild and tame, the common and the huge Muscovite; Guinea fowls, turkeys, geese, and pea-fowls were fat, and fattening for the destined vortex. Here the graceful swan, the mongrels, the black-necked wild goose, partridges, quails, pheasants and pigeons, choice water-fowl, with all their strange varieties, were caught in this huge net. Beef, veal, mutton, and venison, of the most select kinds and quality rolled in bounteous profusion to this grand consumer. The teeming riches of the Chesapeake Bay, its rock perch, drums, crocus, trout, oysters, crabs, and terrapin were drawn hither to adorn the glittering table. The dairy, too, the finest then on the eastern shore of Maryland, supplied by cattle of the best English stock, imported for the express purpose, poured its rich donations of fragrant cheese, golden butter, and delicious cream to heighten the attractions of the gorgeous, unending round of feasting. Nor were the fruits of the earth overlooked. The fertile garden, many acres in size, constituting a separate establishment distinct from the common farm, with its scientific gardener direct from Scotland, a Mr. McDermott, and four men under his direction, was not behind, either in the abundance or in the delicacy of its contributions. The tender asparagus, the crispy celery, and the delicate cauliflower, egg plants, beets, lettuce, parsnips, peas, and French beans, early and late, radishes, cantelopes, melons of all kinds; and the fruits of all climes and of every description, from the hardy apples of the north to the lemon and orange of the south, culminated at this point. Here were gathered figs, raisins, almonds, and grapes from Spain, wines and brandies from France, teas of various flavor from China, and rich, aromatic coffee from Java, all conspiring to swell the tide of high life, where pride and indolence lounged in magnificence and satiety.

Behind the tall-backed and elaborately wrought chairs stood the servants, fifteen in number, carefully selected, not only with a view to their capacity and adeptness, but with special regard to their personal appearance, their graceful agility, and pleasing address. Some of these servants, armed with fans, wafted reviving breezes to the over-heated brows of the alabaster ladies, whilst others watched with eager eye and fawn-like step, anticipating and supplying wants before they were sufficiently formed to be announced by word or sign.

These servants constituted a sort of black aristocracy. They resembled the field hands in nothing except their color, and in this they held the advantage of a velvet-like glossiness, rich and beautiful. The hair, too, showed the same advantage. The delicately-formed colored maid rustled in the scarcely-worn silk of her young mistress, while the servant men were equally well attired from the overflowing wardrobe of their young masters, so that in dress, as well as in form and feature, in manner and speech, in tastes and habits, the distance between these favored few and the sorrow and hunger-smitten multitudes of the quarter and the field was immense.

In the stables and carriage-houses were to be found the same evidences of pride and luxurious extravagance. Here were three splendid coaches, soft within and lustrous without. Here, too, were gigs, phaetons, barouches, sulkeys, and sleighs. Here were saddles and harnesses, beautifully wrought and richly mounted. Not less than thirty-five horses of the best approved blood, both for speed and beauty, were kept only for pleasure. The care of these horses constituted the entire occupation of two men, one or the other of them being always in the stable to answer any call which might be made from the Great House. Over the way from the stable was a house built expressly for the hounds, a pack of twenty-five or thirty, the fare for which would have made glad the hearts of a dozen slaves. Horses and hounds, however, were not the only consumers of the slave's toil. The hospitality practiced at the Lloyd's would have astonished and charmed many a health-seeking divine or merchant from the north. Viewed from his table, and *not* from the field, Colonel Lloyd was, indeed, a model of generous hospitality. His house was literally a hotel for weeks, during the summer months. At those times, especially, the air was freighted with the rich fumes of baking, boiling, roasting, and broiling. It was something to me that I could share these odors with the winds, even if the meats themselves were under a more stringent monopoly. In master Daniel I had a friend at court, who would sometimes give me a cake, and who kept me well informed as to their guests and their entertainments. Viewed from Col. Lloyd's table, who could have said that his slaves were not well clad and well cared for? Who would have said they did not glory in being the slaves of such a master? Who but a fanatic could have seen any cause for sympathy for either master or slave? Alas, this immense wealth, this gilded splendor, this profusion of luxury, this exemption from toil, this life of ease, this sea of plenty were not the pearly gates they seemed to a world of happiness and sweet content. The poor slave, on his hard pine plank, scantily covered with his thin blanket, slept more soundly than the feverish voluptuary who reclined upon his downy pillow. Food to the indolent is poison, not sustenance. Lurking beneath the rich and tempting viands were invisible spirits of evil, which filled the self-deluded gourmandizer with aches and pains, passions uncontrollable, fierce tempers, dyspepsia, rheumatism, lumbago, and gout, and of these the Lloyds had a full share.

I had many opportunities of witnessing the restless discontent and capricious irritation of the Lloyds. My fondness for horses attracted me to the stables much of the time. The two men in charge of this establishment were old and young Barney—father and son. Old Barney was a fine looking, portly old man of a brownish complexion, and a respectful and dignified bearing. He was much devoted to his profession, and held his office as an honorable one. He was a farrier as well as an ostler, and could bleed, remove lampers from their mouths, and administer medicine to horses. No one on the farm knew so well as old Barney what to do with a sick horse; but his office was not an enviable one, and his gifts and acquirements were of little advantage to him. In nothing was Col. Lloyd more unreasonable and exacting than in respect to the management of his horses. Any supposed inattention to these animals was sure to be visited with degrading punishment. His horses and dogs fared better than his men. Their beds were far softer and cleaner than those of his human cattle. No excuse could shield old Barney if the Colonel only suspected something wrong about his horses, and consequently he was often punished when faultless. It was painful to hear the unreasonable and fretful scoldings administered by Col. Lloyd, his son Murray, and his sons-in-law, to this poor man. Three of the daughters of Col. Lloyd were married, and they with their husbands remained at the great house a portion of the year, and enjoyed the luxury of whipping the servants when they pleased. A horse was seldom brought out of the stable to which no objection could be raised. "There was dust in his hair;" "there was a twist in his reins;" "his foretop was not combed;" "his mane did not lie straight;" "his head did not look well;" "his fetlocks had not been properly trimmed." Something was always wrong. However groundless the complaint, Barney must stand, hat in hand, lips sealed, never answering a word in explanation or excuse. In a free State, a master thus complaining without cause, might be told by his ostler: "Sir, I am sorry I cannot please you, but since I have done the best I can and fail to do so, your remedy is to dismiss me." But here the ostler must listen and tremblingly abide his master's behest. One of the most heart-saddening and humiliating scenes I ever witnessed was the whipping of old Barney by Col. Lloyd. These two men were both advanced in years; there were the silver locks of the master, and the bald and toil-worn brow of the slave—superior and inferior here, powerful and weak here, but *equals* before God. "Uncover your head," said the imperious master; he was obeyed. "Take off your jacket, you old rascal!" and off came Barney's jacket. "Down on your knees!" down knelt the old man, his shoulders bare, his bald head glistening in the sunshine, and his aged knees on the cold, damp ground. In this humble and debasing attitude, that master, to whom he had devoted the best years and the best strength of his life, came forward and laid

on thirty lashes with his horse-whip. The old man made no resistance, but bore it patiently, answering each blow with only a shrug of
the shoulders and a groan. I do not think that the physical suffering
from this infliction was severe, for the whip was a light riding-whip;
but the spectacle of an aged man—a husband and a father—humbly
kneeling before his fellow-man, shocked me at the time; and since I
have grown older, few of the features of slavery have impressed me
with a deeper sense of its injustice and barbarity than this exciting
scene. I owe it to the truth, however, to say that this was the first
and last time I ever saw a slave compelled to kneel to receive a
whipping.

Another incident, illustrating a phase of slavery to which I have
referred in another connection, I may here mention. Besides two
other coachmen, Col. Lloyd owned one named William Wilks, and
his was one of the exceptionable cases where a slave possessed a surname, and was recognized by it, by both colored and white people.
Wilks was a very fine-looking man. He was about as white as any
one on the plantation, and in form and feature bore a very striking
resemblance to Murray Lloyd. It was whispered and generally believed that William Wilks was a son of Col. Lloyd, by a highly
favored slave-woman, who was still on the plantation. There were
many reasons for believing this whisper, not only from his personal
appearance, but from the undeniable freedom which he enjoyed over
all others, and his apparent consciousness of being something more
than a slave to his master. It was notorious too that William had a
deadly enemy in Murray Lloyd, whom he so much resembled, and
that the latter greatly worried his father with importunities to sell
William. Indeed, he gave his father no rest, until he did sell him to
Austin Woldfolk, the great slave-trader at that time. Before selling
him, however, he tried to make things smooth by giving William a
whipping, but it proved a failure. It was a compromise, and like
most such, defeated itself,—for soon after Col. Lloyd atoned to William for the abuse by giving him a gold watch and chain. Another
fact somewhat curious was, that though sold to the remorseless Wold-

folk, taken in irons to Baltimore, and cast into prison, with a view to being sent to the South, William outbid all his purchasers, paid for himself, and afterwards resided in Baltimore. How this was accomplished was a great mystery at the time, explained only on the supposition that the hand which had bestowed the gold watch and chain had also supplied the purchase-money, but I have since learned that this was not the true explanation. Wilks had many friends in Baltimore and Annapolis, and they united to save him from a fate which was the one of all others most dreaded by the slaves. Practical amalgamation was however so common at the South, and so many circumstances pointed in that direction, that there was little reason to doubt that William Wilks was the son of Edward Lloyd.

The real feelings and opinions of the slaves were not much known or respected by their masters. The distance between the two was too great to admit of such knowledge; and in this respect Col. Lloyd was no exception to the rule. His slaves were so numerous he did not know them when he saw them. Nor, indeed, did all his slaves know him. It is reported of him, that riding along the road one day he met a colored man, and addressed him in what was the usual way of speaking to colored people on the public highways of the South: "Well, boy, who do you belong to?" "To Col. Lloyd," replied the slave. "Well does the Colonel treat you well?" "No, sir," was the ready reply. "What, does he work you hard?" "Yes, sir." "Well, don't he give you enough to eat?" "Yes, sir, he gives me enough to eat, such as it is." The Colonel rode on; the slave also went on about his business, not dreaming that he had been conversing with his master. He thought and said nothing of the matter, until two or three weeks afterwards, he was informed by his overseer that for having found fault with his master, he was now to be sold to a Georgia trader. He was immediately chained and handcuffed; and thus without a moment's warning, he was snatched away, and forever sundered from his family and friends by a hand as unrelenting as that of death. This was the penalty of telling the simple truth, in answer to a series of plain questions. It was partly in consequence of such facts, that slaves, when inquired of as to their condition and the character of their masters, would almost invariably say that they were contented and their masters kind. Slaveholders are known to have sent spies among their slaves to ascertain if possible their views and feelings in regard to their condition; hence the maxim established among them, that "a still tongue makes a wise head." They would suppress the truth rather than take the consequences of telling it, and in so doing they prove themselves a part of the human family. I was frequently asked if I had a kind master, and I do not remember ever to have given a negative reply. I did not consider myself as uttering that which was strictly untrue, for I always measured the kindness of my master by the standard of kindness set up by the slaveholders around us.

CHARLOTTE FORTEN
(1838-1914)

Outstanding among the Philadelphia Negro families were the Fortens, especially James Forten, an abolitionist leader and a literate, well-to-do sailmaker who had earned a fortune by an invention for handling sails. He fought vigorously to defeat legislative bills to bar free Negroes from Pennsylvania and helped to defeat the African colonization movement.

His granddaughter, Charlotte Forten, had been sent to private schools in order to avoid segregated public schools. As a child she absorbed the reformist ideas of her numerous abolitionist relatives and the distinguished white visitors, Garrison, Wendell Phillips, and John Greenleaf Whittier.

In 1854, when she was sixteen years of age, she moved to Salem to be educated for the teaching profession in a grammar and Normal school. She read voraciously, possessed a talent for writing essays and poetry, and always retained her race-conscious sensitivity, although this did not prevent her from earning the deep affection of both white pupils and parents. Salem knew her not only as a unique Negro teacher of whites but also as an attractive idealistic personality. But her isolated rearing made her a somewhat lonely child, as her recently-published *Journal* reveals.

Almost at the onset of the Civil War, the Union fleet captured the Sea Islands off the coast of South Carolina where some of the largest plantations were located. Federal authorities hastened to organize a Negro regiment at Port Royal Island, South Carolina, and sent Northern teachers to educate the ex-slaves. One of these eager schoolmarms was Charlotte Forten, who came with an introduction from her friend Whittier. The *Atlantic Monthly* was greatly interested in the two articles upon her experences that she sent them. As these selections show, Miss Forten was a keen observer of the process of emancipation and the African speech and customs of the Sea Island Negroes. She was especially sympathetic to the new federal experiment to use the experiences of the Sea Island Reconstruction years as a basis for a national welfare policy for Negroes.

In 1864, she returned to her teaching in the North, wrote for magazines, and took an active part in race questions. Her husband, the Reverend Francis J. Grimké, whom she married in 1878, was the son of a South Carolina planter whose sisters, Sarah and Angelina, were famous Quaker abolitionists. Angelina publicly recognized the ex-slave mulatto intellectual as well as his two colored brothers as members of her family. Both Charlotte and her husband devoted their lives to agitation for racial equality. She died in 1914 at the age of seventy-six.

This *Atlantic Monthly* selection, "Life on the Sea Islands," appeared in May 1864, pages 587-596 and June, 1864, pages 666-676.

It was on the afternoon of a warm, murky day late in October that our steamer, the United States, touched the landing at Hilton Head. A motley assemblage had collected on the wharf,—officers, soldiers, and "contrabands" of every size and hue: black was, however, the prevailing color. The first view of Hilton Head is desolate enough,—a long, low, sandy point, stretching out into the sea, with no visible dwellings upon it, except the rows of small white-roofed houses which have lately been built for the freed people.

After signing a paper wherein we declared ourselves loyal to the Government, and wherein, also, were set forth fearful penalties, should we ever be found guilty of treason, we were allowed to land, and immediately took General Saxton's boat, the Flora, for Beaufort. The General was on board, and we were presented to him. He is handsome, courteous, and affable, and looks—as he is—the gentleman and the soldier.

From Hilton Head to Beaufort the same long, low line of sandy coast, bordered by trees; formidable gunboats in the distance, and the gray ruins of an old fort, said to have been built by the Huguenots more than two hundred years ago. Arrived at Beaufort, we found that we had not yet reached our journey's end. While waiting for the boat which was to take us to our island of St. Helena, we had a little time to observe the ancient town. The houses in the main street, which fronts the "Bay," are large and handsome, built of wood, in the usual Southern style, with spacious piazzas, and surrounded by fine trees. We noticed in one yard a magnolia, as high as some of our largest shade-maples, with rich, dark, shining foliage. A large building which was once the Public Library is now a shelter for freed people from Fernandina. Did the Rebels know it, they would doubtless upturn their aristocratic noses, and exclaim in disgust, "To what base uses," etc. We confess that it was highly satisfactory to us to see how the tables are turned, now that "the whirligig of time has brought about its revenges." We saw the market-place, in which slaves were sometimes sold; but we were told that the buying and selling at auction were usually done in Charleston. The arsenal, a large stone structure, was guarded by cannon and sentinels. The houses in the smaller streets had, mostly, a dismantled, desolate look. We saw no one in the streets but soldiers and freed people. There were indications that already Northern improvements had reached this Southern town. Among them was a wharf, a convenience that one wonders how the Southerners could so long have existed without. The more we know of their mode of life, the more are we inclined to marvel at its utter shiftlessness.

Little colored children of every hue were playing about the streets, looking as merry and happy as children ought to look,—now that the evil shadow of Slavery no longer hangs over them. Some of the officers we met did not impress us favorably. They talked flippantly, and sneeringly of the negroes, whom they found we had come down to teach, using an epithet more offensive than gentlemanly. They assured us that there was great danger of Rebel attacks, that the yellow fever prevailed to an alarming extent, and that, indeed, the manufacture of coffins was the only business that was at all flourishing at present. Although by no means daunted by these alarming stories, we were glad when the announcement of our boat relieved us from their edifying conversation. . . .

The next morning L. and I were awakened by the cheerful voices of men and women, children and chickens, in the yard below. We ran to the window, and looked out. Women in bright-colored handkerchiefs, some carrying pails on their heads, were crossing the yard, busy with their morning work; children were playing and tumbling around them. On every face there was a look of serenity and cheerfulness. My heart gave a great throb of happiness as I looked at them, and thought, "They are free! so long down-trodden, so long crushed to the earth, but now in their old homes, forever free!" And I thanked God that I had lived to see this day.

After breakfast Miss T. drove us to Oaklands, our future home. The road leading to the house was nearly choked with weeds. The house itself was in a dilapidated condition, and the yard and garden had a sadly neglected look. But there were roses in bloom; we plucked handfuls of feathery, fragrant acacia-blossoms; ivy crept along the ground and under the house. The freed people on the place seemed glad to see us. After talking with them, and giving some directions for cleaning the house, we drove to the school, in which I was to teach. It is kept in the Baptist Church,—a brick building, beautifully situated in a grove of live-oaks. These trees are the first objects that attract one's attention here: not that they are finer than our Northern oaks, but because of the singular gray moss with which every branch is heavily draped. This hanging moss grows on nearly all the trees, but on none so luxuriantly as on the live-oak. The pendants are often four or five feet long, very graceful and beautiful, but giving the trees a solemn, almost funereal look. The school was opened in September. Many of the children had, however, received instruction during the summer. It was evident that they had made very rapid improvement, and we noticed with pleasure how bright and eager to learn many of them seemed. They sang in rich, sweet tones, and with a peculiar swaying motion of the body, which made their singing the more effective. They sang "Marching Along," with great spirit, and then one of their own hymns, the air of which is beautiful and touching:—

"My sister, you want to git religion,
　Go down in de Lonesome Valley;
My brudder, you want to git religion,
　Go down in de Lonesome Valley.

CHORUS
"Go down in de Lonesome Valley,
　Go down in de Lonesome Valley, my Lord,

Go down in de Lonesome Valley,
    To meet my Jesus dere!

"Oh, feed on milk and honey,
    Oh, feed on milk and honey, my Lord,
    Oh, feed on milk and honey,
        Meet my Jesus dere!
    Oh, John he brought a letter,
    Oh, John he brought a letter, my Lord,
    Oh, Mary and Marta read 'em,
        Meet my Jesus dere!

CHORUS
"Go down in de Lonesome Valley," etc.

They repeat their hymns several times, and while singing keep perfect time with their hands and feet. . . .

The Sunday after our arrival we attended service at the Baptist Church. The people came in slowly; for they have no way of knowing the hour, except by the sun. By eleven they had all assembled, and the church was well filled. They were neatly dressed in their Sunday attire, the women mostly wearing clean, dark frocks, with white aprons and bright-colored head-handkerchiefs. Some had attained to the dignity of straw hats with gay feathers, but these were not nearly as becoming nor as picturesque as the handkerchiefs. The day was warm, and the windows were thrown open as if it were summer, although it was the second day of November. It was very pleasant to listen to the beautiful hymns, and look from the crowd of dark, earnest faces within, upon the grove of noble oaks without. The people sang, "Roll, Jordan, Roll," the grandest of all their hymns, There is a great, rolling wave of sound through it all.

"Mr. Fuller settin' on de Tree ob Life,
    Fur to hear ven Jordan roll.
    Oh, roll, Jordan! roll, Jordan! roll, Jordan roll!

The first day at school was rather trying. Most of my children were very small, and consequently restless. Some were too young to learn the alphabet. These little ones were brought to school because the older children—in whose care their parents leave them while at work—could not come without them. We were therefore willing to have them come, although they seemed to have discovered the secret of perpetual motion, and tried one's patience sadly. But after some days of positive, though not severe treatment, order was brought out of chaos, and I found but little difficulty in managing and quieting the tiniest and most restless spirits. I never before saw children so eager to learn, although I had had several years' experience in New-England schools. Coming to school is a constant delight and recreation to them. They come here as other children go to play. The older ones, during the summer, work in the fields from early morning until eleven or twelve o'clock, and then come into school, after their hard toil in the hot sun, as bright and as anxious to learn as ever.

Of course there are some stupid ones, but these are the minority. The majority learn with wonderful rapidity. Many of the grown people are desirous of learning to read. It is wonderful how a people who have been so long crushed to the earth, so imbruted as these have been,—and they are said to be among the most degraded negroes of the South,—can have so great a desire for knowledge, and such a capability for attaining it. One cannot believe that the haughty Anglo-Saxon race, after centuries of such an experience as these people have had, would be very much superior to them. And one's indignation increases against those who, North as well as South, taunt the colored race with inferiority while they themselves use every means in their power to crush and degrade them, denying them every right and privilege, closing against them every avenue of elevation and improvement. Were they, under such circumstances, intellectual and refined, they would certainly be vastly superior to any other race that ever existed.

After the lessons, we used to talk freely to the children, often giving them slight sketches of some of the great and good men. Before teaching them the "John Brown" song, which they learned to sing with great spirit, Miss T. told them the story of the brave old man who had died for them. I told them about Toussaint, thinking it well they should know what one of their own color had done for his race. They listened attentively, and seemed to understand. We found it rather hard to keep their attention in school. It is not strange, as they have been so entirely unused to intellectual concentration. It is necessary to interest them every moment, in order to keep their thoughts from wandering. Teaching here is consequently far more fatiguing than at the North. In the church, we had of course but one room in which to hear all the children; and to make one's self heard, when there were often as many as a hundred and forty reciting at once, it was necessary to tax the lungs very severely. . . .

Mr. H.'s store was usually crowded, and Cupid was his most valuable assistant. Gay handkerchiefs for turbans, pots and kettles, and molasses, were principally in demand, especially the last. It was necessary to keep the molasses-barrel in the yard, where Cupid presided over it, and harangued and scolded the eager, noisy crowd, collected around, to his heart's content; while up the road leading to the house came constantly processions of men, women, and children, carrying on their heads cans, jugs, pitchers, and even bottles,— anything, indeed, that was capable of containing molasses. It is wonderful with what ease they carry all sorts of things on their heads, —heavy bundles of wood, hoes and rakes, everything, heavy or light, that can be carried in the hands; and I have seen a woman, with a bucketful of water on her head, stoop down and take up another in her hand, without spilling a drop from either.

We noticed that the people had much better taste in selecting materials for dresses than we had supposed. They do not generally like gaudy colors, but prefer neat, quiet patterns. They are, however, very fond of all kinds of jewelry. I once asked the children in school what their ears were for. "To put ring in," promptly replied one of the little girls.

These people are exceedingly polite in their manner towards each other, each new arrival bowing, scraping his feet, and shaking hands with the others, while there are constant greetings, such as, "Huddy?

How's yer lady?" ("How d' ye do? How's your wife?") The hand-shaking is performed with the greatest possible solemnity. There is never the faintest shadow of a smile on anybody's face during this performance. The children, too, are taught to be very polite to their elders, and it is the rarest thing to hear a disrespectful word from a child to his parent, or to any grown person. They have really what the New-Englanders call "beautiful manners."

We made daily visits to the "quarters," which were a few rods from the house. The negro-houses, on this as on most of the other plantations, were miserable little huts, with nothing comfortable or home-like about them, consisting generally of but two very small rooms,—the only way of lighting them, no matter what the state of the weather, being to leave the doors and windows open. The windows, of course, have no glass in them. In such a place, a father and mother with a large family of children are often obliged to live. It is almost impossible to teach them habits of neatness and order, when they are so crowded. We look forward anxiously to the day when better houses shall increase their comfort and pride of appearance.

Oaklands is a very small plantation. There were not more than eight or nine families living on it. Some of the people interested us much. Celia, one of the best, is a cripple. Her master, she told us, was too mean to give his slaves clothes enough to protect them, and her feet and legs were so badly frozen that they required amputation. She has a lovely face,—well-featured and singularly gentle. In every household where there was illness or trouble, Celia's kind, sympathizing face was the first to be seen, and her services were always the most acceptable.

Harry, the foreman on the plantation, a man of a good deal of natural intelligence, was most desirous of learning to read. He came in at night to be taught, and learned very rapidly. I never saw any one more determined to learn. We enjoyed hearing him talk about the "gun-shoot,"—so the people call the capture of Bay Point and

Hilton Head. They never weary of telling you "how Massa run when he hear de fust gun."

"Why did n't you go with him, Harry?" I asked.

"Oh, Miss, 't was n't 'cause Massa did n't try to 'suade me. He tell we dat de Yankees would shoot we, or would sell we to Cuba, an' do all de wust tings to we, when dey come. 'Bery well, Sar,' says I. 'If I go wid you, I be good as dead. If I stay here, I can't be no wust; so if I got to dead, I might 's well dead here as anywhere. So I'll stay here an' wait for de "dam Yankees."' Lor', Miss, I knowed he was n't tellin' de truth all de time."

"But why did n't you believe him, Harry?"

"Dunno, Miss; somehow we hear de Yankees was our friends, an' dat we'd be free when dey come, an' 'appears like we believe *dat*."

I found this to be true of nearly all the people I talked with, and I thought it strange they should have had so much faith in the Northerners. Truly, for years past, they had had but little cause to think them very friendly. Cupid told us that his master was so daring as to come back, after he had fled from the island, at the risk of being taken prisoner by our soldiers; and that he ordered the people to get all the furniture together and take it to a plantation on the opposite side of the creek, and to stay on that side themselves. "So," said Cupid, "dey could jus' sweep us all up in a heap, an' put us in de boat. An' he telled me to take Patience—dat's my wife— an' de chil'en down to a certain pint, an' den I could come back, if I choose. Jus' as if I was gwine to be sich a goat!" added he, with a look and gesture of ineffable contempt. He and the rest of the people, instead of obeying their master, left the place and hid themselves in the woods; and when he came to look for them, not one of all his "faithful servants" was to be found. A few, principally houseservants, had previously been carried away.

In the evenings, the children frequently came in to sing and shout for us. These "shouts" are very strange,—in truth, almost indescribable. It is necessary to hear and see in order to have any clear idea of them. The children form a ring, and move around in a kind of shuffling dance, singing all the time. Four or five stand apart, and sing very energetically, clapping their hands, stamping their feet, and rocking their bodies to and fro. These are the musicians, to whose performance the shouters keep perfect time. The grown people on this plantation did not shout, but they do on some of the other plantations. It is very comical to see little children, not more than three or four years old, entering into the performance with all their might. But the shouting of the grown people is rather solemn and impressive than otherwise. We cannot determine whether it has a religious character or not. Some of the people tell us that it has, others that it has not. But as the shouts of the group are always in connection with their religious meetings, it is probable that they are the barbarous expression of religion, handed down to them from their African ancestors, and destined to pass away under the influence of Christian teachings. The people on this island have no songs. They sing only hymns, and most of these are sad. Prince, a large black boy from a neighboring plantation, was the principal shouter among the children. It seemed impossible for him to keep still for a moment. His performances were most amusing specimens of Ethiopian gymnastics. Amaretta the younger, a cunning, kittenish little creature of only six years old, had a remarkably sweet voice. Her favorite hymn, which we used to hear her singing to herself as she walked through the yard, is one of the oddest we have heard:—

"What makes ole Satan follow me so?
Satan got nuttin' 't all fur to do wid me.

CHORUS
"Tiddy Rosa, hold your light!
Brudder Tony, hold your light!
All de member, hold bright light
On Canaan's shore!"

This is one of the most spirited shouting-tunes. "Tiddy" is their word for sister.

A very queer-looking old man came into the store one day. He was dressed in a complete suit of brilliant Brussels carpeting. Probably it had been taken from his master's house after the "gun-shoot"; but he looked so very dignified that we did not like to question him about it. The people called him Doctor Crofts,—which was, I believe, his master's name, his own being Scipio. He was very jubilant over the new state of things, and said to Mr. H.,—"Don't hab me feelins hurt now. Used to hab me feelins hurt all de time. But don't hab 'em hurt now no more." Poor old soul! We rejoiced with him that he and his brethren no longer have their "feelins" hurt, as in the old time.

On the Sunday before Thanksgiving, General Saxton's noble Proclamation was read at church. We could not listen to it without emotion. The people listened with the deepest attention, and seemed to understand and appreciate it. Whittier has said of it and its writer,—"It is the most beautiful and touching official document I ever read. God bless him! 'The bravest are the tenderest.'"

General Saxton is truly worthy of the gratitude and admiration with which the people regard him. His unfailing kindness and consideration for them—so different from the treatment they have sometimes received at the hands of other officers—have caused them to have unbounded confidence in General "*Saxby*," as they call him.

After the service, there were six couples married. Some of the dresses were unique. One was particularly fine,—doubtless a cast-off dress of the bride's former mistress. The silk and lace, ribbons, feathers and flowers, were in a rather faded and decayed condition. But, comical as the costumes were, we were not disposed to laugh at them. We were too glad to see the poor creatures trying to lead right and virtuous lives. The legal ceremony, which was formerly scarcely known among them, is now everywhere consecrated. The constant and earnest advice of the minister and teachers has not been given in vain; nearly every Sunday there are several couples married in church. Some of them are people who have grown old together.

Thanksgiving-Day was observed as a general holiday. According to General Saxton's orders, an ox had been killed on each plantation, that the people might that day have fresh meat, which was a great luxury to them, and, indeed, to all of us. In the morning, a large number—superintendents, teachers, and freed people—assembled in the Baptist Church. It was a sight not soon to be forgotten,—that crowd of eager, happy black faces, from which the shadow of Slavery had forever passed. "Forever free! forever free!" those magical words of the Proclamation were constantly singing themselves in my soul. After an appropriate prayer and sermon by Mr. P., and singing by the people, General Saxton made a short, but spirited speech, urging the young men to enlist in the regiment then forming under Colonel Higginson. Mrs. Gage told the people how the slaves in Santa Cruz had secured their liberty. It was something entirely new and strange to them to hear a woman speak in public; but they listened with great attention, and seemed much interested. Before dispersing, they sang "Marching Along," which is an especial favorite with them. It was a very happy Thanksgiving-Day for all of us. The weather was delightful; oranges and figs were hanging on the trees; roses, oleanders, and japonicas were blooming out-of-doors; the sun was warm and bright; and over all shone gloriously the blessed light of Freedom,—Freedom forevermore!

A few days before Christmas, we were delighted at receiving a beautiful Christmas Hymn from Whittier, written by request, especially for our children. They learned it very easily, and enjoyed singing it. We showed them the writer's picture, and told them he was a very good friend of theirs, who felt the deepest interest in them, and had written this hymn expressly for them to sing,—which made them very proud and happy. Early Christmas morning, we were wakened by the people knocking at the doors and windows, and shouting, "Merry Christmas!" After distributing some little presents among them, we went to the church, which had been decorated with holly, pine, cassena, mistletoe, and the hanging moss, and had a very Christmas-like look. The children of our school assembled there, and we gave them the nice, comfortable clothing, and the picture-books, which had been kindly sent by some Philadelphia ladies. There were at least a hundred and fifty children present. It was very pleasant to see their happy, expectant little faces. To them, it was a wonderful Christmas-Day,—such as they had never dreamed of before. There was cheerful sunshine without, lighting up the beautiful moss-drapery of the oaks, and looked in joyously through the open windows; and there were bright faces and glad hearts within. The long, dark night of the Past, with all its sorrows and its fears, was forgotten; and for the Future,—the eyes of these freed children see no clouds in it. It is full of sunlight, they think, and they trust in it, perfectly.

After the distribution of the gifts, the children were addressed by some of the gentlemen present. They then sang Whittier's Hymn, the "John Brown" song, and several of their own hymns, among them a very singular one, commencing,—

> "I wonder where my mudder gone;
>   Sing, O graveyard!
> Graveyard ought to know me;
>   Ring, Jerusalem!
> Grass grow in de graveyard;
>   Sing, O graveyard!
> Graveyard ought to know me;
>   Ring, Jerusalem!"

They improvise many more words as they sing. It is one of the strangest, most mournful things I ever heard. It is impossible to give any idea of the deep pathos of the refrain,—

> "Sing, O graveyard!"

In this, and many other hymns, the words seem to have but little meaning; but the tones,—a whole lifetime of despairing sadness is concentrated in them. They sing, also, "Jehovyah, Hallelujah," which we like particularly:—

> "De foxes hab holes,
>   An' de birdies hab nes',
>   But de Son ob Man he hab not where
>   To lay de weary head.

CHORUS
> "Jehovyah, Hallelujah! De Lord He will purvide!
> Jehovyah, Hallelujah! De Lord He will purvide!"

They repeat the words many times "De foxes hab holes," and the succeeding lines, are sung in the most touching, mournful tones; and then the chorus—"Jehovyah, Hallelujah"—swells forth triumphantly, in glad contrast.

Christmas night, the children came in and had several grand shouts. They were too happy to keep still.

"Oh, Miss, all I want to do is to sing and shout!" said our little pet, Amaretta. And sing and shout she did, to her heart's content.

She read nicely, and was very fond of books. The tiniest children are delighted to get a book in their hands. Many of them already know their letters. The parents are eager to have them learn. They sometimes said to me,—

"Do, Miss, let de chil'en learn eberyting dey can. *We* nebber hab no chance to learn nuttin', but we wants de chil'en to learn."

They are willing to make many sacrifices that their children may attend school. One old woman, who had a large family of children and grandchildren, came regularly to school in the winter, and took her seat among the little ones. She was at least sixty years old. Another woman—who had one of the best faces I ever saw—came daily, and brought her baby in her arms. It happened to be one of the best babies in the world, a perfect little "model of deportment," and allowed its mother to pursue her studies without interruption.

While taking charge of the store, one day, one of the men who came in told me a story which interested me much. He was a carpenter, living on this island, and just before the capture of Port Royal had been taken by his master to the mainland,—"the Main," as the people call it,—to assist in building some houses which were to shelter the families of the Rebels in case the "Yankees" should come. The master afterward sent him back to the island, providing him with a pass, to bring away a boat and some of the people. On his arrival he found that the Union troops were in possession, and determined to remain here with his family instead of returning to his master. Some of his fellow-servants, who had been left on "the Main," hearing that the Federal troops had come, resolved to make their escape to the islands. They found a boat of their master's, out of which a piece six feet square had been cut. In the night they went to the boat, which had been sunk in a creek near the house, measured the hole, and, after several nights' work in the woods, made a piece large enough to fit in. They then mended and sank it again, as they had found it. The next night five of them embarked. They had a perilous journey, often passing quite near the enemy's boats. They travelled at night, and in the day ran close up to the shore out of sight. Sometimes they could hear the hounds, which had been sent in pursuit of them, baying in the woods. Their provisions gave out, and they were nearly exhausted. At last they succeeded in passing all the enemy's boats, and reached one of our gunboats in safety. They were taken on board and kindly cared for, and then sent to this island, where their families, who had no hope of ever seeing them again, welcomed them with great rejoicing.

We were also told the story of two girls, one about ten, the other fifteen, who, having been taken by their master up into the country, on the mainland, at the time of the capture of the islands, determined to try to escape to their parents, who had been left on this island. They stole away at night, and travelled through woods and swamps for two days, without eating. Sometimes their strength gave out, and they would sink down, thinking they could go no farther; but they had brave little hearts, and got up again and struggled on, till at last they reached Port-Royal Ferry, in a state of utter exhaustion. They were seen there by a boatload of people who were also making their escape. The boat was too full to take them in; but the people, on reaching this island, told the children's father of their whereabouts, and he immediately took a boat, and hastened to the ferry. The poor little creatures were almost wild with joy when they saw him. When they were brought to their mother, she fell down "jes' as if she was dead,"—so our informant expressed it,—overpowered with joy on beholding the "lost who were found."

New-Year's-Day—Emancipation-Day—was a glorious one to us. The morning was quite cold, the coldest we had experienced; but we were determined to go to the celebration at Camp Saxton,—the camp of the First Regiment South-Carolina Volunteers,—whither the General and Colonel Higginson had bidden us, on this, "the greatest day in the nation's history." We enjoyed perfectly the exciting scene on board the Flora. There was an eager, wondering crowd of the freed people in their holiday-attire, with the gayest of head-handkerchiefs, the whitest of aprons, and the happiest of faces. The band was playing, the flags streaming, everybody talking merrily and feeling strangely happy. The sun shone brightly, the very waves seemed to partake of the universal gayety, and danced and sparkled more joyously than ever before. Long before we reached Camp Saxton we could see the beautiful grove, and the ruins of the old Huguenot fort near it. Some companies of the First Regiment were drawn up in line under the trees, near the landing, to receive us. A find, soldierly-looking set of men; their brilliant dress against the trees (they were then wearing red pantaloons) invested them with a semibarbaric splendor. It was my good fortune to find among the officers an old friend,—and what it was to meet a friend from the North, in our isolated Southern life, no one can imagine who has not experienced the pleasure. Letters were an unspeakable luxury,—we hungered for them, we could never get enough; but to meet old friends,—that was "too much, too much," as the people here say, when they are very much in earnest. Our friend took us over the camp, and showed us all the arrangements. Everything looked clean and comfortable, much neater, we were told, than in most of the white camps. An officer told us that he had never seen a regiment in which the men were so honest. "In many other camps," said he, "the colonel and the rest of us would find it necessary to place a guard before our tents. We never do it here. They are left entirely unguarded. Yet nothing has ever been touched." We were glad to know that. It is a remarkable fact, when we consider that these men have all their lives been *slaves;* and we know what the teachings of Slavery are.

The celebration took place in the beautiful grove of live-oaks adjoining the camp. It was the largest grove we had seen. I wish it were possible to describe fitly the scene which met our eyes as we sat upon the stand, and looked down on the crowd before us. There were the black soldiers in their blue coats and scarlet pantaloons, the officers of this and other regiments in their handsome uniforms, and crowds of lookers-on,—men, women, and children, of every complexion, grouped in various attitudes under the moss-hung trees. The faces of all wore a happy, interested look. The exercises commenced with a prayer by the chaplain of the regiment. An ode, written for the occasion by Professor Zachos, was read by him, and then sung. Colonel Higginson then introduced Dr. Brisbane, who read the President's Proclamation, which was enthusiastically cheered. Rev. Mr. French presented to the Colonel two very elegant flags, a gift to the regiment from the Church of the Puritans, accompanying them by an appropriate and enthusiastic speech. At its conclusion, before Colonel Higginson could reply, and while he still stood holding the flags in his hand, some of the colored people, of their own accord, commenced singing, "My Country, 't is of thee." It was a touching and beautiful incident, and sent a thrill through all our hearts. The Colonel was deeply moved by it. He said that that reply was far more effective than any speech he could make. But he did make one of those stirring speeches which are "half battles." All hearts swelled with emotion as we listened to his glorious words,— "stirring the soul like the sound of a trumpet."

His soldiers are warmly attached to him, and he evidently feels towards them all as if they were his children. The people speak of him as "the officer who never leaves his regiment for pleasure," but devotes himself, with all his rich gifts of mind and heart, to their interests. It is not strange that his judicious kindness, ready sympathy, and rare fascination of manner should attach them to him strongly. He is one's ideal of an officer. There is in him much of the grand, knightly spirit of the olden time,—scorn of all that is mean and ignoble, pity for the weak, chivalrous devotion to the cause of the oppressed. . . .

L. and I had one day an interesting visit to a plantation about six miles from ours. The house is beautifully situated in the midst of noble pine-trees, on the banks of a large creek. The place was owned by a very wealthy Rebel family, and is one of the pleasantest and healthiest on the island. The vicinity of the pines makes it quite healthy. There were a hundred and fifty people on it,—one hundred of whom had come from Edisto Island at the time of its evacuation by our troops. There were not houses enough to accommodate them, and they had to take shelter in barns, out-houses, or any other place they could find. They afterwards built rude dwellings for themselves, which did not, however, afford them much protection in bad weather. The superintendent told us that they were well-behaved and industrious. One old woman interested us greatly. Her name was Daphne; she was probably more than a hundred years old; had had fifty grandchildren, sixty-five great-grandchildren, and three great-great-grandchildren. Entirely blind, she yet seemed very cheerful and happy. She told us that she was brought with her parents from Africa at the time of the Revolution. A bright, happy old face was hers, and she retained her faculties remarkably well. Fifteen of the people had escaped from the mainland in the previous spring. They were pursued, and one of them was overtaken by his master in the swamps. A fierce grapple ensued,—the master on horseback, the man on foot. The former drew a pistol and shot his slave through the arm, shattering it dreadfully. Still, the heroic man fought desperately, and at last succeeded in unhorsing his master, and beating him until he was senseless. He then made his escape, and joined the rest of the party.

One of the most interesting sights we saw was a baptism among the people. On one Sunday there were a hundred and fifty baptized in the creek near the church. They looked very picturesque in their white aprons and bright frocks and handkerchiefs. As they marched in procession down to the river's edge, and during the ceremony, the spectators, with whom the banks were crowded, sang glad, triumphant songs. The freed people on this island are all Baptists. . . .

In April we left Oaklands, which had always been considered a particularly unhealthy place during the summer, and came to "Seaside," a plantation on another and healthier part of the island. The place contains nearly a hundred people. The house is large and comparatively comfortable. Notwithstanding the name, we have not even a distant glimpse of the sea, although we can sometimes hear its roar. At low tide there is not a drop of water to be seen,—only dreary stretches of marsh-land, reminding us of the sad outlook of Mariana in the Moated Grange,—

"The level waste and rounding gray."

But at night we have generally a good sea-breeze, and during the hottest weather the air is purer and more invigorating than in many parts of the island.

On this, as on several other large plantations, there is a "Praise-House," which is the special property of the people. Even in the old days of Slavery, they were allowed to hold meetings here; and they still keep up the custom. They assemble on several nights of the week, and on Sunday afternoons. First, they hold what is called the "Praise-Meeting," which consists of singing, praying, and preaching. We have heard some of the old negro preachers make prayers that were really beautiful and touching. In these meetings they sing only the church-hymns which the Northern ministers have taught them, and which are far less suited to their voices than their own. At the close of the Praise-Meeting they all shake hands with each other in the most solemn manner. Afterward, as a kind of appendix, they have a grand "shout," during which they sing their own hymns. Maurice, an old blind man, leads the singing. He has a remarkable voice, and sings with the greatest enthusiasm. The first shout that we witnessed in the Praise-House impressed us very much. The large, gloomy room, with its blackened walls—the wild, whirling dance of the shouters,—the crowd of dark, eager faces gathered around,—the figure of the old blind man, whose excitement could hardly be controlled, and whose attitude and gestures while singing were very fine, —and over all, the red glare of the burning pine-knot, which shed a circle of light around it, but only seemed to deepen and darken the shadows in the other parts of the room,—these all formed a wild, strange, and deeply impressive picture, not soon to be forgotten.

Maurice's especial favorite is one of the grandest hymns that we have yet heard:—

> "De tallest tree in Paradise
> De Christian calls de Tree ob Life,
> An' I hope dat trumpet blow me home
> To my New Jerusalem.

CHORUS
> "Blow, Gabriel! trumpet, blow louder, louder!
> An' I hope dat trumpet blow me home
> To my New Jerusalem!

> "Paul and Silas jail-bound
> Sing God's praise both night and day,
> An' I hope dat trumpet blow me home
> To my new Jerusalem.

CHORUS
> "Blow, Gabriel! trumpet blow louder, louder!

An' I hope dat trumpet blow me home
To my New Jerusalem!"

The chorus has a glad, triumphal sound, and in singing it the voice of old Maurice rings out in wonderfully clear, trumpet-like tones. His blindness was caused by a blow on the head from a loaded whip. He was struck by his master in a fit of anger. "I feel great distress when I become blind," said Maurice; "but den I went to seek de Lord; and eber since I know I see in de next world, I always hab great satisfaction." We are told that the master was not a "hard man" except when in a passion, and then he seems to have been very cruel.

One of the women on the place, Old Bess, bears on her limbs many marks of the whip. Some of the scars are three and four inches long. She was used principally as a house-servant. She says, "Ebery time I lay de table I put cowskin on one end, an' I git beatin' and thumpin' all de time. Hab all kinds o' work to do, and sich a gang [of children] to look after! One person couldn't git along wid so much work, so it go wrong, and den I git beatin'."

But the cruelty of Bess's master sinks into insignificance, when compared with the far-famed wickedness of another slave-holder, known all over the island as "Old Joe Eddings." There seem to have been no bounds to his cruelty and licentiousness; and the people tell tales of him which make one shudder. We were once asking some questions about him of an old, half-witted woman, a former slave of his. The look of horror and loathing which overspread her face was perfectly indescribable, as, with upraised hands, she exclaimed, "What! Old Joe Eddings? Lord, Missus, he second to none in de world but de Debil!" She had, indeed, good cause to detest him; for, some years before, her daughter, a young black girl, maddened by his persecutions, had thrown herself into the creek and been drowned, after having been severely beaten for refusing to degrade herself. Outraged, despised, and black, she yet preferred death to dishonor. But these are things too heart-sickening to dwell upon. God alone

Daily the long-oppressed people of these islands are demonstrating their capacity for improvement in learning and labor. What they have accomplished in one short year exceeds our utmost expectations. Still the sky is dark; but through the darkness we can discern a brighter future. We cannot but feel that the day of final and entire deliverance, so long and often so hopelessly prayed for, has at length begun to dawn upon this much-enduring race. An old freedman said to me one day, "De Lord make me suffer long time, Miss. 'Peared like we nebber was gwine to git troo. But now we's free. He bring us all out right at las'." In their darkest hours they have clung to Him, and we know He will not forsake them.

> "The poor among men shall rejoice,
> For the terrible one is brought to nought."

While writing these pages I am once more nearing Port Royal. The Fortunate Isles of Freedom are before me. I shall again tread the flower-skirted woodpaths of St. Helena, and the sombre pines and bearded oaks shall whisper in the sea-wind their grave welcome. I shall dwell again among "mine own people." I shall gather my scholars about me, and see smiles of greeting break over their dusky faces. My heart sings a song of thanksgiving, at the thought that even I am permitted to do something for a long-abused race, and aid in promoting a higher, holier, and happier life on the Sea Islands.

TESTIMONY
OF THE
CANADIAN FUGITIVES

Benjamin Drew, a Boston abolitionist acting in cooperation with officers of the Canadian Anti-Slavery Society, visited various towns of Upper Canada around the middle 1850's, interviewing scores of refugees from the slave states and copying their words soon after they were spoken. For reasons of safety, he protected the identity of his informants and used fictitious names. There were about 30,000 Negroes at that time in Upper Canada, mostly adults who had once been slaves. John P. Jewett, the prominent abolitionist-minded publisher of Boston who had unexpectedly reaped a fortune from printing *Uncle Tom's Cabin* in 1852, vouched for the integrity and intelligence of Drew.

The testimony tends to stress well-known gross abuses, but some of the ex-slaves offer fresh insights into the working of the plantation system. These selections come from Benjamin Drew (ed.), *The Refugee: Narratives of Fugitive Slaves in Canada Related by Themselves* (Boston, 1856), pages 260-270, 276-280, 301-305, 314-320.

EDWARD HICKS

I was born and raised in old Virginia, Lunenburg county, and was sold when a well-grown boy—was put on the block at the court house and sold. I was frightened at being up there on the block, and was afraid of being carried out of the country. A trader on his way to New Orleans bought me. He took me to his pen at Brunswick court house. I being very obedient, he thought I wouldn't run; but I determined to run if I could, for I thought if I got to New Orleans, I *was* at the shutting-up place. He waited a day or two to attend another sale fifty miles off, taking us with him—perhaps forty or fifty. We went by stages. I being so obedient, he turned me out to bring water and do errands in general, while he waited for the sale at Brunswick court house. In this time I thought about my mother and brother in the place where I was raised, and thought 't was about time to run. I ran; but did not know what way to go, and took into the pines. Now, after I had done this, I began to study what I should do for something to eat: then I was in a strange country. I continued there for four days without any food except sassafras leaves, and I found water. After that, I found an old colored man. I told him how the case was with me, and asked for a bit of bread. He told me to come to his house at night, at a certain hour, and he would give me a mouthful to eat. I went to the house, got some food; and, behold, the patrollers were out that night, and they came within one of catching me. Just as I had stepped out of the house, they came right in. The old man came out a little before day and whistled. I went to him, and he put me on the way to Lunenburg.

I travelled on about twelve miles, when it was so dark I dared not walk any further. I made for the bush, and laid a stick with the big end the way I was to go. That night about dark, I got up and started again. I went on, and struck a creek near midnight, called Earn's Creek,—from Earn's Creek, I came to Stony Creek. Day overtaking me, I had to make into the willows on the creek. The bloodhounds that day, of their own accord, having such knowledge, gave me a little race: I went down into the creek, nothing out but my head, among big water moccasin snakes, which I kept off with a stick. The dogs I saw,—they heard me, but there was no one to hearken them on. At night I left the creek, and went up into the neighborhood of the house where I was born and raised: I saw some of my friends and brothers there, and I got something to eat. I was then advised (as the advertisement was just out from the *nigger*-trader) to go on to an old house where cotton was kept, and there stay until the advertisement was over. For they drive for runaways there with bloodhounds, and a great many men moving abreast, so that they will have a man unless he is a long distance under the ground. I went to the cotton house, and got under the cotton, and stayed till the drive was over—some two or three days.

I came out then, and made for the bush. I stayed till that trader went down with that company of colored people, and sold them and came back. I was out all the winter in caves and barns. In the spring the trader came back. There was a white man in Lunenburg, that wanted to buy me. The trader heard of it, and said, "I'll sell him, if you think you can get him: a *nigger* that will stay in the woods all winter, I won't have him. What will you give me for him?" It was settled at eight hundred dollars: then he sent out some of his boys to tell me, and in a few days I went to him.

He had four farms. I commenced to work right at the great house. I stayed there three years, I guess: then he died. Then every man had to come up to be appraised: about sixty of us were appraised. The same old trader (S—— N——) came up to buy me again, chains and handcuffs all in his hand. He swore that the "nigger" that ran away from him, was the one he'd have, and the chains should not leave him, till he'd got him to Orleans. At twelve o'clock, I went to the kitchen to get my breakfast, and stepped right on, out into the bush. The sale was coming on in about a week, and the trader had come on to brag what he would do,—I stepped out right in the bush.

I was appraised and given to a young lady who thought it necessary to hire me out, right in the bush, where I was. A man hired
me at about half price. He was a good man,—no bad man will hire
one in the bush, because he won't come to him to save his life, and
only the big traders can afford to have driving done. After I got to
him, he put me to work at the great house, and he liked me so
well, he bought me.

He got a man to oversee at the great house, who was determined
to make more than any farmer in that country. He began to fight,
kick, and knock over. We were going along, suckering tobacco one
day; a couple of worms were found—these big, horned worms—
lying on the ground in the rows: we had not seen them as we were
breaking the suckers. He called the two men who went by them, and
made each take one of the worms and bite its head off. I passed a
small worm,— "G— d— you," says he, "you bite the worm's head,
and suck the stuff out of him: you may run away,—you've got to a
place now, where if you run nine miles into h—, we'll go in for you
up to our armpits. You've made three runs, now you've made a
bad stand." I told him I shouldn't bite the worm's head off: it was a
thing I never had done, and I wasn't used to it, and wouldn't do it.
He made to me with his bull whip, very long, and struck me three
or four times; the third or fourth time, I got hold of it. He then
turned to strike me with the butt,—but being too anxious, he let
too much of it go over my shoulder, and I caught the other part,
that he was going to knock me down with. S—— H——, if he gets
hold of that paper, he'll know all about it. He hollowed for help,—
he wanted the other colored people to help him. They all passed on
with their rows, but would not. I then having hold of both ends of
the whip, jerked it out of his hands and ran. I did not intend to
carry the whip far, but there was no stop for *me* then. I went on
to the bush; he mounted his horse, and started off for men and
bloodhounds. He then came back with the company and the
hounds, stripped the head man and whipped him, because he did

not help take me. I was then preparing to keep the bloodhounds from following me. I had gathered up some wild onions, and knew what to do.

The master now came home. He tells the overseers, that he shall pay a dollar a day for every day that I was gone, for he had no business to make that disturbance among the people. They chased me that day, but could not follow me beyond the place where I had put on the onions. It takes a mighty old hound to follow that track. I stayed three weeks, and then went in home. When I got home, the old man got hold of it then, and I was not flogged. At the end of the year, my lost time was brought against the overseer. The overseer left, and went to oversee for another man, named S—— S——, at the edge of Brunswick Co. My master being sickly, in some way, his boys being sportsmen, and gambled, got involved, and had to sell part of his hands, at sheriff's sale I suppose. I was again put on the block and sold, and that overseer, S— H——, persuaded his employer, S——, to buy me, so he could get his spite of me. S—— bought me and sent me on to the quarter: put on leg goggles, a band of thin iron round each ancle, with a piece of wood, banded with iron, sticking from each with a rivet. A man cannot run with them on: the iron plays round and the long piece whips his legs as he runs. Each goggle weighs about three pounds. The overseer put them right on, as soon as I got there.

The master had plenty of dogs, four of which were regular "nigger bloodhounds," worth one hundred dollars or more apiece. That was the first time I began studying head-work. I had been running about in the bush without much object, but now I began studying head-work: while in this condition, it put my mind off to study what to do now. Every day I was sure of my whipping though—that was sure—with the loaded bull whip—loaded at both ends: every blow would cut through the skin. I could n't run—could n't get away. I lay down studying, and got up studying, how to get out of the condition I was placed in.

One night it came to my mind that I would go to the blacksmith's shop. After every person was asleep, and every thing appeared still, I got into the window and got a rasp. I put it away where I could get hold of it, knowing that if I cut it part through, they would see it, and band me stronger. That night I studied that I would go down deep, right there in the yard, where they machine cotton and pack cotton right down among the seeds—way down—five feet I guess I went down,—and that the bloodhounds would not find me, as they would look round for me outside. I studied that as hard as a Philadelphia lawyer ever studied a case: if he studies as hard as I studied that, he'll give a right judgment.

I went down the night after I got the rasp, taking the rasp with me. The cotton seed and motes tumbled in after me as I went down, and buried me up entirely. They walked over me: I could feel the rattling over me. I could not rifle in there. The next night I came out, and commenced rifling to get off the goggles. They had been out all day with some drivers and the bloodhounds, expecting, as I had the goggles on, to catch me directly. I sat up on the upper floor, where I could see by the light of the moon or stars, and there I rifled away; I rifled faithfully, and got one off that night,—but I had to break it away some, and got the skin off my leg. Before day I went down into the hole again.

The next night I came out and rifled off the other: it came off easier than the other. Now I've got to go down again. Into the same hole I went—'t would n't do to come out yet. They had driven the second day, and I was afraid they would the third. I had eaten nothing all this time, nor drank a drop. The next night about dark, I jumped out and went into the bush. I knew all about that neighborhood, and which way to go. I got me an old scythe-blade, and broke off a piece and made me a knife. This I found at the machine as I was on the way to the bush. Then I killed me a pig, took him on my back and walked five miles. I dressed him, singed off the hair, and before he was fairly dressed, I had his ears on the coals broiling.

Another consideration struck me now. It would be death to go back to that place: I must get to a free land now. I had got the irons off—that I knew. I came out of that county, went into a neighboring county, into the bush, and staid out six months. I heard of some free people coming on to the Ohio, and I thought I would get in the crowd. We came on with a white man who had formed an attachment to a colored girl, and as she was coming, he determined to leave too, although he was a regular patroller. I came on with him as a waiter and servant, and very faithfully I worked too. We travelled with horses and wagons, but some had to walk. I had to pull at the baggage,—I would have pulled a wagon all through myself but what I'd have come. I was concealed the first part of the way; all the food and clothes piled on me in the wagon, which was very uncomfortable. You do n't know how much I endured. At night I would get out and walk. We succeeded until we got to Point Pleasant; within three or four miles of the ferry, we met men at different times, telling this tale— "If you take your slaves this way they'll all get free,—for you'll get 'em on the Ohio side: I would n't take that man; if you want to sell him, you can get your money right in this place," etc.

He began to fear that they'd think he was running away slaves. "Look here," says he, "to-night you'd better take a skiff and cross the river—these folks have got passes to show, and you have not." This made me uneasy—I knew nothing about padding a skiff: I might get off into the middle of the river, and then paddle back to the same shore. I then said to him, "It is a matter of course that we go on, and I go on as you said, and you've a right to take your slave wherever you please." Now he told me, "Do you go off, and come up to us when we get to the ferry-place." I said, "That won't do." We reasoned considerably about it: he was a man that would hear to a little reason, and so we reasoned. Now he told me, "Suppose I sell you, and I come back and steal you, and we divide the money?" He was turning now; he'd been into the town that day: enough wanted to buy me, but they did n't want the women. I told him, that would n't do—that was n't our bargain—I had worked for him all the way, and his agreement was to take me over the ferry, and go on to the farm he was to take, and work for him one year at clearing, etc. We came on, all hands, down to the ferry at Point Pleasant,—some were for putting me in the wagon, and covering me; but they would search the wagon. So I walked with the rest.

At the ferry, the guard who watches all who cross the ferry—a great, big white man, who looked rather severe, quizzed my master, whether I was his slave, and questioned so close, that the white man began to grow weak in the knees, and I saw it: he trembled. I was scared for him, and I was scared about being taken myself—it was a scaring time. The guard told him the consequences—of going to the penitentiary, if he were going off with another man's slave. He trembled, and got weak, so that he did not get over it, till he got way out into the Ohio. We were commanded to get aboard the ferry-boat, and over we went. I walked on behind him, as he went up the hill: he yet trembled, and so did I, not knowing what might take place yet. I felt joyful that I had got over, but it was no time to rejoice there. We put the man in the wagon, and dragged him: he was more scared than he ought to have been.

I went to work with him in Ohio, according to promise. After we had begun, it got clear back to where I started from, that I was in Ohio. I made out that I was a man from Cincinnati, and was hired for money: but it got back home, that I was in Ohio. He then told me to leave. I understood that there was a reward of five hundred dollars offered to any one who would take me over the river to the Kentucky side. I had been there as near as I can tell about six months when I got this news. I left him and was concealed at Gallipolis, at old man Isaac Browner's house—he is dead now, and 't wont do any hurt to mention his name. He put me in a bedtick on which he placed his children, who were sick of measles. I was in the straw-tick, the feather-bed was above me, and then the children. This was so, that if they came to search for the sake of the reward, they might not move the sick. I stayed there one day: I cared nothing for the heat, discomfort, nor sickness. All I thought of was to get off clear. At night-fall, I all alone came to the wharf to hail a boat—he told me how—to hollow "passenger." The boat was for the salt-works at Kanawha. If I had gone on board they would have taken me sure, because the boat was going to the place I did not want to go. The boat did not, however, put in for me, and I had to go back and get concealed again. The next day, they disguised me,—I went down to the wharf—a boat was coming which was bound for Pittsburg: it touched the wharf-boat,—there was no freight and only three passengers; a gentleman and a lady, and myself; they stepped aboard, and so did I,—a little bell rung, and away went the boat: when, looking back, I saw two men whom I knew, standing on a place, where they could see every man who came down to the boat. But they did not know me and the boat came on.

The river was high, and we came on slowly. I did not sleep for four nights at all—dozed a little in daytime. There was another boat coming behind,—"Clipper, No. 2,"—and I was afraid she was in pursuit of me. I fired up harder on that account: although I expected to get nothing for my work, I worked sharp. After we had started out, the clerk came round with his book and pen. I tried to dodge, but when he touched me, I thought I was gone. But he only wanted the money: I gave him all I had, and he returned me ten cents. I had my victuals for my work. At Pittsburg, I left a handkerchief of victuals, which I had put up, I was in such a hurry. I went up into the town, and inquired for the country, where I could get work. I worked not many miles from Pittsburg, and got a little money, and then concluded to come to Canada, where I would be safe.

I have been here about six years. I like Canada well,—I am satisfied with it. I have got a little property together, worth some two thousand dollars.

Liquor is right along the road here, and some make fools of themselves: but I mind my business, and am doing well.

My opinion of slavery is, that it ought to be broken down. If the white people were to set the slaves free, and offer to hire them, they would jump at the chance: they would n't cut throats.

We have got some good white friends in the United States. If it had not been for them, I would not have got here.

HENRY BLUE

I learned the trade of a blacksmith in Kentucky. I should have been perfectly miserable to have had to work all my life for another man for nothing. As soon as I had arrived to years of discretion, I felt determined that I would not be a slave all my days. My master was a kind and honorable man; purchased no slaves himself: what he had, came by marriage. He used to say it was wrong to hold slaves, and a good many who hold them say the same. It's a habit—they mean, they say, to set them free at such a time, or such a time,—by and by they die, and the children hold on to the slaves.

I purchased my freedom, and remained in Kentucky awhile; then removed to Cincinnati; thence to Chatham. Every thing goes well with me in Canada; I have no reason to complain.

I think that if a slaveholder offers his servant freedom, on condition that he will earn and pay a certain sum, and the slave accepts freedom on that condition, he is bound in honor to pay the sum promised.

Some poor, ignorant fellows may be satisfied with their condition as slaves, but, as a general thing, they are not satisfied with being slaves.

THOMAS HEDGEBETH

I was born free, in Halifax Co. North Carolina, where I lived thirty-five years. About ten years ago, I removed to Indiana. My father was a farmer, half white, who ran through his farm. If a white man there brings a great account, the white man would carry it against the colored,—the law there does not favor colored people. I cannot read or write. A free-born man in North Carolina is as much oppressed, in one sense, as the slave: I was not allowed to go to school. I recollect when I was a boy, a colored man came from Ohio, and opened a school, but it was broken up. I was in the field ploughing with my father,—he said he wished we could go and learn. I think it an outrageous sin and shame, that a free colored man could not be taught. My ignorance has a very injurious effect on my prospects and success. I blame the State of North Carolina—the white people of that State—for it. I am now engaged in a troublesome lawsuit, about the title to my estate, which I would not have got into, had I known how to read and write.

There were lots of slaves in the neighborhood where I was raised. After I grew up to take notice of things, I found I was oppressed as well as they. I thought it a sin then, for one man to hold another. I never was allowed to visit among the slaves,—had I been caught visiting them, I should have been fined: if a slave had visited me, he would have been whipped. This prevented my having much intercourse with them, except when I was hired to work by the masters. The conversation among the slaves was, that they worked hard, and got no benefit,—that the masters got it all. They knew but little about the good of themselves,—they often grumbled about food and clothing,—that they had not enough. I never heard a colored man grumbling about that here. They were generally religious,— they believed in a just God, and thought the owners wrong in punish-

ing them in the way they were punished. A good many were so ignorant that they did not know any better, than to suppose that they
were made for slavery, and the white men for freedom. Some, however, would talk about freedom, and think they ought to be free.

I have often been insulted, abused, and imposed upon, and had
advantage taken of me by the whites in North Carolina, and could
not help myself.

When I was twenty-one, I went to vote, supposing it would be
allowed. The 'Squire, who held the box objected, and said no colored
man was allowed to vote. I felt very badly about it,—I felt cheap,
and I felt vexed: but I knew better than make an answer,—I would
have been knocked down certain. Unless I took off my hat, and made
a bow to a white man, when I met him, he would rip out an oath,—
"d—n you, you mulatto, ain't you got no politeness? do n't you
know enough to take off your hat to a white man?" On going into a
store, I was required to take off my hat.

I have seen slaves with whom I worked, nearly starved out, and
yet stripped and whipped; blood cut out of them. It makes my flesh
creep now to think of it—such gashes as I've seen cut in them.
After a whipping, they would often leave and take to the woods for a
month or two, and live by taking what they could find. I've often
heard it said that's the cause of colored people in the South being
dishonest, because they are brought up so as to be obliged to steal. But
I do not consider it dishonest—I always thought it right for a
slave to take and eat as much as he wanted where he labored.

At some places where I have worked, I have known that the
slaves had not a bite of meat given them. They had a pint of corn
meal unsifted, for a meal,—three pints a day. I have seen the white
men measure it and the cook bake it, and seen them eat: that was
all they had but water—they might have as much of that as they
wanted. This is no hearsay—I've seen it through the spring, and
on until crop time: three pints of meal a day and the bran and
nothing else. I heard them talk among themselves about having got
a chicken or something, and being whipped for it. They were a bad

looking set—some twenty of them—starved and without clothing enough for decency. It ought to have been a disgrace to their master, to see them about his house. If a man were to go through Canada so, they'd stop him to know what he meant by it—whether it was poverty or if he was crazy,—and they'd put a suit of clothes on him. I have seen them working out in the hot sun in July or August without hats—bareheaded. It was not from choice,—they could n't get hats.

I have seen families put on the block and sold, some one way, some another way. I remember a family about two miles from me, —a father and mother and three children. Their master died, and they were sold. The father went one way, the mother another, with one child, and the other two children another way. I saw the sale— I was there—I went to buy hogs. The purchaser examined the persons of the slaves to see if they were sound,—if they were "good niggers." I was used to such things, but it made me feel bad to see it. The oldest was about ten or eleven years. It was hard upon them to be separated—they made lamentations about it. I never heard a white man at a sale express a wish that a family might be sold together.

On removing to Indiana, the white people did not seem so hostile altogether, nor want the colored people to knuckle quite so low. There were more white people who were friendly than in North Carolina. I was not allowed my vote nor my oath. There were more who wished colored people to have their rights than in North Carolina,—I mean there were abolitionists in Indiana.

I came here a year last spring, to escape the oppression of the laws upon the colored men. After the fugitive slave bill was passed, a man came into Indianapolis, and claimed John Freeman, a free colored man, an industrious, respectable man, as his slave. He brought *proofs* enough. Freedman was kept in jail several weeks,—but at last it turned out that the slave sought, was not Freeman, but a colored man in Canada, and F. was released. The danger of being taken as Freeman was, and suffering from a different decision, worked on my mind. I came away into Canada in consequence, as did many others. There were colored people who could have testified to Freeman's being free from his birth, but their oath would not be taken in Indiana.

In regard to Canada, I like the country, the soil, as well as any country I ever saw. I like the laws, which leave a man as much freedom as a man can have,—still there is prejudice here. The colored people are trying to remove this by improving and educating themselves, and by industry, to show that they are a people who have minds, and that all they want is cultivating.

I do not know how many colored people are here—but last summer five hundred and twenty-five were counted leaving the four churches.

HARRY THOMAS

I was born in Brunswick, partly raised in Southampton, ten miles below Bethlehem, Virginia. Was then bought by a "nigger-trader," J—— B——, and was sold to J—— S——, in South Carolina. The treatment there was barbarous. At sixteen years old, they gave me a task, splitting rails, which I did in the time, then went to take my rest. His wife was harder than he was,—she told me to make lights in the road, setting fire to rubbish, it being a new place. I got through at ten o'clock: boss came home, I went in again. She ordered me to put on water to scour the floors, etc. I would n't,—I went over to her father's "nigger-house" all night. Next morning, the master came for me, took me home, stripped me stark naked, made a paddle of thick oak board, lashed me across a pine log, secured my hands and feet, and whipped me with the paddle. His little boy saw it and cried,—he cursed him away,—his wife came,—he cursed her away. He whipped till he broke the paddle. After that, he took me to the house, and hit me with a hickory stick over the head and shoulders, a dozen times or more: then he got salt and water, and a corn cob, and scrubbed me. Then he sent me to water the hogs, naked as I was, in January. I ran into the woods, and went back to the same house, and the colored people gave me some old rags to keep me from freezing.

I recovered from that beating, and at length ran away again, because he refused to let me go to see my friends. I was caught by a colored man, who took me to my master's step-father's,—he whipped me till he was satisfied, then master came, and whipped me with a leather strap. I ran right off again; was caught and put in a potato house. After that I was put in the field to knock along the best way I could, but I was not able to work.

My master removed to Mississippi, taking me with him, the year before Gen. Jackson commenced fighting the Creek Indians.

This big scar on my left cheek, I got in a runaway scrape. A man who got up with me, jabbed me with the muzzle of a gun, which knocked me back into the mud: then he tied me. That time, I received three hundred lashes; one of the slaves who helped tie me, fainted at seeing me so abused. I have a cut with a knife made by J—— S—— after I had worked for him all day, because he could not flog me, as he liked.

I staid awhile, then ran away again,—then a man caught me, and another came with him home, who wished to buy me. I was a smart-looking boy—he offered one thousand dollars for me: master would n't sell. For running away, I received a hundred lashes on the bare back. I was then sold to his cousin, J—— Y——, in Mississippi. I lived with him ten years; I suppose I must have been about thirty-two. At first, Y.'s treatment was fair. I was foreman. He got rich, and grew mean, and I left him. I was caught and taken back again. He took me to the blacksmith's shop and had a ring made of axe-bar iron, which I wore on my right leg from the middle of May to the middle of September. I worked with it on, and slept with it on all that time.

After he got it off, I worked awhile,—again I went off, went into Alabama, was out from October to March,—then was put in jail, where I lay three months, as they could not hear from my owner,

who had moved off to the Choctaw purchase. My boss came and
took me out of jail, chained me to his horse with plough traces,
and was taking me on his way, when Gen. S——, of Georgia bought
me. He put me in his kitchen to cook for him. But I was not satisfied with him, although he used me well. The fact is, I wanted to
be free. I ran away and left him,—he had me caught, and sold me
to S—— N——, who took me to New Orleans. Nobody there liked
my countenance at all—no one would give a cent for me. N——
took me to Natchez and sold me, after a week, to a young man
named G—— S——, who had a cotton plantation a few miles
above Natchez. He treated me well at first. He would not allow any
to leave the place to see their friends without a pass from him or
the overseer. I went out to see my friends, and was flogged with a
bull whip on the bare back—a whip heavier and larger than a horse-
whip, with a buck-skin cracker on the lash. I ran away again—they
caught me and put plough traces around my body, and put me to
work hoeing cotton and corn. Not long after, they put on an iron
collar. I made an errand—went to the woods—and the overseer sent
all hands to hunt for me. They found me, and brought me back to
the driver. The old driver gave me two blows with the bull whip;
the young driver stopped him. The overseer came up and knocked
me down with his fist by a blow on the head. I fainted, was taken
to a tree, and when I came to, the overseer was bleeding me. Word
came to the overseer, from my master's grandmother, the same day,
that my master was gone away, and unless he took off my chains, I
would die before his return. The overseer took them all off.

At night, I dressed up and started off, steering by the north star.
I walked seven hundred and fifty miles nights,—then, in Kentucky,
I was betrayed by a colored man, and lay in jail fifteen months. I
would n't tell them where I belonged. Then, under terror of the
whip, I told them all about it. A Dr. J—— N—— had bought the
chance of me,—he took me to Nashville, where I waited on him, his
partner, and took care of his horses about four years. I started to
run away from him on his partner's horse—I had one hundred and

fifty dollars with me. He overtook me and took away my money. Then he put me in jail and sold me to an old broken down trader. I left him, proceeded north, was caught in Indiana, and taken to Evansville jail. They would not receive me there, and I was taken to Henderson, on the Kentucky side, and put in jail there. My owner put on handcuffs and locked me into the wagon besides with plough chains. I travelled three days thus in succession—he chaining me at night to his bedstead. On the third night, I was eating in the tavern kitchen where we stopped; I concluded to try for the North once more, I went out and hammered off my chains—found some assistance to get off my cuffs, and came on my way, travelling altogether nights by the north star, and lying by in the day. In Ohio, I found the best kind of friends, and soon reached Canada. When I first came, I joined the soldiers just after the rebellion: then practised up and down the province as a physician, from the knowledge I had obtained from a colored man in Mississippi, who knew roots and herbs,—but there were many kinds I wanted which I could not find here.

I am now hiring a piece of land in Buxton. My calculation is, if I live, to own a farm if I can. My health is good, and the climate agrees with me—and it does with colored men generally.

Slavery is barbarous. In my view, slaveholders, judged by the way they treat colored people, are the worst persons on earth.

WILLIAM A. HALL

I was born seven miles from Nashville, Tenn., Davidson county. I lived one year in Mississippi. I saw there a great deal of cotton-growing and persecution of slaves by men who had used them well in Tennessee. No man would have thought there could have been such a difference in treatment, when the masters got where they could make money. They drove the hands severely. My mother and brothers and sisters, when they changed their country, changed their position from good to bad. They were in Mississippi the last I heard of them, and I suppose they are there yet. It makes me miserable to consider that they are there: for their condition has been kept fresh in my memory, by seeing so much suffering and enduring so much. I went from Mississippi to Bedford county, Tenn. My master died here, and I was in hopes to go to see my mother. The doctor who attended my master had me sold at auction, and bought me himself, and promised he would never sell me to anybody; but in six months he tried to sell me. Not making out, he sent me to his father's farm in Tennessee, where I was treated tolerably well.

I remained there one year, then he took me horse-driving to Louisiana and back.

I saw some of the dreadfulest treatment on the sugar farms in the sugar-making season. The mill did not stop only to gear horses. People would come to my master and beg money to buy a loaf of bread. I saw them chained. I saw twelve men chained together, working on the levees. I saw three hundred that speculators had, dressing them up for sale. The overseers were about the mills, carrying their long whips all the time and using them occasionally. When they wanted to whip severely, they put the head and hands in stocks in a stooping posture.

The last two years I was in Tennessee, I saw nine persons at different times, made fast to four stakes, and whipped with a leather strap from their neck to their heels and on the bottoms of their feet, raising blisters: then the blisters broken with a plaited whip, the overseer standing off and fetching hard blows. I have seen a man faint under this treatment. I saw one about eighteen years old, as smart as you would see on the foot, used in this way: seven weeks after he fainted in consequence; his nerves were so shattered that he seemed like a man of fifty.

The overseer tied me to a tree, and flogged me with the whip. Afterwards he said he would stake me down, and give me a farewell whipping, that I would always remember. While he was eating supper,

I got off my shoe, and slipped off a chain and ran: I ran, I suppose, some six hundred yards: then hearing a dog, which alarmed me, I climbed a hill, where I sat down to rest. Then I heard a shouting, hallooing, for dogs to hunt me up. I tried to understand, and made out they were after me. I went through the woods to a road on a ridge. I came to a guide-board—in order to read it, I pulled it up, and read it in the moonlight, and found I was going wrong—turned about and went back, travelling all night: lay by all day, travelled at night till I came where Duck River and Tennessee come together. Here I found I was wrong,—went back to a road that led down Tennessee River, the way I wanted to go. This was Monday night,— the day before they had been there for me. A colored man had told them, "For God's sake to tell me not to get caught, for they would kill me:" but that I knew before. I got something to eat, and went on down the river, and travelled until Saturday night at ten, living on green corn and watermelons. Then I came to a house where an old colored man gave me a supper: another kept me with him three days. My clothes were now very dirty: I got some soap of a woman, and went to a wash-place, and washed my clothes and dried them. A heavy rain came on at daybreak, and I went down to the river for a canoe—found none—and went back for the day,—got some bread, and at night went on down the river; but there were so many roads, I could not make out how to go. I laid all day in a corn field. At night I found a canoe, 12 feet long, and travelled down the river several days, to its mouth. There I got on an island, the river being low. I took my canoe across a tongue of land,—a sand-bar—into the Ohio, which I crossed into Illinois. I travelled three nights, not daring to travel days, until I came to Golconda, which I recognized by a description I had been given on a previous attempt,—for this last time when I got away was my fourth effort. I went on to three forks in the road, took the left, travelled through the night, and lay by. At two, I ventured to go on, the road not being travelled much. But it seemed to go too far west: I struck through the woods, and went on till so tired I could walk no further.

I got into a tobacco-pen, and stayed till morning. Then I went through the woods, and came to where a fire had been burning—I kindled it up, roasted a lot of corn, then travelled on about three miles completely lost. I now came to a house, and revolved in my mind some hours whether to go or not, to ask. At last I ventured, and asked the road—got the information—reached Marion: got bewildered, and went wrong again, and travelled back for Golconda, —but I was set right by some children. At dark I went on, and at daybreak got to Frankfort—13 miles all night long, being weak from want of food. A few miles further on I found an old friend, who was backward about letting me in, having been troubled at night by white children. At last he let me in, and gave me some food, which I much needed. The next night he gave me as much as I could carry with me.

I went on to within five miles of Mount Vernon. At 4 A.M., I lay down, and slept till about noon. I got up and tried to walk, but every time I tried to stoop under the bushes, I would fall down. I was close to a house, but did not dare to go to it; so I laid there and was sick —vomited, and wanted water very bad. At night I was so badly off that I was obliged to go to the house for water. The man gave me some, and said, "Are you a runaway?" I said, "No—I am walking away." "Where do you live?" "I live here now." "Are you a free man?" "Why should I be here, if I am not a free man?—this is a free country." "Where do you live, anyhow?" "I live here, do n't you understand me?" "You are a free man, are you?" "Do n't you see he is a free man, who walks in a free country?" "Show me your pass —I s'pose you've got one." "Do you suppose men need a pass in a free country? this is a free country." "I suppose you run away—a good many fugitives go through here, and do mischief." Said I, "I am doing no mischief—I am a man peaceable, going about my own business; when I am doing mischief, persecute me,—while I am peaceable, let no man trouble me." Said he, "I'll go with you to Mount Vernon." "You may go, if you have a mind to: I am going, if it is the Lord's will that I shall get there. Good evening;" and I started out of the gate. He said, "Stop!" Said I, "Man, do n't bother me,—I'm sick, and do n't feel like being bothered." I kept on: he followed me,—"Stop, or I'll make you stop!" "Man, did n't I tell you I was sick, and do n't want to be bothered." I kept on,—he picked up a little maul at a wood-pile, and came with me, his little son following, to see what was going on.

He walked a mile and a quarter with me, to a neighbor of his— called—there came out three men. He stated to them, "Here's a runaway going to Mount Vernon: I think it would be right to go with him." I made no reply. He said, "We'll go in with him, and if he be correct, we'll not injure him,—we'll not do him no harm, no-how." I stood consulting with myself, whether to fight or run; I concluded to run first, and fight afterward. I ran a hundred yards: one ran after me to the edge of the woods, and turned back. I sat down to rest,—say an hour. They had gone on ahead of me on horses. I took a back track, and found another road which led to Mount Vernon, which I did not reach until daybreak, although he said 't was only five miles. I hastened on very quick through town, and so got off the track again: but I found a colored friend who harbored me three days, and fulfilled the Scriptures in one sense to perfection. I was hungry, and he fed me; thirsty, and he gave me drink; weary, and he ministered to my necessities; sick, and he cared for me till I got relieved: he took me on his own beast, and carried me ten miles, and his wife gave me food for four days' travel. His name was Y——. I travelled on three nights, and every morning found myself close to a town. One was a large one. I got into it early,—I was scared, for people was stirring,—but I got through it by turning to my right, which led me thirty miles out of my way. I was trying to get to Springfield. Then I went on to Taylorville. I lay out all day, two miles out, and while there, a man came riding on horseback within two feet of me. I thought he *would* see me, but he wheeled his horse, and away he went. At dark I got up and started on. It rained heavily. I went on to the town. I could discover nothing—the ground was black, the sky was cloudy. I travelled a while by the lights in the windows; at last ventured to ask the way, and got a direction for Springfield. After the rain the wind blew cold; I was chilled: I went into a calf-lot, and scared up the calves, and lay where they had been lying, to warm myself. It was dark yet. I stayed there half an hour, trying to get warm, then got up, and travelled on till daybreak. It being in a prairie, I had to travel very fast to get a place to hide myself. I came to a drain between two plantations, and got into it to hide. At sundown I went on, and reached Springfield, as near as I could guess, at 3 o'clock. I got into a stable, and lay on some boards in the loft.

When I awoke, the sun was up, and people were feeding horses in the stable. I found there was no chance to get out, without being discovered, and I went down and told them that I was a stranger, knowing no one there; that I was out until late, and so went into the stable. I asked them if there was any harm. They said "No." I thanked them and pursued my way. I walked out a little and found a friend who gave me breakfast. Then I was taken sick, and could not get a step from there for ten days: then I could walk a little, and had to start.

I took directions for Bloomington,—but the directions were wrong, and I got thirty miles out of my way again: so that when I reached Bloomington, I was too tired to go another step. I begged for a carriage, and if they had not got one, the Lord only knows what would have happened. I was conveyed to Ottawa, where I found an abolitionist who helped me to Chicago. From about the middle of August to the middle of November, I dwelt in no house except in Springfield, sick,—had no bed till I got to Bloomington. In February, I cut wood in Indiana,—I went to Wisconsin, and staid till harvest was over; then came to a particular friend, who offered me books. I had no money for books: he gave me a Testament, and gave me good instruction. I had worn out two Testaments in slavery, carrying them with me trying to get some instruction to carry me through life. "Now," said he, "square up your business, and go to the lake, for there are men here now, even here where you are living, who would betray you for half a dollar if they knew where your master is. Cross the lake: get into Canada." I thanked him for the book, which I have now; settled up and came to Canada.

I like Canada. If the United States were as free as Canada, I would still prefer to live here. I can do as much toward a living here in three days, as there in six.

PART TWO

THE VIEWS
OF THE
NORTHERNERS
AND THE
BRITISH

ISAAC WELD
(*1774-1856*)

This Dublin-born topographer was the son of a well-to-do customs official and owed his education to excellent private schools and a stimulating home cultural environment. In 1795 he resolved to explore the resources and life of the United States and Canada. Beginning in November of that year he embarked upon a two-year journey, accompanied by a servant, through the forests and along the river courses of America, often on foot, on horseback, or by canoe, and occasionally guided by Indians. In his visit to the tobacco plantations, he met George Washington and apparently peered critically at the slave cabins of an otherwise well-operated enterprise. As the following selection indicates, he concluded that slave exploitation was much worse on the smaller farms than on the large plantations. These observations were recorded at length in *Travels Through the States of North America and the Provinces of Upper and Lower Canada* (2 vols., London, 1799). So popular was this work that a second edition quickly appeared and so did French, German, and Dutch translations. His reputation as a topographer and scientist grew to national and international proportions during his long lifetime.

This is taken from volume I, 145-152 (Letter XI).

This part of Virginia, situated between the Patowmac and Rappahannock rivers, is called the Northern Neck, and is remarkable for having been the birth place of many of the principal characters which distinguished themselves in America during the war by their great talents, General Washington at their head. It was here that numbers of English gentlemen, who migrated when Virginia was a young colony, fixed their residence; and several of the houses which they built, exactly similar to the old manor houses in England, are still remaining, particularly in the counties of Richmond and Weftmoreland. Some of these, like the houses in Maryland, are quite in ruins; others are kept in good repair by the present occupiers, who live in a style which approaches nearer to that of English country gentlemen than what is to be met with any where else on the continent, some other parts of Virginia alone excepted.

Amongst the inhabitants here and in the lower parts of Virginia there is a disparity unknown elsewhere in America, excepting in the large towns. Instead of the lands being equally divided, immense estates are held by a few individuals, who derive large incomes from them, whilst the generality of the people are but in a state of mediocrity. Most of the men also, who possess these large estates, having received liberal educations, which the others have not, the distinction between them is still more observable: I met with several in this neighborhood who had been brought up at the public schools and universities in England, where, until the unfortunate war which separated the colonies from her, the young men were very generally educated; and even still a few are sent there, as the veneration for that country from whence their ancestors came, and with which they were themselves for a long time afterwards connected, is by no-means yet extinguished.

There is by no means so great a disparity now, however, amongst the inhabitants of the Northern Neck, as was formerly, and it is becoming less and less perceptible every year, many of the large estates having been divided in consequence of the removal of the proprietors to other parts of the country that were more healthy, and many more on account of the present laws of Virginia, which do not permit any one son to inherit the landed estates of the father to the exclusion of his brothers.

The principal planters in Virginia have nearly every thing they can want on their own estates. Amongst their slaves are found taylors, shoemakers, carpenters, smiths, turners, wheelwrights, weavers, tanners, &c. I have seen patterns of excellent coarse woollen cloth made in the country by slaves, and a variety of cotton manufactures, amongst the rest good nankeen. Cotton grows here extremely well; the plants are often killed by frost in winter, but they always produce abundantly the first year in which they are sown. The cotton from which nankeen is made is of a particular kind, naturally of a yellowish colour.

The large estates are managed by stewards and overseers, the proprietors just amusing themselves with seeing what is going forward. The work is done wholly by slaves, whose numbers are in this part of the country more than double that of white persons. The slaves on the large plantations are in general very well provided for, and treated with mildness. During three months nearly that I was in Virginia, but two or three instances of ill treatment towards them came under my observation. Their quarters, the name whereby their habitations are called, are usually situated one or two hundred yards from the dwelling house, which gives the appearance of a village to the residence of every planter in Virginia; when the estate, however, is so large as to be divided into several farms, then separate quarters are attached to the house of the overseer on each farm. Adjoining their little habitations, the slaves commonly have small gardens and yards for poultry, which are all their own property; they have ample time to attend to their own concerns, and their gardens are generally found well stocked, and their flocks of poultry numerous. Besides the food they raise for themselves, they are allowed liberal rations of salted pork and Indian corn. Many of their little huts are comfortably furnished, and they are themselves, in general, extremely well clothed. In short, their condition is by no means so wretched as might be imagined. They are forced to work certain hours in the day; but in return they are clothed, dieted, and lodged comfortably, and saved all anxiety about provision for their offspring. Still, however, let the condition of a slave be made ever so comfortable, as long as he is conscious of being the property of another man, who has it in his power to dispose of him according to the dictates of caprice; as long as he hears people around him talking of the blessings of liberty, and considers that he is in a state of bondage, it is not to be supposed that he can feel equally happy with the freeman. It is immaterial under what form slavery presents itself, whenever it appears there is ample cause for humanity to weep at the sight, and to lament that men can be found so forgetful of their own situations, as to live regardless of the feelings of their fellow creatures.

With respect to the policy of holding slaves in any country, on account of the depravity of morals which it necessarily occasions, besides the many other evil consequences attendant upon it, so much has already been said by others, that it is needless here to make any comments on the subject.

The number of the slaves increases most rapidly, so that there is scarcely any estate but what is overstocked. This is a circumstance complained of by every planter, as the maintenance of more than are requisite for the culture of the estate is attended with great expence. Motives of humanity deter them from selling the poor creatures, or turning them adrift from the spot where they have been born and brought up, in the midst of friends and relations.

What I have here said, respecting the condition and treatment of slaves, appertains, it must be remembered, to those only who are upon the large plantations in Virginia; the lot of such as are unfortunate enough to fall into the hands of the lower class of white people, and of hard task-masters in the towns, is very different. In the Carolinas and Georgia again, slavery presents itself in very different colours from what it does even in its worst form in Virginia. I am told, that it is no uncommon thing there, to see gangs of negroes staked at a horse race, and to see these unfortunate beings bandied about from one set of drunken gamblers to another for days together. How much to be deprecated are the laws which suffer such abuses to exist! yet these are the laws enacted by people who boast of their love of liberty and independence, and who presume to say, that it is in the breasts of Americans alone that the blessings of freedom are held in just estimation.

The Northern Neck, with the exception of some few spots only, is flat and sandy, and abounds with pine and cedar trees. Some parts of it are well cultivated, and afford good crops; but these are so intermixed with extensive tracts of waste land, worn out by the culture of tobacco, and which are almost destitute of verdure, that on the whole the country has the appearance of barrenness.

This is the case wherever tobacco has been made the principal object of cultivation. It is not, however, so much owing to the great share of nutriment which the tobacco plant requires that the land is impoverished, as to the particular mode of cultivating it which renders it necessary for people to be continually walking between the plants from the moment they are set out, so that the ground about each plant is left exposed to the burning rays of the sun all the summer, and becomes at the end of the season a hard beaten pathway. A ruinous system has prevailed also of working the same piece of land year after year, till it was totally exhausted; after this it was left neglected, and a fresh piece of land was cleared, that always produced good crops for one or two seasons; but this in its turn was worn out and afterwards left waste. Many of the planters are at length beginning to see the absurdity of wearing out their lands in this manner, and now raise only one crop of tobacco upon a piece of new land, then they sow wheat for two years, and afterwards clover. They put on from twelve to fifteen hundred bushels of manure per acre at first, which is found to be sufficient both for the tobacco and wheat; the latter is produced at the rate of about twenty bushels per acre.

In some parts of Virginia, the lands left waste in this manner throw up, in a very short time, a spontaneous growth of pines and cedars; in which case, being shaded from the powerful influence of the sun, they recover their former fertility at the end of fifteen or twenty years; but in other parts many years elapse before any verdure appears upon them. The trees springing up in this spontaneous manner usually grow very close to each other; they attain the height of fifteen or twenty feet, perhaps, in the same number of years; there is, however, but very little sap in them, and in a short time after they are cut down they decay. . . .

BASIL HALL
(*1788-1844*)

Captain Basil Hall of the British Navy was born in Edinburgh, the son of a noted geologist, and became a prolific writer on his travels in America and Asia. Like so many British visitors to the United States, he had pronounced anti-slavery views, although he sought to set forth the planter's position as fairly as he could.

Among his books was *An Account of a Voyage of Discovery to the West Coast of Corea* . . . (1818), which dealt with his cruise in the sloop *Lyra* in 1816, a voyage which took Lord Amherst's embassy to China. Another book appeared in 1824, this time a journal of a trip along the coasts of Chile, Peru, and Mexico. Then in 1829 he published *Travels in North America in 1827 and 1828* from which these selections are taken, (specifically pages 34-40, 74-79, 188-199, and 204-208).

At various times in his active life he issued sections of a nine-volume *Fragments of Voyages and Travels*. His vivid descriptions and observations attracted wide comment, although proslavery writers resented his strictures on the slave institution.

Although the debates in the National Legislature formed the chief object of interest at Washington, many other incidental matters arose, from time to time, to vary the picture.

The following advertisement caught my eye, in one of the newspapers:—

MARSHAL'S SALE.

By authority of a writ of fieri facias, issued from the Clerk's Office of the Circuit Court, in this district for the county of Washington, to me directed, I shall expose to sale, for cash, on Tuesday, the 15th instant, Negro GEORGE, a slave for life, and about sixteen years old. Seized and taken in execution of, as the goods and chattels of Zachariah Hazle, and will be sold to satisfy a debt due by him to William Smith.

Sale to be at the County Court-House Door, and to commence at 12 o'clock, M.

TENCH RINGGOLD,

jan 10 dts   Marshal District of Columbia.

I had often, in the course of my life, in the British West India possessions, and elsewhere, seen slavery in full operation; but as I had never happened to be actually present at the sale of a negro, I resolved to witness it for once, and in a place where, at first sight, such an incident might least of all have been looked for.

I repaired to the County Court-House, accordingly, at noon, on the 15th of January, 1827, and having found my way along an empty passage, I reached a door, from which people were departing and others entering, like bees crowding in and out of a hive. This was the Court of Justice. But the matters under discussion were either so completely technical, or my head was so full of the black boy, that I could not follow what was going on.

I came again into the passage, and walked along to the front door, which nearly faces the Capitol, distant about one-third of a mile. The flags were just hoisted on the top of the building, which intimate that the Senate and the House of Representatives had assembled to discuss the affairs of this free nation—slavery amongst the rest.

The only man I could see in the passage, was a great heavy-looking black fellow, who appeared so much downcast and miserable, that I settled within myself that this must needs be no other than Negro George, placed there for inspection. But the Deputy-marshal, who entered at this moment, holding in one hand the advertisement copied above, and in the other the writ of fieri facias alluded to therein, undeceived me, by saying that the man I pointed to was a slave indeed, though not for sale, but that I should see the other immediately.

It was soon buzzed about, I suspect, amongst the purchasers, that a suspicious-looking stranger was making enquiries respecting the boy; for a tall man, wrapped in a cloak, whom I had observed for some time cutting large junks of tobacco from a lump which he drew from his waistcoat pocket, and thrusting them into his mouth, evidently in a fidget, now came up to me, and said, with an air of affected carelessness, "Do you mean to buy the lad, sir?"

"I? Oh, no!" I exclaimed.

The tall man drew a satisfied breath on hearing this, and said, in a more natural tone, "I am glad of it, sir—for I do; and am very anxious to succeed, because I know the chap well, and have become interested in him, and he himself—ah! there he stands—wishes to become my property."

"How is that?"

"Why," said he, "you must know that his owner was indebted to me fifty dollars, and would not or could not pay me, so I had a lien upon this boy, and the Court allowed me to have him latterly, pending the litigations. There have been three or four law-suits about him, and he has been knocking about from hand to hand ever since March, 1822—five years—and he is now to be sold to satisfy this debt."

"What says the boy to all this?" I asked.

"Come here, George," he called, and the lad joined us. "Don't be scared, my boy," said the gentleman, "there is no one going to hurt you."

"O, I am not scared," answered the boy, though he trembled all the while. He looked very ill at ease, I thought, and I soon found out the cause, in his apprehension of being purchased by a person, of whom, I suppose, he had some previous knowledge, and whose looks certainly were as little inviting as any thing could well be. He was a short, lean man, with a face deeply wrinkled, not so much with age or care, as with the deep seams of intemperance. His two little eyes were placed so far back in his head, that you could not see them in profile, and when viewed in front through a pair of enormous spectacles, sparkled in a very ominous manner; while his straight, scanty, and disordered hair, formed an appropriate sky-line to the picture. I began to take considerable interest in the little fellow's fate, and whispered to my tall companion, that I hoped he would get the boy.

After various delays, the slave was put up to auction, at the end of the passage, near which four or five persons had by this time collected. There was a good deal of laughing and talking amongst the buyers, and several jests were sported on the occasion, of which their little victim took no more notice, than if he had been a horse or a dog. In fact, he was not a chubby shining little negro, with a flat nose, thick lips, and woolly hair, but a slender, delicate-looking youth, more yellow than black, with an expression every way suitable, I thought, with the forlorn situation in which he was placed— for both his parents, and all his brothers and sisters, he told me, had been long ago sold into slavery, and sent to the Southern States —Florida or Alabama—he knew not where!

"Well, gentlemen," cried the Deputy-marshal, "will you give us a bid? Look at him—as smart a fellow as ever you saw—works like a tiger!"

One of the spectators called out, "Come, I'll say 25 dollars;" another said 35—another said 40—and at last 100 dollars were bid for him.

From the spot where I was standing, in the corner, behind the rest of the party, I could see all that was passing. I felt my pulse accelerating at each successive offer, and my cheek getting flushed—for the scene was so very new that I almost fancied I was dreaming.

The interest, after a time, took a different character, to which, however, I by no means wished to give utterance, or in any shape to betray; but at this moment, the Deputy-marshal, finding the price to hang at 100 dollars, looked over to me, and said, "Do give us a bid, sir—won't you?"

My indignation was just beginning to boil over at this juncture, and I cried out, in answer to this appeal, with more asperity than good sense or good breeding,—"No! no! I thank God we don't do such things in my country!"

"And I wish, with all my heart," said the auctioneer, in a tone that made me sorry for having spoken so hastily—"I wish we did not do such things here."

"Amen!" said several voices.

The sale went on.

"We can't help it, however," observed the Marshal; "we must do our duty. 100 dollars are bid, gentlemen! One—hundred—dollars!"

The ominous personage with the deep-set eyes now called out, to my horror, and that of the poor boy, "120!"

Just at this moment a farmer, who had come from the country, and seemed pleased with the looks of the youth, nodded to the auctioneer, and said, "130."

My tall friend now said, "140," which was echoed by the new comer with, "142!"

Upon which these two bidders having exchanged looks, walked

apart for a couple of minutes, whispering something, which I did not hear. I observed the farmer nod several times, as if assenting to some compromise. They now returned, and the tall gentleman said, "I will give 143 dollars for him," while the other, though more than once appealed to by the auctioneer, spoke no more.

"143 dollars are bid for this lad! One hundred and forty-three dollars—once! twice!—Are you all done, gentlemen?—Thrice!—The lad is yours, sir,—a slave for life!"

I patted the boy on the head, wished his new master, my tall friend, all joy of his bargain, and ran off as fast as I could down one of the avenues, hoping, by change of place, to get rid of the entanglement of many unpleasant thoughts which crowded upon me during the sale; and perhaps willing, by a good scamper over the ground, to satisfy myself of the identity of my own freedom. . . .

SLAVE PATROLS AND TOBACCO

In walking round the Capitol at Richmond, in the course of the morning, my eyes were struck with the unusual sight of a sentinel marching in front of the building, with his musket on his shoulder. "Bless me!" I exclaimed, "has your legislature a guard of honour? —that is something new."

"Oh, no, no!" cried my companion, "that soldier is one of the guard stationed near the Capitol;—there are the barracks."

"I do not understand."

"It is necessary," he continued, "or at all events it is customary in these States to have a small guard always under arms;—there are only fifty men here. It is in consequence of the nature of our coloured population; but is done more as a preventive check than any thing else—it keeps all thoughts of insurrection out of the heads of the slaves, and so gives confidence to those persons amongst us who may be timorous. But in reality, there is no cause for alarm, as it is sixteen years since such a thing was attempted here, and the blacks have become more and more sensible every day of their want of power."

On enquiring further into these matters, I learnt that there was in all these towns a vigorous and active police, whose rule is not to take for granted that any thing is secure which vigilance can watch. No negro, for example, is allowed to be out of doors after sunset, without a written pass from his master explaining the nature of his errand. If, during his absence from home, he be found wandering from the proper line of his message, he is speedily taken up and corrected accordingly.

I had many opportunities of investigating the slavery question, during my stay in Virginia, for I always found the planters in that State, and I may add in every other, extremely fair and communicative; and so far from their being touchy or prone to take offence when talked to upon this subject, as I had often been told they were, they seemed to me quite willing to discuss it frankly. The essential impediment, however, which I found in the way of getting at the truth, on this and many other subjects, consisted less in any reserve on the part of the natives, than in the difficulty I found in removing the shell or husk of prejudice which surrounded my own mind, and gave me a constant desire to distort my observation, in order that I might see things in the particular light under which I had preconceived they ought to be viewed.

On the slavery question, this difficulty is perhaps greater than on most others; for there our feelings enter into contest so often with the judgment, that sober reason, political necessity, established usage, and so forth, have sometimes no fair play.

My sincere wish, however, even when I commenced these researches, undoubtedly was to meet this great topic as boldly and fairly as possible, by giving due weight to all I should hear on both sides. In the end I hope I have done so; though at first nothing can be conceived more difficult. A stranger, quite unaccustomed to the actual presence of slavery, is naturally very shy of admitting any thing, even to himself, which shall look like approving of the principle of such degradation of any part of his species; and it requires considerable time, and a knowledge of many details, before he can be sure that he is doing the subject justice. Ignorance, unfortunately, is so apt to usurp the place of knowledge, that, by a strange perversity, fresh information often appears unnecessary, and is not unfrequently resisted as intrusive.

The subject was, at all events, full of interest and novelty, and contributed, along with many other circumstances at this stage of our journey, to make us feel that we were verging towards the region of the tropics. Tobacco, cotton, and rice fields, met our eyes, by the road side, everywhere. The mildness of the climate, too, the colour of the population, and the tone of their voices, were all so characteristic of countries quite dissimilar from those we had left, that almost for the first time we felt fairly on our travels.

On the 4th of February, I accompanied a gentleman to his plantation some miles out of town on the banks of James's river, where I had a most agreeable and advantageous opportunity of seeing the arrangements on a well managed estate, the working of several coalpits, and the operations along the line of a magnificent canal, recently formed in order to improve the internal communications of Virginia, at a point where the river, by passing over rapids, is rendered unnavigable.

What interested me most, however, was a party of a dozen negroes, squatted on the floor of a tobacco house. They were placed, men, women, and children, in a circle, drawing the leaves from the stalk. In the centre stood two men, who, on receiving the leaves from the pickers, distributed them in heaps according to their quality. There seem to be three qualities of tobacco. The lower leaves, or those which touch the ground, are liable to get dirty and torn, but on the higher parts of the same stalk, two different sorts of leaves are found, one yellow, and one brown. These being carefully separated, and made up into little bunches, somewhat thicker than a man's thumb, are tied round with a thong, formed out of the leaf itself. The bunches are then slung, in pairs, across bars of wood, stretching from side to side of the roof, not unlike herrings in a drying house. In the course of time, the house becomes so completely filled with these bars, carrying bunches of tobacco, that there is barely left space enough for a man to creep under them to trim the fires, kept constantly burning on the mud floor to dry the leaves.

The next process is to pack it into the large hogsheads which every one has seen before the door of a tobacconist's shop. This operation is performed by means of long levers worked by hand, which force it into a compact mass.

The slaves looked wonderfully cheerful and healthy, and though scantily clad, were not unseasonably so, for the air was quite mild, notwithstanding it was now the depth of winter. Of 110 slaves on this plantation, I was told not one, old or young, knew how to read or write. . . .

A RICE PLANTATION

The cultivation of rice was described to me as by far the most unhealthy work in which the slaves were employed; and, in spite of every care, that they sank under it in great numbers. The causes of this dreadful mortality, are the constant moisture and heat of the atmosphere, together with the alternate floodings and dryings of the fields, on which the negroes are perpetually at work, often ankle deep in mud, with their bare heads exposed to the fierce rays of the sun. At such seasons every white man leaves the spot, as a matter of course, and proceeds inland to the high grounds; or, if he can afford it, he travels northward to the springs of Saratoga, or the Lakes of Canada.

Each plantation is furnished with a mill; and in most cases that fell in my way, the planters contrived to make this and every thing else, or very nearly every thing else which they require, on their own estates. All the blacksmiths' and carpenters' work, for example, was done by the slaves of each plantation; nor did it appear, from all I could learn, that there was any deficiency of intellect in the negro, so far as these mechanical operations went. The contrary is stoutly maintained in the non-slave-holding States; but this, I think, is in some degree to be accounted for by the admitted fact, of the free negro population—with which alone persons in the north are personally acquainted—being a degraded, dissolute class. But on a well regulated plantation, such as the one I am describing, where the proprietor is a man of sense, temper, and discrimination, and where he has somewhat more than a thousand slaves to choose from, the experiment—as to the lower walks of intellect, at least—has more fair play given it. The negroes themselves feel this very strongly, I was told, and whenever they are under the management of such a person as our judicious host, they exert themselves greatly from the hope of being distinguished. While he and I were in the act of discussing this topic, I happened to break the bolt joining the triple legs of the camp stool I used when drawing with the Camera Lucida. "Do you think, now," I said, "you have any man on your plantation who could repair this, for it is rather a nice matter?"

"O yes.—Cæsar! come here," he called out to the blacksmith. "Don't you see this bolt is broken—can you put it to rights?"

"I can, sir," was his answer; and though he was rather hurried, he executed the job in a very neat and business-like style. The rest of the party having walked on, I staid to have some conversation with Cæsar, whose correct acquaintance not only with his own mechanical operations, but with many other things, surprised me a good deal, and I left the smithy, with my opinion of the whole black race raised in the scale by this trivial incident. Of such flimsy materials is prejudice built!

I think it right to mention, that as far as my own experience has gone, I have invariably noticed that precisely in proportion as the negro has a fair chance given him, so he proves himself equal in capacity to the white man. Perhaps the only place in the world where a black has, to all intents and purposes, an equal chance with the rest of mankind, is on board a ship-of-war. He is there subjected to the same discipline, has the same favour shown if he behaves well, and suffers a like punishment for the like faults. I think it is generally allowed in the English navy, that under like circumstances, black seamen are as useful and as trust-worthy as the rest of the crew. I am led to infer, also, from a recent American work—the Red Rover [by J. Fenimore Cooper]—that the author, who is a naval officer, agrees with me in this view of the matter. At all events, he makes his admirable seaman, 'Fid,' not superior, if equal, to his sable companion 'Guinea,'—both characters, however, being so exquisitely drawn, that it would almost be worth a landsman's while to make a voyage or two merely to understand them.

Generally speaking, though by no means always, I found the most sensible planters of opinions, that there was not naturally and essentially any intellectual difference between the two races.

Our hospitable friend next showed us the slave village of his plantation, where every thing was neat and comfortable. In answer to our questions, he told us, that he interfered as little as possible with their domestic habits, except in matters of police. "We don't care what they do when their tasks are over—we lose sight of them till next day. Their morals and manners are in their own keeping. The men may have, for instance, as many wives as they please, so long as they do not quarrel about such matters."

I asked if they had any religion?

"I know little about that," he said; "there may perhaps be one or two methodists in a hundred. Preachers are never prevented, by me at least, from coming amongst the negroes, upon a distinct and express stipulation, however, that they do not interfere with the duties of the slaves, towards their master."

"Can any of them read and write?"

"Certainly none," he answered; "that is entirely contrary to usage here, and contrary to law in some places. Such things would only make them discontented with their lot, and in fact would be quite repugnant to the whole system of slave discipline in this country."

Domestic slaves, he told me, were better fed and clothed, and generally better treated, than those employed out of doors; but, what was odd enough, he added, that every where the slaves preferred the field-work, chiefly, as far as I could learn, from its being definite in amount, which left them a certain portion of the day entirely to themselves. This privilege has become, virtually, a right in many places; and so far, is a spark of freedom in their dark night of bondage; whereas the house slave, from being liable to every call, early and late, sometimes fancies himself less free. A negro, however, who has been regularly bred in that line, generally becomes so much attached to the children and to the other members of the family, and falls so completely into the ways of the house, that he would feel it an intolerable hardship to be sent to the field-work.

The laws direct that the overseer of the plantation shall always be a white man. He is a very important personage, as may be supposed, since much of the success of an estate, as well as the happiness or misery of the negroes—which appears to be nearly the same thing—depend upon his character. The details of superintendence pass under his eye, and he has the power of directing punishments, which ought always to be inflicted in his presence on the spot, by the driver. It is very disagreeable to think of such things, but it is obvious to every one who has reflected at all on this painful subject, that there must be a certain amount of prompt and vigorous discipline exercised over people who are influenced by so few of the ordinary motives to exertion.

It is the popular fashion in America, and I think elsewhere, to abuse these overseers as a class. But none of my enquiries led me to think so ill of them by any means as I had heard them reported. Their interest, as well as that of the planters, in the long run, is, unquestionably, to use the slaves well. An overseer who acquires a character for undue severity, is much scouted, and sooner or later discovers that his services are not valued or sought after, merely because he produces less effective work than a more judicious person

would do. Negroes, like many other people, may be driven to perform a certain portion of labour; but as no amount of tyranny can
carry things permanently beyond that point, custom seems to have
established in the slave-holding States of America, a particular
method of treatment, which is found to produce the greatest result. I
have much satisfaction, accordingly, in stating, that after many careful enquiries, I have no reason to suppose unnecessary severity is
by any means general in America.

The idea of cultivating the sea-coast, and indeed any part of the
low districts of the Southern States, by white labour, I regret to say,
appears quite visionary; and I only mention it because such notions
are sometimes brought forward by the opponents of slavery. Every
thing I heard in the South respecting the climate, showed this to be
impossible. Whether my informants were planters, or merchants, or
medical men, or strangers, or advocates for slavery, or the contrary,
one uniform opinion was expressed on this point. There seems, therefore, to be no choice left between abandoning the fertile countries
in question, or having them cultivated by negroes.

Over considerable tracts of some of the United States, such as the
northern parts of Virginia, where the soil is poor, the slaves do not
reproduce by their labour as much as they consume in the shape of
food. Consequently, they are a source of loss to their masters, or
rather they would be so, if other methods were not fallen upon to
turn them to account. This state of things has been partly brought
about by a curious circumstance, which would not strike one at first
as being likely to cause so great an effect as I have been told it does.
If human beings till the ground, and, at the same time, are fed
upon vegetable productions, the grain, or whatever it be, which they
eat, must, in order to be nutritive, be allowed to remain growing till
it comes to maturity. In so doing, however, the soil is deteriorated in
a manner which does not take place if cattle be fed off the same
ground; because their food being green, is used at a stage antecedent
to the period in which the scourging process, agriculturally speaking,
begins. While the ground, therefore, is not injured by being grazed

upon, it is liable to be worn out if tilled by slaves, whose food must be allowed to ripen.

Many fine-looking districts were pointed out to me in Virginia, formerly rich in tobacco and Indian corn, which had been completely exhausted by the production of crops for the maintenance of slaves. In thickly peopled countries, where great towns are at hand, the fertility of such soils may be recovered, and even improved, by manuring; but over the tracts of country I now speak of, no such advantages are within the farmer's reach.

If this state of things, instead of being local, were general over the Southern States, it is quite obvious that slavery must die a sort of natural death, as nobody would go on permanently maintaining negroes at a greater cost than the value of the crops they could be made to raise, over and above those necessary for their own maintenance. But whether this be so or not, it is now useless to enquire, since a more ready and infinitely more profitable way has been found of escaping from the dilemma. The climate as well as the soil of the extreme Southern States, Georgia, Alabama, and Louisiana, together with the territory of Florida, are quite unlike those which are found in the northern districts of the slave-holding portion of the Union, such as Maryland, Virginia, and Kentucky. In the southern section, as the labour of the negro is highly productive, the settlers in that new and fertile country are willing to give large prices for slaves. A sure and profitable market is thus furnished for the sale of the blacks reared, in that express view, on the more northern plantations above described.

The new States bordering on the Gulf of Mexico, as well as those which are watered by the Mississippi, are at present the chief markets to which the slaves bred in the North are sent. But great numbers are also absorbed by South Carolina and Georgia, where the cultivation of rice thins the black population so fast, as to render a constant fresh supply of negroes indispensable, in order to meet the increasing demand for that great staple production of the country. The enormous increased consumption of cotton, also, has brought down multitudes of negroes to turn up the fertile soils of those burning regions—the sea-island districts—well known to commerce. The progress of sugar cultivation, in like manner, in the alluvial lands forming the vast Delta of the Mississippi, is a further attraction to the slave-dealers, and must, like the others, long continue in operation as a productive field for slave labour. These combined causes have set a-going, and will probably keep in motion, for a long period of time to come, one of the most extensive slave-trades in the world, in the very heart of the United States.

I have no data to enable me to state the exact amount of this traffic, but it is undoubtedly very great. During certain seasons of the year, I am informed, all the roads, steam-boats, and packets, are crowded with troops of negroes on their way to the great slave markets of the South. As it is perfectly useless, however, merely to speculate on what might be desirable, we ought, if we wish to do good, fairly to look at the thing as it stands, in order to see what can be done to lessen an evil which it is utterly impossible to remove.

It is quite clear, that the pecuniary interest of the slave-holders in the more northern districts, above alluded to, is to rear as many negroes as possible, since they are quite sure of a favourable market for them, so long as the crowds of fresh inhabitants in the new States of the South, who are daily bringing more capital, industry, high hopes, and great determination, to bear upon the virgin soil of those regions, are unceasing in their demands for more labourers.

The ideas connected with a deliberate slave-trade were at first so revolting to the Americans, that, in most of the Southern legislatures, laws were passed forbidding the traffic; that is to say, rendering the open, notorious trade in human beings illegal. These laws were made in perfectly good faith, but, like the laws of other countries prohibiting the export of specie, or the import of silks, they were soon evaded, and having become utterly inefficient, were necessarily abandoned altogether, leaving the trade as free as that between the coast of Africa and the Brazils.

I ought to mention, that it was never at any time intended by the

Governments of the Southern States, by these enactments against the importation of slaves, to prevent persons who came to settle there from bringing their own negroes with them, since, if it had been otherwise arranged, and that no settler could import his slaves, the ground must have remained uncultivated to this hour. The laws alluded to were directed against the mere thoroughpaced slave-trader. The permission, however, for new comers to import their own gangs of negroes, opened so easy a door for evading the law, that the State legislatures, after a time, discovered the inefficiency of their enactments, and gave up the point. This great internal slave-trade is carried on by sea as well as by land. I saw a brig from Baltimore, lying alongside of the Levée at New Orleans, with upwards of two hundred negroes on board. Her decks presented a scene which forcibly reminded me of Rio Janeiro. In the one case, however, the slaves were brought from the savage regions of Africa; in the other, from the very heart of a free country. To the poor negro the distinction is probably no great matter!

The Americans are perpetually taunting England with having entailed slavery upon their country. The charge, indeed, may be true, and there is no denying that it was every way disgraceful in the British Ministry of former times to thwart the wishes of the Colonists, if indeed they sincerely desired to avoid the incipient evil which has fallen so heavily upon their descendants. The whole case, however, as far as the two nations are concerned, has completely altered its character of late years, by the acquisition of Florida and Louisiana, countries which must be worked by slaves, or not at all; and still more by the introduction of Missouri into the Union as a State, where no such necessity on account of climate exists, or was even pretended to exist. . . .

Instead of seeing my way better as I went on, I found my ideas on the intricate and formidable subject of slavery, becoming rather less clear than I fancied they had formerly been. The different accounts which different people gave me of the actual condition of the negroes, sorely distracted every general conclusion I ventured to draw; while a multiplicity of local circumstances, daily coming to my knowledge, cast adrift all my own theories on the subject. I daresay that I listened to nearly as many methods of remedying this evil, as I heard speculative cures for the frightful mischiefs incident to the Presidential election. Almost every gentleman I met with in the South, had some project or other for mitigating the national oppression arising from this incubus, as they frequently called it, or believed he had discovered some nostrum for removing a great portion of its bad effects. But I never met a man who was hardy enough to suppose it could be entirely removed. To the hideous moral evils that pervade this dismal subject, must be added a long catalogue of diseases and death, which thin the ranks of the unhappy sufferers, and drain the profits of their owners. A medical gentleman at Savannah told me, that pulmonary complaints are those which prove most fatal to the negroes, especially to such as cultivate the rice-grounds. The Blacks, he said, are not nearly so liable to intermittents as the Whites are, but pleurisy is more frequent amongst them, and generally proves fatal. On the cotton plantations, according to his account, the negroes are generally healthy,—all the work being of a dry kind; but on rice-estates, the hospitals are often quite crowded in autumn. He told me of a friend of his who had lost 40 out of 300 slaves last year.

This sickness is brought on chiefly by circumstances inevitably connected with the cultivation of rice, the negroes being almost constantly working in the water, or ankle deep in mud, ditching, drawing, or weeding, or turning over wet ground. They are sometimes overworked, in order to 'meet the season,' as it is called, and upon these occasions they sink rapidly under their complicated hardships. The slaves, I was told, are so well aware of the amount of work which they are competent to perform, that the imposition of a greater task seldom produces a greater final result. If additional labour, beyond the ordinary measure, be assigned them, they first become sulky, then sick, often droop and die, or if not, they are seized with despair and run away, only to be caught again and punished. Thus they are sometimes, but not often, worried and harassed, to no good purpose. All experience, therefore, I was assured, went to prove that moderate tasks, strict superintendence, with uniform kindness, in the ordinary style of the country, was by far the best way to get useful service out of the negroes—it being always borne in mind, that a slave will work as little as he can. I was much gratified by finding that these generous and politic principles were very generally acted upon by the American planters. The exceptions—it was curious to hear—are most frequently found amongst the new comers from the Northern States of the Union, or from England—those very persons who, on their first arrival, have had least patience with slavery under any modification! People who are inconsiderate enough to abuse a whole system without taking the pains to distinguish between what is inevitable, and what is remediable, are not likely to be more reflecting when these distinctions become apparent.

I made particular enquiries as to the fact of parents and children being separated as well as husbands and wives, when families are sold. And I was glad to find, that this is discouraged as much as possible, not only as a matter of feeling and propriety, but as a matter of interest.

I was sometimes amused, if this be a proper word to apply to such things, on observing how adroitly the inhabitants of the different States in America shifted the blame off their own shoulders to those of their neighbours. The Virginians told sad stories of the way in which the South Carolinians used their negroes. But when I reached that State, I heard such language as follows:—

"Wait till you go into Georgia," said the planters of Carolina, "there you will see what the slaves suffer."

On reaching Savannah, however, the ball was tossed along to the westward.

"O, sir, you have no idea how ill the slaves are used in Louisiana; there, amongst the sugar plantations, they have to work day and night, Sundays and all!"

The real truth, however, I believe to be this: Men of sense and feeling use their slaves well in every State, not only because it is much more agreeable to be kind than cruel to them, but because the pecuniary advantages are always greater. Men who have no sense or command of temper, are sure to disregard the feelings of those over whom they have such unlimited authority. Consequently, wherever there is slavery, there must be more or less cruelty and injustice, if —as in America—the checks to the intemperate use of irresponsible power are merely nominal. But I have no idea that Georgia is worse in this respect than Virginia, or Louisiana than either. The laws in those States vary, it is true; but, really, nothing is to be made out in these respects from the written laws, since, under any system of legislative arrangement in America, as far as I could learn, the negroes must, in every case, be left almost entirely to the control of their masters, or with no appeal that deserves the name. . . .

FRANCES (FANNY)
ANNE KEMBLE
(1809-1893)

American playgoers warmly admired the vivacious English-born actress Fanny Kemble who often played key Shakespearian roles opposite her distinguished father, Charles Kemble, in the Park Theatre Company in New York. She retired from the stage in 1834 at the age of 25 after marrying Pierce Butler of Germantown, Pennsylvania, who had inherited a large Georgia plantation. But her experiences caused a revulsion in feeling in her both against human bondage and her husband, the slavemaster, whom she eventually divorced in 1849 in a much publicized proceeding.

Before going to Georgia, she published a mildly critical book on American customs, *Journal of a Residence in America* (1835), which made local reviewers unhappy. But she was so shocked by her plantation life during the winter of 1838-39 on her husband's slave estate that her second journal expressed deep bitterness. However, this was not published until 1863, when she decided that this might convince Britons of the evils of slavery at a critical time. *The Journal of a Residence on a Georgian Plantation* (1863), from which these selections are taken, reveals her acute mind and realistic observations. She returned to the English stage, gave interpretive public readings, and wrote autobiographical books, plays, and lyrical poems up to her death in 1893. Her *Journal* has become one of the most fascinating documents of antebellum plantation life.

(The pages reproduced are 27-46 of her *Journal*).

I mentioned to you just now that two of the carpenters had made a boat in their leisure time. I must explain this to you, and this will involve the mention of another of Miss Martineau's mistakes with regard to slave labor, at least in many parts of the Southern States. She mentions that on one estate of which she knew, the proprietor had made the experiment, and very successfully, of appointing to each of his slaves a certain task to be performed in the day, which once accomplished, no matter how early, the rest of the four-and-twenty hours were allowed to the laborer to employ as he pleased. She mentions this as a single experiment, and rejoices over it as a decided amelioration in the condition of the slave, and one deserving of general adoption. But in the part of Georgia where this estate is situated, the custom of task labor is universal, and it prevails, I believe, throughout Georgia, South Carolina, and parts of North Carolina; in other parts of the latter state, however—as I was informed by our overseer, who is a native of that state—the estates are small, rather deserving the name of farms, and the laborers are much upon the same footing as the laboring men at the North, working from sunrise to sunset in the fields with the farmer and his sons, and coming in with them to their meals, which they take immediately after the rest of the family. In Louisiana and the new southwestern slave states, I believe, task labor does not prevail; but it is in those that the condition of the poor human cattle is most deplorable; as you know it was there that the humane calculation was not only made, but openly and unhesitatingly avowed, that the planters found it, upon the whole, their most profitable plan to work off (kill with labor) their whole number of slaves about once in seven years, and renew the whole stock. By-the-by, the Jewish institution of slavery is much insisted upon by the Southern upholders of the system;

perhaps this is their notion of the Jewish jubilee, when the slaves
were by Moses's strict enactment to be all set free.* Well, this task
system is pursued on this estate; and thus it is that the two carpenters were enabled to make the boat they sold for sixty dollars.
These tasks, of course, profess to be graduated according to the sex,
age, and strength of the laborer; but in many instances this is not the
case, as I think you will agree when I tell you that on Mr. ——'s first
visit to his estates he found that the men and the women who labored
in the fields had the same task to perform. This was a noble admission of female equality, was it not?—and thus it had been on the
estate for many years past. Mr. ——, of course, altered the distribution of the work, diminishing the quantity done by the women.

I had a most ludicrous visit this morning from the midwife of the
estate—rather an important personage both to master and slave, as
to her unassisted skill and science the ushering of all the young negroes into their existence of bondage is intrusted. I heard a great
deal of conversation in the dressing-room adjoining mine while performing my own toilet, and presently Mr. ——opened my room
door, ushering in a dirty, fat, good-humored looking old negress, saying, "The midwife, Rose, wants to make your acquaintance." "Oh
massa!" shrieked out the old creature, in a paroxysm of admiration,
"where you get this lilly alabaster baby!" For a moment I looked
round to see if she was speaking of my baby; but no, my dear, this
superlative apostrophe was elicited by the fairness of *my skin:* so
much for degrees of comparison. Now I suppose that if I chose to
walk arm in arm with the dingiest mulatto through the streets of
Philadelphia, nobody could possibly tell by my complexion that I
was not his sister, so that the mere quality of mistress must have
had a most miraculous effect upon my skin in the eyes of poor Rose.
But this species of outrageous flattery is as usual with these people
as with the low Irish, and arises from the ignorant desire, common to
both the races, of propitiating at all costs the fellow-creature who

* [A reference to Leviticus xxv, 39-55. ED.]

is to them as a Providence—or rather, I should say, a fate—for 'tis a heathen and no Christian relationship. Soon after this visit, I was summoned into the wooden porch or piazza of the house, to see a poor woman who desired to speak to me. This was none other than the tall, emaciated-looking negress who, on the day of our arrival, had embraced me and my nurse with such irresistible zeal. She appeared very ill to-day, and presently unfolded to me a most distressing history of bodily afflictions. She was the mother of a very large family, and complained to me that, what with childbearing and hard field labor, her back was almost broken in two. With an almost savage vehemence of gesticulation, she suddenly tore up her scanty clothing, and exhibited a spectacle with which I was inconceivably shocked and sickened. The facts, without any of her corroborating statements, bore tolerable witness to the hardships of her existence. I promised to attend to her ailments and give her proper remedies; but these are natural results, inevitable and irremediable ones, of improper treatment of the female frame; and, though there may be alleviation, there can not be any cure when once the beautiful and wonderful structure has been thus made the victim of ignorance, folly, and wickedness.

After the departure of this poor woman, I walked down the settlement toward the Infirmary or hospital, calling in at one or two of the houses along the row. These cabins consist of one room, about twelve feet by fifteen, with a couple of closets smaller and closer than the state-rooms of a ship, divided off from the main room and each other by rough wooden partitions, in which the inhabitants sleep. They have almost all of them a rude bedstead, with the gray moss of the forests for mattress, and filthy, pestilential-looking blankets for covering. Two families (sometimes eight and ten in number) reside in one of these huts, which are mere wooden frames pinned, as it were, to the earth by a brick chimney outside, whose enormous aperture within pours down a flood of air, but little counteracted by the miserable spark of fire, which hardly sends an attenuated thread of lingering smoke up its huge throat. A wide ditch runs immediately at the back of these dwellings, which is filled and emptied daily by the tide. Attached to each hovel is a small scrap of ground for a garden, which, however, is for the most part untended and uncultivated. Such of these dwellings as I visited to-day were filthy and wretched in the extreme, and exhibited that most deplorable consequence of ignorance and an abject condition, the inability of the inhabitants to secure and improve even such pitiful comfort as might yet be achieved by them. Instead of the order, neatness, and ingenuity which might convert even these miserable hovels into tolerable residences, there was the careless, reckless, filthy indolence which even the brutes do not exhibit in their lairs and nests, and which seemed incapable of applying to the uses of existence the few miserable means of comfort yet within their reach. Firewood and shavings lay littered about the floors, while the half-naked children were cowering round two or three smouldering cinders. The moss with which the chinks and crannies of their ill-protecting dwellings might have been stuffed was trailing in dirt and dust about the ground, while the back door of the huts, opening upon a most unsightly ditch, was left wide open for the fowls and ducks, which they are allowed to raise, to travel in and out, increasing the filth of the cabin by what they brought and left in every direction. In the midst of the floor, or squatting round the cold hearth, would be four or five little children from four to ten years old, the latter all with babies in their arms, the care of the infants being taken from the mothers (who are driven afield as soon as they recover from child labor), and devolved upon these poor little nurses, as they are called, whose business it is to watch the infant, and carry it to its mother whenever it may require nourishment. To these hardly human little beings I addressed my remonstrances about the filth, cold, and unnecessary wretchedness of their room, bidding the elder boys and girls kindle up the fire, sweep the floor, and expel the poultry. For a long time my very words seemed unintelligible to them, till, when I began to sweep and make up the fire, etc., they first fell to laughing, and then imitating me. The incrustations of dirt on their hands, feet, and faces were my next object of attack, and the stupid negro practice (by-the-by, but a short time since nearly universal in enlightened Europe) of keeping the babies with their feet bare, and their heads, already well capped by nature with their woolly hair, wrapped in half a dozen hot, filthy coverings. Thus I traveled down the "street," in every dwelling endeavoring to awaken a new perception, that of cleanliness, sighing, as I went, over the futility of my own exertions, for how can slaves be improved? Nathless, thought I, let what can be done; for it may be that, the two being incompatible, improvement may yet expel slavery; and so it might, and surely would, if, instead of beginning at the end, I could but begin at the beginning of my task. If the mind and soul were awakened, instead of mere physical good attempted, the physical good would result, and the great curse vanish away; but my hands are tied fast, and this corner of the work is all that I may do. Yet it can not be but, from my words and actions, some revelations should reach these poor people; and going in and out among them perpetually, I shall teach, and they learn involuntarily a thousand things of deepest import. They must learn, and who can tell the fruit of that knowledge alone, that there are beings in the world, even with skins of a different color from their own, who have sympathy for their misfortunes, love for their virtues, and respect for their common nature—but oh! my heart is full almost to bursting as I walk among these most poor creatures.

The Infirmary is a large two-story building, terminating the broad orange-planted space between the two rows of houses which form the first settlement; it is built of whitewashed wood, and contains four large-sized rooms. But how shall I describe to you the spectacle which was presented to me on entering the first of these? But half the casements, of which there were six, were glazed, and these were obscured with dirt, almost as much as the other windowless ones were darkened by the dingy shutters, which the shivering inmates had fastened to in order to protect themselves from the cold. In the enormous chimney glimmered the powerless embers of a few sticks of wood, round which, however, as many of the sick women as could approach were cowering, some on wooden settles, most of them on the ground, excluding those who were too ill to rise; and these last poor wretches lay prostrate on the floor, without bed, mattress, or pillow, buried in tattered and filthy blankets, which, huddled round them as they lay strewed about, left hardly space to move upon the floor. And here, in their hour of sickness and suffering, lay those whose health and strength are spent in unrequited labor for us— those who, perhaps even yesterday, were being urged on to their unpaid task—those whose husbands, fathers, brothers, and sons were even at that hour sweating over the earth, whose produce was to buy for us all the luxuries which health can revel in, all the comforts which can alleviate sickness. I stood in the midst of them, perfectly unable to speak, the tears pouring from my eyes at this sad spectacle of their misery, myself and my emotion alike strange and incomprehensible to them. Here lay women expecting every hour the terrors and agonies of childbirth, others who had just brought their doomed offspring into the world, others who were groaning over the anguish and bitter disappointment of miscarriages—here lay some burning with fever, others chilled with cold and aching with rheumatism, upon the hard cold ground, the draughts and dampness of the atmosphere increasing their sufferings, and dirt, noise, and stench, and every aggravation of which sickness is capable, combined in their condition—here they lay like brute beasts, absorbed in physical suffering; unvisited by any of those Divine influences which may ennoble the dispensations of pain and illness, forsaken, as it seemed to me, of all good; and yet, O God, Thou surely hadst not forsaken them! Now pray take notice that this is the hospital of an estate where the owners are supposed to be humane, the overseer efficient and kind, and the negroes remarkably well cared for and comfortable. As soon as I recovered from my dismay, I addressed old Rose the midwife, who had charge of this room, bidding her open the shutters of such windows as were glazed, and let in the light. I next proceeded to make up the fire; but, upon my lifting a log for that purpose, there was one universal outcry of horror, and old Rose, attempting to snatch it from me, explained, "Let alone, missis—let be; what for you lift wood? you have nigger enough, missis, to do it!" I hereupon had to explain to them my view of the purposes for which hands and arms were appended to our bodies, and forthwith began making Rose tidy up the miserable apartment, removing all the filth and rubbish from the floor that could be removed, folding up in piles the blankets of the patients who were not using them, and placing, in rather more sheltered and comfortable positions, those who were unable to rise. It was all that I could do, and having enforced upon them all my earnest desire that they should keep their room swept, and as tidy as possible, I passed on to the other room on the ground floor, and to the two above, one of which is appropriated to the use of the men who are ill. They were all in the same deplorable condition, the upper rooms being rather the more miserable, inasmuch as none of the windows were glazed at all, and they had, therefore, only the alternative of utter darkness, or killing draughts of air from the unsheltered casements. In all, filth, disorder, and misery abounded; the floor was the only bed, and scanty begrimed rags of blankets the only covering. I left this refuge for Mr. ——'s sick dependents with my clothes covered with dust, and full of vermin, and with a heart heavy enough, as you will well believe. My morning's work had fatigued me not a little, and I was glad to return to the house, where I gave vent to my indignation and regret at the scene I had just witnessed to Mr. ——and his overseer, who, here, is a member of our family. The latter told me that the condition of the hospital had appeared to him, from his first entering upon his situation (only within the last year), to require a reform, and that he had proposed it to the former manager, Mr. K——, and Mr. ——'s brother, who is part proprietor of the estate, but, receiving no encouragement from them, had supposed that it was a matter of indifference to the owners, and had left it in the condition in which he had found it, in which condition it has been for the last nineteen years and upward.

This new overseer of ours has lived fourteen years with an old Scotch gentleman, who owns an estate adjoining Mr. ——'s, on the island of St. Simon's, upon which estate, from every thing I can gather, and from what I know of the proprietor's character, the slaves are probably treated with as much humanity as is consistent with slavery at all, and where the management and comfort of the hospital in particular had been most carefully and judiciously attended to. With regard to the indifference of our former manager upon the subject of the accommodation for the sick, he was an excellent overseer, *videlicet* the estate returned a full income under his management, and such men have nothing to do with sick slaves: they are tools, to be mended only if they can be made available again; if not, to be flung by as useless, without farther expense of money, time, or trouble.

I am learning to row here, for circumscribed, as my walks necessarily are, impossible as it is to resort to my favorite exercise on horseback upon these narrow dikes, I must do something to prevent my blood from stagnating; and this broad brimming river, and the beautiful light canoes which lie moored at the steps, are very inviting persuaders to this species of exercise. My first attempt was confined to pulling an oar across the stream, for which I rejoiced in sundry aches and pains altogether novel, letting alone a delightful row of blisters on each of my hands.

I forgot to tell you that in the hospital were several sick babies, whose mothers were permitted to suspend their field labor in order to nurse them. Upon addressing some remonstrances to one of these, who, besides having a sick child, was ill herself, about the horribly dirty condition of her baby, she assured me that it was impossible for them to keep their children clean; that they went out to work at daybreak, and did not get their tasks done till evening, and that then they were too tired and worn out to do any thing but throw themselves down and sleep. This statement of hers I mentioned on my return from the hospital, and the overseer appeared extremely annoyed by it, and assured me repeatedly that it was not true.

In the evening Mr. ——, who had been over to Darien, mentioned that one of the storekeepers there had told him that, in the course of a few years, he had paid the negroes of this estate several thousand dollars for moss, which is a very profitable article of traffic with them: they collect it from the trees, dry and pick it, and then sell it to the people in Darien for mattresses, sofas, and all sorts of stuffing purposes, which, in my opinion, it answers better than any other material whatever that I am acquainted with, being as light as horse-hair, as springy and elastic, and a great deal less harsh and rigid. It is now bedtime, dear E——, and I doubt not it has been sleepy time with you over this letter long ere you came thus far. There is a preliminary to my repose, however, in this agreeable residence, which I rather dread, namely, the hunting for, or discovering without hunting, in fine relief upon the whitewashed walls of my bedroom, a most hideous and detestable species of *reptile* called centipedes, which come out of the cracks and crevices of the walls, and fill my very heart with dismay. They are from an inch to two inches long, and appear to have not a hundred, but a thousand legs. I can not ascertain very certainly from the negroes whether they sting or not, but they look exceedingly as if they might, and I visit my babies every night in fear and trembling, lest I should find one or more of these hateful creatures mounting guard over them. Good-night; you are well to be free from centipedes—better to be free from slaves.

Dear E——,—This morning I paid my second visit to the Infirmary, and found there had been some faint attempt at sweeping and cleaning, in compliance with my entreaties. The poor woman Harriet, however, whose statement with regard to the impossibility of their attending properly to their children had been so vehemently denied by the overseer, was crying bitterly. I asked her what ailed her, when, more by signs and dumb show than words, she and old Rose informed me that Mr. O—— had flogged her that morning for having told me that the women had not time to keep their children clean. It is part of the regular duty of every overseer to visit the Infirmary at least once a day, which he generally does in the morning, and

Mr. O——'s visit had preceded mine but a short time only, or I might have been edified by seeing a man horsewhip a woman. I again and again made her repeat her story, and she again and again affirmed that she had been flogged for what she told me, none of the whole company in the room denying it or contradicting her. I left the room because I was so disgusted and indignant that I could hardly restrain my feelings, and to express them could have produced no single good result. In the next ward, stretched upon the ground, apparently either asleep or so overcome with sickness as to be incapable of moving, lay an immense woman; her stature, as she cumbered the earth, must have been, I should think, five feet seven or eight, and her bulk enormous. She was wrapped in filthy rags, and lay with her face on the floor. As I approached, and stooped to see what ailed her, she suddenly threw out her arms, and, seized with violent convulsions, rolled over and over upon the floor, beating her head violently upon the ground, and throwing her enormous limbs about in a horrible manner. Immediately upon the occurrence of this fit, four or five women threw themselves literally upon her, and held her down by main force; they even proceeded to bind her legs and arms together, to prevent her dashing herself about; but this violent coercion and tight bandaging seemed to me, in my profound ignorance, more likely to increase her illness by impeding her breathing and the circulation of her blood, and I bade them desist, and unfasten all the strings and ligatures not only that they had put round her limbs, but which, by tightening her clothes round her body, caused any obstruction. How much I wished that, instead of music, and dancing, and such stuff, I had learned something of sickness and health, of the conditions and liabilities of the human body, that I might have known how to assist this poor creature, and to direct her ignorant and helpless nurses! The fit presently subsided, and was succeeded by the most deplorable prostration and weakness of nerves, the tears streaming down the poor woman's cheeks in showers, without, however, her uttering a single word, though she moaned incessantly. After bathing her forehead, hands, and chest with vinegar, we raised her up, and I sent to the house for a chair with a back (there was no such thing in the hospital), and we contrived to place her in it. I have seldom seen finer women than this poor creature and her younger sister, an immense strapping lass called Chloe —tall, straight, and extremely well made—who was assisting her sister, and whom I had remarked, for the extreme delight and merriment which my cleansing propensities seemed to give her, on my last visit to the hospital. She was here taking care of a sick baby, and helping to nurse her sister Molly, who, it seems, is subject to those fits, about which I spoke to our physician here—an intelligent man residing in Darien, who visits the estate whenever medical assistance is required. He seemed to attribute them to nervous disorder, brought on by frequent childbearing. This woman is young, I suppose at the outside not thirty, and her sister informed me that she had had ten children—ten children, E——! Fits and hard labor in the fields, unpaid labor, labor exacted with stripes—how do you fancy that? I wonder if my mere narration can make your blood boil as the facts did mine? Among the patients in this room was a young girl, apparently from fourteen to fifteen, whose hands and feet were literally rotting away piecemeal, from the effect of a horrible disease, to which the negroes are subject here, and I believe in the West Indies, and when it attacks the joints of the toes and fingers, the pieces absolutely decay and come off, leaving the limb a maimed and horrible stump! I believe no cure is known for this disgusting malady, which seems confined to these poor creatures. Another disease, of which they complained much, and which, of course, I was utterly incapable of accounting for, was a species of lock-jaw, to which their babies very frequently fall victims in the first or second week after their birth, refusing the breast, and the mouth gradually losing the power of opening itself. The horrible diseased state of head, common among their babies, is a mere result of filth and confinement, and therefore, though I never any where saw such distressing and disgusting objects as some of these poor little woolly skulls presented, the cause was sufficiently obvious. Pleurisy, or a tendency to it, seems very common among them; also peripneumonia, or inflammation of the lungs, which is terribly prevalent, and generally fatal. Rheumatism is almost universal; and as it proceeds from exposure, and want of knowledge and care, attacks indiscriminately the young and old. A great number of the women are victims to falling of the womb and weakness in the spine; but these are necessary results of their laborious existence, and do not belong either to climate or constitution.

I have ingeniously contrived to introduce bribery, corruption, and pauperism, all in a breath, upon this island, which, until my advent, was as innocent of these pollutions, I suppose, as Prospero's isle of refuge. Wishing, however, to appeal to some perception, perhaps a little less dim in their minds than the abstract loveliness of cleanliness, I have proclaimed to all the little baby nurses that I will give a cent to every little boy or girl whose baby's face shall be clean, and one to every individual with clean face and hands of their own. My appeal was fully comprehended by the majority, it seems, for this morning I was surrounded, as soon as I came out, by a swarm of children carrying their little charges on their backs and in their arms, the shining, and, in many instances, wet faces and hands of the latter bearing ample testimony to the ablutions which had been inflicted upon them. How they will curse me and the copper cause of all their woes in their baby bosoms! Do you know that, little as grown negroes are admirable for their personal beauty (in my opinion, at least), the black babies of a year or two old are very pretty; they have, for the most part, beautiful eyes and eyelashes, the pearly perfect teeth, which they retain after their other juvenile graces have left them; their skins are all (I mean of blacks generally) infinitely finer and softer than the skins of white people. Perhaps you are not aware that among the white race the *finest grained* skins generally belong to persons of dark complexion. This, as a characteristic of the black race, I think might be accepted as some compensation for the coarse woolly hair. The nose and mouth, which are so peculiarly displeasing in their conformation in the face of a negro man or woman, being the features least developed in a baby's countenance, do not at first present the ugliness which they assume as they become more marked; and when the very unusual operation of washing has been performed, the blood shines through the fine texture of the skin, giving life and richness to the dingy color, and displaying a species of beauty which I think scarcely anybody who observed it would fail to acknowledge. I have seen many babies on this plantation who were quite as pretty as white children, and this very day stooped to kiss a little sleeping creature that lay on its mother's knees in the Infirmary—as beautiful a specimen of a sleeping infant as I ever saw. The caress excited the irrepressible delight of all the women present—poor creatures! who seemed to forget that I was a woman, and had children myself, and bore a woman's and a mother's heart toward them and theirs; but, indeed, the Honorable Mr. Slumkey could not have achieved more popularity by his performances in that line than I by this exhibition of feeling; and, had the question been my election, I am very sure nobody else would have had a chance of a vote through the island. But wisely is it said that use is second nature, and the contempt and neglect to which these poor people are used make the commonest expression of human sympathy appear a boon and gracious condescension. While I am speaking of the negro countenance, there is another beauty which is not at all unfrequent among those I see here—a finely-shaped oval face—and those who know (as all painters and sculptors, all who understand beauty do) how much expression there is in the outline of the head, and how very rare it is to see a well-formed face, will be apt to consider this a higher matter than any coloring, of which, indeed, the red and white one so often admired is by no means the most rich, picturesque, or expressive. At first the dark color confounded all features to my eye, and I could hardly tell one face from another. Becoming, however, accustomed to the complexion, I now perceive all the variety among these black countenances that there is among our own race, and as much difference in features and in expression as among the same number of whites. There is another peculiarity which I have remarked among the women here—very considerable beauty in the make of the hands; their feet are very generally ill made, which must be a natural, and not an acquired defect, as they seldom injure their feet by wearing shoes. The figures of some of the women are handsome, and their carriage, from the absence of any confining or tightening clothing, and the habit they have of balancing great weights on their heads, erect and good.

At the upper end of the row of houses, and nearest to our overseer's residence, is the hut of the head driver. Let me explain, by the way, his office. The negroes, as I before told you, are divided into troops or gangs, as they are called; at the head of each gang is a driver, who stands over them, whip in hand, while they perform their daily task, who renders an account of each individual slave and his work every evening to the overseer, and receives from him directions for their next day's tasks. Each driver is allowed to inflict a dozen lashes upon any refractory slave in the field, and at the time of the offense; they may not, however, extend the chastisement, and if it is found ineffectual, their remedy lies in reporting the unmanageable individual either to the head driver or the overseer, the former of whom has power to inflict three dozen lashes at his own discretion, and the latter as many as he himself sees fit, within the number of fifty; which limit, however, I must tell you, is an arbitrary one on this plantation, appointed by the founder of the estate, Major ——, Mr. ——'s grandfather, many of whose regulations, indeed I believe most of them, are still observed in the government of the plantation. Limits of this sort, however, to the power of either driver, head driver, or overseer, may or may not exist elsewhere; they are, to a certain degree, a check upon the power of these individuals; but in the absence of the master, the overseer may confine himself within the limit or not, as he chooses; and as for the master himself, where is his limit? He may, if he likes, flog a slave to death, for the laws which pretend that he may not are a mere pretense, inasmuch as the testimony of a black is never taken against a white; and upon this plantation of ours, and a thousand more, the overseer is the *only* white man, so whence should come the testimony to any crime of his? With regard to the oft-repeated statement that it is not the owner's interest to destroy his human property, it answers nothing; the instances in which men, to gratify the immediate impulse of passion, sacrifice not only their eternal, but their evident, palpable, positive worldly interest, are infinite. Nothing is commoner than for a man under the transient influence of anger to disregard his worldly advantage; and the black slave, whose preservation is indeed supposed to be his owner's interest, may be, will be, and is occasionally sacrificed to the blind impulse of passion.

To return to our head driver, or, as he is familiarly called, head man, Frank—he is second in authority only to the overseer, and exercises rule alike over the drivers and the gangs in the absence of the sovereign white man from the estate, which happens whenever Mr. O—— visits the other two plantations at Woodville and St. Simon's. He is sole master and governor of the island, appoints the work, pronounces punishments, gives permission to the men to leave the island (without it they never may do so), and exercises all functions of undisputed mastery over his fellow-slaves, for you will observe that all this while he is just as much a slave as any of the rest. Trustworthy, upright, intelligent, he may be flogged to-morrow if Mr. O—— or Mr. —— so please it, and sold the next day, like a cart-horse, at the will of the latter. Besides his various other responsibilities, he has the key of all the stores, and gives out the people's rations weekly; nor is it only the people's provisions that are put under his charge—meat, which is only given out to them occasionally, and provisions for the use of the family, are also intrusted to his care. Thus you see, among these *inferior* creatures, their own masters yet look to find, surviving all their best efforts to destroy them, good sense, honesty, self-denial, and all the qualities, mental and moral, that make one man worthy to be trusted by another. From the imperceptible but inevitable effect of the sympathies and influences of human creatures toward and over each other, Frank's intelligence has become uncommonly developed by intimate communion in the discharge of his duty with the former overseer, a very intelligent man, who has only just left the estate, after managing it for nineteen years; the effect of this intercourse, and of the trust and responsibility laid upon the man, are that he is clear-headed, well judging, active, intelligent, extremely well mannered, and, being respected, he respects himself. He is as ignorant as the rest of the slaves; but he is always clean and tidy in his person, with a courteousness of demeanor far removed from servility, and exhibits a strong instance of the intolerable and wicked injustice of the system under which he lives, having advanced thus far toward improvement, in spite of all the bars it puts to progress; and here being arrested, not by want of energy, want of sense, or any want of his own, but by being held as another man's property, who can only thus hold him by forbidding him farther improvement. When I see that man, who keeps himself a good deal aloof from the rest, in his leisure hours looking, with a countenance of deep thought, as I did today, over the broad river, which is to him as a prison wall, to the fields and forest beyond, not one inch or branch of which his utmost industry can conquer as his own, or acquire and leave an independent heritage to his children, I marvel what the thoughts of such a man may be. I was in his house to-day, and the same superiority in cleanliness, comfort, and propriety exhibited itself in his dwelling as in his own personal appearance and that of his wife—a most active, trustworthy, excellent woman, daughter of the oldest, and probably most highly respected of all Mr. ——'s slaves. To the excellent conduct of this woman, and, indeed, every member of her family, both the present and the last overseer bear unqualified testimony.

As I was returning toward the house after my long morning's lounge, a man rushed out of the blacksmith's shop, and, catching me by the skirt of my gown, poured forth a torrent of self-gratulations on having at length found the "right missis." They have no idea, of course, of a white person performing any of the offices of a servant, and as throughout the whole Southern country the owner's children are nursed and tended, and sometimes *suckled* by their slaves (I wonder how this inferior milk agrees with the lordly *white* babies?), the appearance of M—— with my two children had immediately suggested the idea that she must be the missis. Many of the poor negroes flocked to her, paying their profound homage under this impression; and when she explained to them that she was not their owner's wife, the confusion in their minds seemed very great— Heaven only knows whether they did not conclude that they had two mistresses, and Mr. —— two wives; for the privileged race must seem, in their eyes, to have such absolute masterdom on earth, that perhaps they thought polygamy might be one of the sovereign white men's numerous indulgences. The ecstasy of the blacksmith on discovering the "right missis" at last was very funny, and was expressed with such extraordinary grimaces, contortions, and gesticulations, that I thought I should have died of laughing at this rapturous identification of my most melancholy relation to the poor fellow.

Having at length extricated myself from the group which forms round me whenever I stop but for a few minutes, I pursued my voyage of discovery by peeping into the kitchen garden. I dared do no more; the aspect of the place would have rejoiced the very soul of Solomon's sluggard of old—a few cabbages and weeds innumerable filled the neglected-looking inclosure, and I ventured no farther than the entrance into its most uninviting precincts. You are to understand that upon this swamp island of ours we have quite a large stock of cattle, cows, sheep, pigs, and poultry in the most enormous and inconvenient abundance. The cows are pretty miserably off for pasture, the banks and pathways of the dikes being their only grazing ground, which the sheep perambulate also, in earnest search of a nibble of fresh herbage; both the cows and sheep are fed with rice flour in great abundance, and are pretty often carried down for change of air and more sufficient grazing to Hampton, Mr. ——'s estate, on the island of St. Simon's, fifteen miles from this place, farther down the river—or rather, indeed, I should say in the sea, for 'tis salt water all round, and one end of the island has a noble beach open to the vast Atlantic.

FREDERICK LAW OLMSTED
(1822-1903)

Few visitors were as objective and expert as Frederick Law Olmsted in appraising the plantation system. This Hartford-born scientific farmer was the son of a prosperous merchant, who afforded him the opportunity of studying agricultural science and engineering at Yale. As a result of a stay in England he published the interesting *Walks and Talks of an American Farmer in England* (1852), noting rural life and city workmen, particularly the Liverpool working class. Much of the time he cultivated a 130-acre farm on Staten Island, which was devoted in large part to fruit trees. By the time he came to study the plantation system, he had a practicing expert's knowledge of farming.

Olmsted had already made up his mind about the evils of slavery before he accepted a journalistic assignment to visit the slave states extended by a fellow Free-Soiler, Henry Raymond, editor of the *New York Daily Times*. On December 11, 1852, he set out on a fourteen-month tour starting from Virginia down through the Deep South to Texas. He wrote his newspaper articles as he went along, and these became the substance of a trilogy of books, *A Journey in the Seaboard Slave States* (1856), *A Journey Through Texas* (1857), and *A Journey in the Back Country* (1860). These were condensed and considerably revised in *The Cotton Kingdom* (1861), just before the outbreak of war. In future years, Olmsted was to embark on a brilliant career as one of America's foremost landscape architects, designer of New York's Central Park and the White City at the Chicago's World Fair.

He hoped by his writings to convince planters that slavery did not pay —a mission not unlike that of Hinton R. Helper's *The Impending Crisis of the South* (1857), which appeared shortly after Olmsted's first book; but Olmsted's was a far more reliable and descriptive work than the polemic volume of the North Carolinian rebel. His acute interviews, his highly readable dialog, and his evaluative skill made his work easily the best account extant of the Old South and plantation slavery.

Taken from *A Journey in the Seaboard Slave States* (1856), pp. 88-115.

Half an hour after this I arrived at the negro-quarters—a little hamlet of ten or twelve small and dilapidated cabins. Just beyond them was a plain farm-gate, at which several negroes were standing; one of them, a well-made man, with an intelligent countenance and prompt manner, directed me how to find my way to his owner's house. It was still nearly a mile distant; and yet, until I arrived in its immediate vicinity, I saw no cultivated field, and but one clearing. On the edge of this clearing, a number of negroes, male and female, lay stretched out upon the ground near a small smoking charcoal pit. Their master afterwards informed me that they were burning charcoal for the plantation blacksmith, using the time allowed them for holidays—from Christmas to New Year's—to earn a little money for themselves in this way. He paid them by the bushel for it. When I said that I supposed he allowed them to take what wood they chose for this purpose, he replied that he had five hundred acres covered with wood, which he would be very glad to have any one burn, or clear off in any way. Cannot some Yankee contrive a method of concentrating some of the valuable properties of this old-field pine, so that they may be profitably brought into use in more cultivated regions? Charcoal is now brought to New York from Virginia; but when made from pine it is not very valuable, and will only bear transportation from the banks of the navigable rivers, whence it can be shipped, at one movement, to New York. Turpentine does not flow in sufficient quantity from this variety of the pine to be profitably collected, and for lumber it is of very small value.

Mr. W.'s house was an old family mansion, which he had himself remodeled in the Grecian style, and furnished with a large wooden portico. An oak forest had originally occupied the ground where it stood; but this having been cleared and the soil worn out in cultivation by the previous proprietors, pine woods now surrounded it in every direction, a square of a few acres only being kept clear immediately about it. A number of the old oaks still stood in the rear of the house, and, until Mr. W. commenced his improvements, there had been some in its front. These, however, he had cut away, as interfering with the symmetry of his grounds, and in place of them had planted ailanthus trees in parallel rows.

On three sides of the outer part of the cleared square there was a row of large and comfortable-looking negro-quarters, stables, tobacco-houses, and other offices, built of logs.

Mr. W. was one of the few large planters, of his vicinity, who still made the culture of tobacco their principal business. He said there was a general prejudice against tobacco, in all the tide-water region of the State, because it was through the culture of tobacco that the once fertile soils had been impoverished; but he did not believe that, at the present value of negroes, their labor could be applied to the culture of grain, with any profit, except under peculiarly favorable circumstances. Possibly, the use of guano might make wheat a paying crop, but he still doubted. He had not used it, himself. Tobacco required fresh land, and was rapidly exhausting, but it returned more money, for the labor used upon it, than anything else; enough more, in his opinion, to pay for the wearing out of the land. If he was well-paid for it, he did not know why he should not wear out his land.

His tobacco-fields were nearly all in a distant and lower part of his plantation; land which had been neglected before his time, in a great measure, because it had been sometimes flooded, and was, much of the year, too wet for cultivation. He was draining and clearing it, and it now brought good crops.

He had had an Irish gang draining for him, by contract. He thought a negro could do twice as much work, in a day, as an Irishman. He had not stood over them and seen them at work, but judged entirely from the amount they accomplished: he thought a good gang of negroes would have got on twice as fast. He was sure they must have "trifled" a great deal, or they would have accomplished more than they had. He complained much, also, of their sprees and quarrels. I asked why he should employ Irishmen, in preference to doing the work with his own hands. "It's dangerous work (unhealthy?), and a negro's life is too valuable to be risked at it. If a negro dies, it's a considerable loss, you know."

He afterwards said that his negroes never worked so hard as to tire themselves—always were lively, and ready to go off on a frolic at night He did not think they ever did half a fair day's work. They could not be made to work hard: they never would lay out their strength freely, and it was impossible to make them do it.

This is just what I have thought when I have seen slaves at work—they seem to go through the motions of labor without putting strength into them. They keep their powers in reserve for their own use at night, perhaps.

Mr. W. also said that he cultivated only the coarser and lower-priced sorts of tobacco, because the finer sorts required more painstaking and discretion than it was possible to make a large gang of negroes use. "You can make a nigger work," he said, *but you cannot make him think.*"

Although Mr. W. was very wealthy (or, at least, would be considered so anywhere at the North), and was a gentleman of education, his style of living was very farmer-like, and thoroughly Southern. On their plantations, generally, the Virginia gentlemen seem to drop their full-dress and constrained town-habits, and to live a free, rustic, shooting-jacket life. We dined in a room that extended out, rearwardly, from the house, and which, in a Northern establishment, would have been the kitchen. The cooking was done in a detached log-cabin, and the dishes brought some distance, through the open air, by the servants. The outer door was left constantly open though there was a fire in an enormous old fire-place, large enough, if it could have been distributed sufficiently, to have lasted a New York seamstress the best part of the winter. By the door, there was indiscriminate admittance to negro children and fox-hounds, and, on an average, there were four of these, grinning or licking their chops, on either side of my chair, all the time I was at the table. A stout woman acted as head waitress, employing two handsome little mulatto boys as her aids in communicating with the kitchen, from which relays of hot corn-bread, of an excellence quite new to me, were brought at frequent intervals. There was no other bread, and but one vegetable served—sweet potato, roasted in ashes, and this, I thought, was the best sweet potato, also, that I ever had eaten; but there were four preparations of swine's flesh, besides fried fowls, fried eggs, cold roast turkey, and opossum, cooked I know not how, but it somewhat resembled baked sucking-pig. The only beverages on the table were milk and whisky.

I was pressed to stay several days with Mr. W., and should have been glad to have accepted such hospitality, had not another engagement prevented. When I was about to leave, an old servant was directed to get a horse, and go with me, as guide, to the rail-road station at Col. Gillin's. He followed behind me, and I had great difficulty in inducing him to ride near enough to converse with me. I wished to ascertain from him how old the different stages of the old-field forest-growth, by the side of our road, might be; but, for a long time, he was, or pretended to be, unable to comprehend my questions. When he did so, the most accurate information he could give me was, that he reckoned such a field (in which the pines were now some sixty feet high) had been planted with tobacco the year his old master bought him. He thought he was about twenty years old then, and that now he was forty. He had every appearance of being seventy.

He frequently told me there was no need for him to go any further, and that it was a dead, straight road to the station, without any forks. As he appeared very eager to return, I was at length foolish enough to allow myself to be prevailed upon to dispense with his guidance; gave him a quarter of a dollar for his time that I had employed, and went on alone. The road, which for a short distance further was plain enough, soon began to ramify, and, in half an hour, we were stumbling along a dark wood-path, looking eagerly for a house. At length, seeing one across a large clearing, we went through a long lane, opening gates and letting down bars, until we met two negroes, riding a mule, who were going to the plantation near the school-house, which we had seen the day before. Following them thither, we knew the rest of the way (Jane gave a bound and neighed, when we struck the old road, showing that she had been lost, as well as I, up to the moment).

It was twenty minutes after the hour given in the time-table for the passage of the train, when I reached the station, but it had not arrived; nor did it make its appearance for a quarter of an hour longer; so I had plenty of time to deliver Tom's wife's message and take leave of Jane. I am sorry to say she appeared very indifferent, and seemed to think a good deal more of Tom than of me. Mr. W. had told me that the train would, probably, be half an hour behind its advertised time, and that I had no need to ride with haste, to reach it. I asked Col. Gillin if it would be safe to always calculate on the train being half an hour late: he said it would not; for, although usually that much behind the time-table, it was sometimes half an hour ahead of it. So those, who would be safe, had commonly to wait an hour. People, therefore, who wished to go not more than twenty miles from home, would find it more convenient, and equally expeditious, taking all things into account, to go in their own conveyances—there being but few who lived so near the station that they would not have to employ a horse and servant to get to it.

A FREE-LABOR FARM IN VIRGINIA

I have been visiting a farm, cultivated entirely by free-labor. The proprietor told me that he was first led to disuse slave-labor, not from any economical considerations, but because he had become convinced that there was an essential wrong in holding men in forced servitude with any other purpose than to benefit them alone, and because he was not willing to allow his own children to be educated as slave-masters. His father had been a large slave-holder, and he felt very strongly the bad influence it had had on his own character. He wished me to be satisfied that Jefferson uttered a great truth when he asserted that slavery was more pernicious to the white race than the black. Although, therefore, a chief part of his inheritance had been in slaves, he had liberated them all.

Most of them had, by his advice, gone to Africa. These he had frequently heard from. Except a child that had been drowned, they were, at his last account, all alive, in general good health, and satisfactorily prospering. He had lately received a letter from one of them, who told him that he was "*trying* to preach the Gospel," and who had evidently greatly improved, both intellectually and morally, since he left here. With regard to those going North, and the common opinion that they encountered much misery, and would be much better off here, he said that it entirely depended on the general character and habits of the individual: it was true of those who were badly brought up, and who had acquired indolent and vicious habits, especially if they were drunkards, but, if of some intelligence and well-trained, they generally represented themselves to be successful and contented.

He mentioned two remarkable cases, that had come under his own observation, of this kind. One was that of a man who had been free, but, by some fraud and informality of his papers, was reënslaved. He ran away, and afterwards negotiated, by correspondence, with his master, and purchased his freedom. This man he had accidentally met fifteen years afterwards, in a Northern city; he was engaged in profitable and increasing business, and showed him, by his books, that he was possessed of property to the amount of ten thousand dollars. He was living a great deal more comfortably and wisely than ever his old master had done. The other case was that of a colored woman, who had obtained her freedom, and who became apprehensive that she also was about to be fraudulently made a slave again. She fled to Philadelphia, where she was nearly starved, at first. A little girl, who heard her begging in the streets to be allowed to work for bread, told her that her mother was wanting some washing done, and she followed her home. The mother, not knowing her, was afraid to trust her with the articles to be washed. She prayed so earnestly for the job, however—suggesting that she might be locked into a room until she had completed it—that it was given her.

So she commenced life in Philadelphia. Ten years afterwards he had accidentally met her there; she recognized him immediately, recalled herself to his recollection, manifested the greatest joy at seeing him, and asked him to come to her house, which he found a handsome three-story building, furnished really with elegance; and she pointed out to him, from the window, three houses in the vicinity that she owned and rented. She showed great anxiety to have her children well educated, and was employing the best instructors for them which she could procure in Philadelphia.

This gentleman, notwithstanding his anti-slavery sentiments, by no means favors the running away of slaves, and thinks the Abolitionists have done immense harm to the cause they have at heart. He wishes Northerners would mind their business, and leave Slavery alone, say but little about it—nothing in the present condition of affairs at the South—and never speak of it but in a kind and calm manner. He would not think it right to return a fugitive slave; but he would never assist one to escape. He has several times purchased slaves, generally such as his neighbors were obliged to sell, and who would otherwise have been taken South. This he had been led to do by the solicitation of some of their relatives. He had retained them in his possession until their labor had in some degree returned their cost to him, and he could afford to provide them with the means of going to Africa or the North, and a small means of support after their arrival. Having received some suitable training in his family, they had, without exception, been successful, and had frequently sent him money to purchase the freedom of relatives or friends they had left in slavery.

He considered the condition of slaves to have much improved since the Revolution, and very perceptibly during the last twenty years. The original stock of slaves, the imported Africans, he observed, probably required to be governed with much greater severity, and very little humanity was exercised or thought of with regard to them. The slaves of the present day are of a higher character; in fact, he did not think more than half of them were full-blooded Africans. Public sentiment condemned the man who treated his slaves with cruelty. The owners were mainly men of some cultivation, and felt a family attachment to their slaves, many of whom had been the playmates of their boyhood. Nevertheless, they were frequently punished severely, under the impulse of temporary passion, often without deliberation, and on unfounded suspicion. This was especially the case where they were left to overseers, who, though sometimes men of intelligence and piety, were more often coarse, brutal, and licentious; drinking men, wholly unfitted for the responsibility imposed on them.

He had read "Uncle Tom's Cabin;" mentioned several points in which he thought it wrong—that Uncle Tom was too highly painted, for instance; that such a character could not exist in, or spring out of Slavery, and that no gentleman of Kentucky or Virginia would have allowed himself to be in the position with a slave-dealer in which Mr. Shelby is represented—but he acknowledged that cases of cruelty and suffering, equal to any described in it, might be found. In his own neighborhood, some time ago, a man had been whipped to death; and he recollected several that had been maimed for life, by harsh and hasty punishment; but the whole community were indignant when such things occurred, and any man guilty of them would be without associates, except of similar character.

The opinions of this gentleman must not, of course, be considered as representative of those of the South in general, by any means; but as to facts, he is a competent, and, I believe, a wholly candid and unprejudiced witness. He is much respected, and on terms of friendship with all his neighbors, though they do not like his views on this subject. He told me, however, that one of them, becoming convinced of their correctness some time ago, freed his slaves, and moved to Ohio. As to "Uncle Tom," it is generally criticised very severely, and its representations of Slavery indignantly denied. I observe that it is not placarded outside the booksellers' stores, though the whole fleet of gunboats that have been launched after it show their colors bravely. It must, however, be a good deal read here, as I judge from the frequent allusions I hear made to it.

With regard to the value of slave-labor, this gentleman is confident that, at present, he has the advantage in employing freemen instead of it. It has not been so until of late, the price of slaves having much advanced within ten years, while immigration has made free white laborers more easy to be procured.

He has heretofore had some difficulty in obtaining hands when he needed them, and has suffered a good deal from the demoralizing influence of adjacent slave-labor, the men, after a few months' residence, inclining to follow the customs of the slaves with regard to the amount of work they should do in a day, or their careless mode of operation. He has had white and black Virginians, sometimes Germans, and latterly Irish. Of all these, he has found the Irish on the whole the best. The poorest have been the native white Virginians; next, the free blacks: and though there have been exceptions, he has not generally paid these as high as one hundred dollars a year, and has thought them less worth their wages than any he has had. At present, he has two white natives and two free colored men, but both the latter were brought up in his family, and are worth twenty dollars a year more than the average. The free black, he thinks, is generally worse than the slave, and so is the poor white man. He also employs, at present, four Irish hands, and is expecting two more to arrive, who have been recommended to him, and sent for by those he has. He pays the Irishmen $120 a year, and boards them.

He has had them for $100; but these are all excellent men, and well worth their price. They are less given to drinking than any men he has ever had; and one of them first suggested improvements to him in his farm, that he is now carrying out with prospects of considerable advantage. House-maids, Irish girls, he pays $3 and $6 a month.

He does not apprehend that in future he shall have any difficulty in obtaining steady and reliable men, that will accomplish much more work than any slaves. There are some operations, such as carting and spreading dung, and all work with the fork, spade, or shovel, at which his Irishmen will do, he thinks, over fifty per cent more in a day than any negroes he has ever known. On the whole, he is satisfied that at present free-labor is more profitable than slave-labor, though his success is not so evident that he would be willing to have attention particularly called to it. His farm, moreover, is now in a transition state from one system of husbandry to another, and appearances are temporarily more unfavorable on that account.

The wages paid for slaves, when they are hired for agricultural labor, do not differ at present, he says, from those which he pays for his free laborers. In both cases the hiring party boards the laborer, but, in addition to money and board, the slave-employer has to furnish clothing, and is subject, without redress, to any losses which may result from the carelessness or malevolence of the slave. He also has to lose his time if he is unwell, or when from any cause he is absent or unable to work.

The slave, if he is indisposed to work, and especially if he is not treated well, or does not like the master who has hired him, will sham sickness—even make himself sick or lame—that he need not work. But a more serious loss frequently arises, when the slave, thinking he is worked too hard, or being angered by punishment or unkind treatment, "getting the sulks," takes to "the swamp," and comes back when he has a mind to. Often this will not be till the year is up for which he is engaged, when he will return to his owner, who, glad to find his property safe, and that it has not died in the swamp, or gone to Canada, forgets to punish him, and immediately sends him for another year to a new master.

"But, meanwhile, how does the negro support life in the swamp?" I asked.

"Oh, he gets sheep and pigs and calves, and fowls and turkeys; sometimes they will kill a small cow. We have often seen the fires, where they were cooking them, through the woods, in the swamp yonder. If it is cold, he will crawl under a fodder-stack, or go into the cabins with some of the other negroes, and in the same way, you see, he can get all the corn, or almost anything else he wants."

"He steals them from his master?"

"From any one; frequently from me. I have had many a sheep taken by them."

"It is a common thing, then?"

"Certainly, it is, very common, and the loss is sometimes exceedingly provoking. One of my neighbors here was going to build, and hired two mechanics for a year. Just as he was ready to put his house up, the two men, taking offense at something, both ran away, and did not come back at all, till their year was out, and then their owner immediately hired them out again to another man."

These negroes "in the swamp," he said, were often hunted after, but it was very difficult to find them, and, if caught, they would run again, and the other negroes would hide and assist them. Dogs to track them he had never known to be used in Virginia.

RECREATION AND LUXURY AMONG THE SLAVES

Saturday, Dec. 25. From Christmas to New-Year's Day, most of the slaves, except house servants, enjoy a freedom from labor; and Christmas is especially holiday, or Saturnalia, with them. The young ones began last night firing crackers, and I do not observe that they are engaged in any other amusement to-day; the older ones are generally getting drunk, and making business for the police. I have seen large gangs coming in from the country, and these contrast much in their general appearance with the town negroes. The latter are dressed expensively, and frequently more elegantly than the whites. They seem to be spending money freely, and I observe that they, and even the slaves that wait upon me at the hotel, often have watches, and other articles of value.

The slaves have a good many ways of obtaining "spending money," which, though in law belonging to their owner, as the property of a son under age does to his father, they are never dispossessed of, and use for their own gratification, with even less restraint than a wholesome regard for their health and moral condition may be thought to require. A Richmond paper, complaining of the liberty allowed to slaves in this respect, as calculated to foster an insubordinate spirit, speaks of their "champagne suppers." The police broke into a gambling cellar a few nights since, and found about twenty negroes at "high play," with all the usual accessories of a first-class "Hell." It is mentioned that, among the number taken to the watch-house, and treated with lashes the next morning, there were some who had previously enjoyed a high reputation for piety, and others of a very elegant or foppish appearance.

Passing two negroes in the street, I heard the following:

"——Workin' in a tobacco factory all de year roun', an' come Christmas, only twenty dollars! Workin' mighty hard, too—up to 12 o'clock o' night very often—an' then to hab a nigger oberseah!"

"A nigger!"

"Yes—dat's it, yer see. Wouldn't care if 'twarnt for dat. Nothin' but a dirty nigger! orderin' 'round, jes' as if he was a wite man!"

It is the custom of tobacco manufacturers to hire slaves and free negroes at a certain rate of wages per year. A task of 45 lbs. per day is given them to work up, and all that they choose to do more than this they are paid for—payment being made once a fortnight; and invariably this over-wages is used by the slave for himself, and is usually spent in drinking, licentiousness and gambling. The man was grumbling that he had saved but $20 to spend at the holidays. One of the manufacturers offered to show me, by his books, that nearly all gained by overwork $5 a month, many $20, and some as much as $28.

INGENUITY OF THE NEGRO

Sitting with a company of smokers last night, one of them, to show me the manner in which a slave of any ingenuity or cunning would manage to avoid working for his master's profit, narrated the following anecdote. He was executor of an estate in which, among other negroes, there was one very smart man, who, he knew perfectly well, ought to be earning for the estate $150 a year, and who could do it if he chose, yet whose wages for a year, being let out by the day or job, had amounted to but $18, while he had paid for medical attendance upon him $45. Having failed in every other way to make him earn anything, he proposed to him that he should purchase his freedom and go to Philadelphia, where he had a brother. He told him if he would earn a certain sum ($400 I believe), and pay it over to the estate for himself, he would give him his free papers. The man agreed to the arrangement, and by his overwork in a tobacco factory, and some assistance from his free brother, soon paid the sum agreed upon, and was sent to Philadelphia. A few weeks afterwards he met him in the street, and asked him why he had returned. "Oh, I don't like dat Philadelphy, massa; ant no chance for colored folks dere; spec' if I'd been a runaway, de wite folks dere take care o' me; but I couldn't git anythin' to do, so I jis borrow ten dollar of my broder, and cum back to old Virginny."

"But you know the law forbids your return. I wonder that you are not afraid to be seen here; I should think Mr. —— (an officer of police) would take you up."

"Oh! I look out for dat, Massa, I juss hire myself out to Mr. —— himself, ha! ha! He tink I your boy."

And so it proved, the officer, thinking that he was permitted to hire himself out, and tempted by the low wages at which he offered himself, had neglected to ask for his written permission, and had engaged him for a year. He still lived with the officer, and was an active, healthy, good servant to him.

QUALITIES AS A LABORER

A well-informed capitalist and slave-holder remarked, that negroes could not be employed in cotton factories. I said that I understood they were so in Charleston, and some other places at the South.

"It may be so, *yet*," he answered, "but they will have to give it up."

The reason was, he said, that the negro could never be trained to exercise judgment; he cannot be made to use his mind; he always depends on machinery doing its own work, and cannot be made to watch it. He neglects it until something is broken or there is great waste. "We have tried reward and punishments, but it makes no difference. It's his nature and you cannot change it. All men are indolent and have a disinclination to labor, but this is a great deal stronger in the African race than in any other. In working niggers, we just always calculate that they will not labor at all except to avoid punishment, and they will never do more than just enough to save themselves from being punished, and no amount of punishment will prevent their working carelessly and indifferently. It always seems on the plantation as if they took pains to break all the tools and spoil all the cattle that they possibly can, even when they know they'll be directly punished for it."

As to rewards, he said, "They only want to support life, they will not work for anything more; and in this country it would be hard to prevent their getting that." I thought this opinion of the power of rewards was not exactly confirmed by the narrative we had just heard, but I said nothing. "If you could move," he continued, "all the white people from the whole seaboard district of Virginia and give it up to the negroes that are on it now, just leave them to themselves, in ten years time there would not be an acre of land cultivated, and nothing would be produced, except what grew spontaneously."

The Hon. Willoughby Newton, by the way, seems to think that if it had not been for the introduction of guano, a similar desolation would have soon occurred without the Africanization of the country. He is reported to have said:

"I look upon the introduction of guano, and the success attending its application to our barren lands, in the light of a special interposition of Divine Providence, to save the northern neck of Virginia from reverting entirely into its former state of wilderness and utter desolation. Until the discovery of guano—more valuable to us than the mines of California—I looked upon the possibility of renovating our soil, of ever bringing it to a point capable of producing remunerating crops, as utterly hopeless. Our up-lands were all worn out, and our bottom-lands fast failing, and if it had not been for guano, to revive our last hope, a few years more and the whole country must have been deserted by all who desired to increase their own wealth, or advance the cause of civilization by a proper cultivation of the earth."

IMPROVEMENT OF THE NEGRO IN SLAVERY

"But are they not *improving?*" said I; "that is a point in which I am much interested, and I should be glad to know what is your observation? Have they not, as a race, improved during the last hundred years, do you not think?"

"Oh, yes indeed, very greatly. During my time—I can remember how they were forty years ago—they have improved *two thousand per cent.!* Don't you think so?" he asked another gentleman.

"Yes; certainly."

"And you may find them now, on the isolated old plantations in the back country, just as I recollect them when I was a boy, stupid and moping, and with no more intelligence than when they first came from Africa. But all about where the country is much settled their condition is vastly ameliorated. They are treated much better, they are fed better, and they have much greater educational privileges."

EDUCATIONAL PRIVILEGES

"Educational privileges?" I asked, in surprise.

"I mean by preaching and religious instruction. They have the Bible read to them a great deal, and there is preaching for them all over the country. They have preachers of their own; right smart ones they are, too, some of them."

"Do they?" said I. "I thought that was not allowed by law."

"Well, it is not—that is, they are not allowed to have meetings without some white man is present. They must not preach unless a white man hears what they say. However, they do. On my plantation, they always have a meeting on Sundays, and I have sometimes, when I have been there, told my overseer,—'You must go up there to the meeting, you know the law requires it;' and he would start as if he was going, but would just look in and go by; he wasn't going to wait for them."

A DISTINGUISHED DIVINE

He then spoke of a minister, whom he owned, and described him as a very intelligent man. He knew almost the whole of the Bible by heart. He was a fine-looking man—a fine head and a very large frame. He had been a sailor, and had been in New Orleans and New York, and many foreign ports. "He could have left me at any time for twenty years, if he had wished to," he said. "I asked him once how he would like to live in New York? Oh, he did not like New York at all! niggers were not treated well there—there was more distinction made between them and white folks than there was here. 'Oh, dey ain't no place in de worl like Ole Virginny for niggers, massa,' says he."

Another gentleman gave similar testimony.

HOW THEY ARE FED

I said I supposed that they were much better off, more improved intellectually, and more kindly treated in Virginia than further South. He said I was mistaken in both respects—that in Louisiana, especially, they were more intelligent, because the amalgamation of the races was much greater, and they were treated with more familiarity by the whites; besides which, the laws of Louisiana were much more favorable to them. For instance, they required the planter to give slaves 200 pounds of pork a year: and he gave a very apt anecdote, showing the effect of this law, but which, at the same time, made it evident that a Virginian may be accustomed to neglect providing sufficient food for his force, and that they sometimes suffer greatly for want of it. I was assured, however, that this was very rare—that, generally, the slaves were well provided for—always allowed a sufficient quantity of meal, and, generally, of pork—were permitted to raise pigs and poultry, and in summer could always grow as many vegetables as they wanted. It was observed, however, that they frequently neglected to provide for themselves in this way, and live mainly on meal and bacon. If a man does not provide well for his slaves, it soon becomes known, he gets the name of a "nigger killer," and loses the respect of the community.

The general allowance of food was thought to be a peck and a half of meal, and three pounds of bacon a week. This, it was observed, is as much meal as they can eat, but they would be glad to have more bacon; sometimes they receive four pounds, but it is oftener that they get less than three. It is distributed to them on Saturday nights; or, on the better managed plantations, sometimes, on Wednesday, to prevent their using it extravagantly, or selling it for whisky on Sunday. This distribution is called the "drawing," and is made by the overseer to all the heads of families or single negroes. Except on the smallest plantations, where the cooking is done in the house of the proprietor, there is a cook-house, furnished with a large copper for boiling, and an oven. Every night the negroes take their "mess," for the next day's breakfast and dinner, to the cook, to be prepared for the next day. Custom varies as to the time it is served out to them; sometimes at morning and noon, at other times at noon and night. Each negro marks his meat by cuts, so that he shall know it from the rest, and they observe each other's rights with regard to this, punctiliously.

After breakfast has been eaten early in the cabins, at sunrise or a little before in winter, and perhaps a little later in summer, they go to the field. At noon dinner is brought to them, and, unless the work presses, they are allowed two hours' rest. Very punctually at sunset they stop work and are at liberty, except that a squad is detached once a week for shelling corn, to go to the mill for the next week's drawing of meal. Thus they work in the field about eleven hours a day on an average. Returning to the cabins, wood "ought to have been" carted for them; but if it has not been, they then go to the woods and "tote" it home for themselves. They then make a fire—a big, blazing fire at this season, for the supply of fuel is unlimited—and cook their own supper, which will be a bit of bacon fried, often with eggs, corn-bread baked in the spider after the bacon, to absorb the fat, and perhaps some sweet potatoes roasted in the ashes. Immediately after supper they go to sleep, often lying on the floor or a bench in preference to a bed. About two o'clock they very generally rouse up and cook and eat, or eat cold, what they call their "mornin' bit;" then sleep again till breakfast.

I think the slaves generally (no one denies that there are exceptions) have plenty to eat; probably are fed better than the proletarian class of any other part of the world. I think that they generally save from their ration of meal. My informant said that commonly as much as five bushels of meal was sent to town by his hands every week, to be sold for them. Upon inquiry, he almost always found that it belonged to only two or three individuals, who had traded for it with the rest; he added, that too often the exchange was for whisky, which, against his rules, they obtained of some rascally white people in the neighborhood, and kept concealed. They were very fond of whisky, and sometimes much injured themselves with it.

To show me how well they were supplied with eggs, he said that once a vessel came to anchor, becalmed, off his place, and the captain came to him and asked leave to purchase some eggs of his people. He gave him permission, and called the cook to collect them for him. The cook asked how many she should bring. "Oh, all you can get," he answered—and she returned after a time, with several boys assisting her, bringing nearly two bushels, all the property of the slaves, and which they were willing to sell at four cents a dozen.

One of the smokers explained to me that it is very bad economy, not to allow an abundant supply of food to "a man's force." The negroes are fond of good living, and, if not well provided for, know how to provide for themselves. It is, also, but simple policy to have them well lodged and clothed. If they do not have comfortable cabins and sufficient clothing, they will take cold, and be laid up. He lost a very valuable negro, once, from having neglected to provide him with shoes.

LODGINGS

The houses of the slaves are usually log-cabins, of various degrees of comfort and commodiousness. At one end there is a great open fire-place, which is exterior to the wall of the house, being made of clay in an inclosure, about eight feet square and high, of logs. The chimney is sometimes of brick, but more commonly of lath or split sticks, laid up like log-work and plastered with mud. They enjoy great roaring fires, and, as the common fuel is pitch pine, the cabin, at night when the door is open, seen from a distance, appears like a fierce furnace. The chimneys often catch fire, and the cabin is destroyed. Very little precaution can be taken against this danger. Several cabins are placed near together, and they are called "the quarters." On a plantation of moderate size there will be but one "quarters." The situation chosen for it has reference to convenience of obtaining water from springs and fuel from the woods. On some of the James River plantations there are larger houses, boarded and made ornamental. In these, eight families, each having a distinct sleeping-room and lock-up closets, and every two having a common kitchen or living-room, are accommodated.

CLOTHING

As to the clothing of the slaves on the plantations, they are said to be usually furnished by their owners or masters, every year, each with a coat and trousers, of a coarse woolen or woolen and cotton stuff (mostly made, especially for this purpose, in Providence, R. I.), for Winter, trousers of cotton osnaburghs for Summer, sometimes with a jacket also of the same; two pairs of strong shoes, or one pair of strong boots and one of lighter shoes for harvest; three shirts; one blanket, and one felt hat.

The women have two dresses of striped cotton, three shifts, two pairs of shoes, etc. The women lying-in are kept at knitting short sacks, from cotton which, in Southern Virginia, is usually raised, for this purpose, on the farm, and these are also given to the negroes. They also purchase clothing for themselves, and, I notice especially, are well supplied with handkerchiefs which the men frequently, and the women nearly always, wear on their heads. On Sundays and holidays they usually look very smart, but when at work, very ragged and slovenly.

At the conclusion of our bar-room session, some time after midnight, as we were retiring to our rooms, our progress up stairs and along the corridors was several times impeded, by negroes lying fast asleep, in their usual clothes only, upon the floor. I asked why they were not abed, and was answered by a gentleman, that negroes never wanted to go to bed; they always preferred to sleep upon the floor.

FRATERNITY

As I was walking in the outskirts of the town this morning, I saw squads of negro and white boys together, pitching pennies and firing crackers in complete fraternization. The white boys manifested no superiority, or assumption of it, over the dark ones.

An old, palsied negro-woman, very thinly and very raggedly clad, met me and spoke to me. I could not, from the trembling incoherency of her voice, understand what she said, but she was evidently begging, and I never saw a more pitiable object of charity at the North. She was, perhaps, a free person, with no master and no system to provide for her.

I saw, for the first time in my life, two or three young white women smoking tobacco in clay pipes. From their manner it was evidently a well-formed habit, and one which they did not suspect there was occasion for them to practice clandestinely, or be ashamed of.

RELIGIOUS CONDITION

With regard to the moral and religious condition of the slaves, I cannot, either from what I observe, or from what is told me, consider it in any way gratifying. They are forbidden by law to meet together for worship, or for the purpose of mutual improvement. In the cities, there are churches especially for them, in which the exercises are conducted by white clergymen. In the country, there is usually a service, after that for the whites especially, in all the churches which, by the way, are not very thickly scattered. In one parish, about twenty miles from Richmond, I was told that the colored congregation in the afternoon is much smaller than that of the whites in the morning; and it was thought not more than one-fifth of the negroes living within a convenient distance were in the habit of attending it; and of these many came late, and many more slept through the greater part of the service.

A goodly proportion of them, I am told, "profess religion," and are received into the fellowship of the churches; but it is evident, of the greater part even of these, that their idea of religion, and the standard of morality which they deem consistent with a "profession" of it, is very degraded. That they are subject to intense excitements, often really maniacal, which they consider to be religious, is true; but as these are described, I cannot see that they indicate anything but a miserable system of superstition, the more painful that it employs some forms and words ordinarily connected with true Christianity.

A Virginia correspondent of the *N. Y. Times,* writing upon the general religious condition of the State, and of the comparative strength and usefulness of the different churches, says:

"The Baptists also number (in Eastern Virginia) 44,000 colored members. This makes a great difference. Negroes join the church—perhaps in a great majority of cases—with no ideas of religion. I have but little confidence in their religious professions. Many of them I hope are very pious; but many of them are great scoundrels—perhaps the great majority of them—regardless of their church profession as a rule of conduct. They are often baptized in great numbers, and the Baptist Church (so exemplary in so much) is to blame, I fear, in the ready admission it gives to the negroes.

"The Baptist Church generally gets the negroes—where there are no Baptists, the Methodist. *Immersion* strikes their fancy. It is a palpable, overt act, that their imagination can take hold of. The ceremony mystically impresses them, as the ceremonies of Romanism affect the devotees of that connection. They come up out of the water, and believe they see 'the Lord.' In their religion, negroes are excessively superstitious. They have all sorts of 'experiences,' and enjoy the most wonderful revelations. Visions of the supernatural are of nightly occurrence, and the most absurd circumstances are invested with some marvelous significance. I have heard that the great ordeal, in their estimation, a 'seeker' had to pass, was being *held over the infernal flames by a thread or a hair*. If the thread does not break, the suspendee is 'in the Lord.'

"It is proper, therefore, I think, to consider this circumstance, in estimating the strength of a Church, whose communicants embrace such a number of negroes. Of the Methodists, in Eastern Virginia, some six or seven thousand are colored."

This condition of the slaves is not necessarily a reproach to those whose duty it more particularly is to instruct and preach the true Gospel to them. It is, in a great degree, a necessary result of the circumstances of their existence. The possession of arbitrary power has always, the world over, tended irresistibly to destroy humane sensibility, magnanimity, and truth. . . .

CHARLES MACKAY
(*1814-1889*)

Among the thoughtful English critics of slavery was the internationally famous poet, composer, and journalist Charles Mackay, editor of the *Glasgow Argus,* who visited the United States during 1857-1858. Americans already knew where he stood, for 20,000 copies of his song of John Brown of Osawatomie had been bought. Newspapers praised his lecture tour on "Songs, National, Historical, and Popular." Out of his visit came a book that was both analytical and readable, *Life and Liberty in America* (1859) which appeared just at the moment of John Brown's raid on Harper's Ferry.

Mackay thought that slavery and the Southern climate had enervated the slaveholder's character—a common view of the time—and pointed out the dangerous implications for freedom of all races in George Fitzhugh's proslavery propaganda.

Below is all of Chapter 28 of *Life and Liberty in America.*

THE SOCIAL AND POLITICAL
ASPECTS OF SLAVERY

Washington, March 25, 1859

No traveler in the United States who desires to record his free, unbiased opinions can give the go-by to the question of slavery. That question has long been a sore in the bosom of the Great Republic, but has not pressed at any time for immediate solution. It has been a difficult and complicated, as well as an exasperating subject. It has been the battle-ground of parties—the touchstone of political life— the theme of the senate, the platform, the pulpit, and the press; but it has involved too many personal and national interests, and been of too vital an importance to the integrity of the Union to be driven even by the most zealous friends of negro freedom to such a point as to force a deliverance. If, on the one hand, there were slavery to be abolished, there was, upon the other, the union of the thirty-two republics which lend a star each to the banner of the states to be maintained inviolate. Many abolitionists have been prepared for the *fiat justitia,* but not for the *ruat coelum;* and the few able and earnest men who have avowed themselves ready to confront all con-sequences, however ominous or fatal, have been in such a minority as to render their action hopeless for the present, and to adjourn it into the indefinite future, where all hopes grow, and where all theories gradually transform themselves into facts.

In the District of Columbia slavery is not offensive in its outward manifestations; and Washington contains a large number of free negroes. But the fact that slavery is permitted to exist within the district is made a particular grievance by the abolitionists of the free North. "You have slavery in your own states," they say to the people of the slave-holding South, "and, unfortunately, we have not the power to interfere with you; but we know of no right that you have to introduce the objectionable and criminal system into Columbia and the City of Washington, which belong to the whole Union, and not to the South, and to us quite as much as to you." The South has replied by insisting on as much right to maintain slavery as the North has to abolish it; that possession is nine points of the law, and that, being in possession, they are determined to remain so. Several attempts have been made by the abolition party to carry a law through Congress to free the national capital and its small surrounding district from the "domestic institution" of the South, but hitherto in vain. The fact, however, suggests the opportunity to say a few words on the social and political aspects of this great question, not simply as affecting the national metropolis, but as affecting both the white and the black races in every part of the Union.

It was intended by the original framers of the Declaration of Independence that all the United States should be free. Wiser at this time than the monarchy, whose yoke they so gallantly threw off, they thought to repudiate slavery, and all that appertained to it. It was their wish to set an example to the world. They desired to proclaim that "a man was a man for a' that," and that the accident of his color made no difference in his rights or his responsibilities. But a timid and unwise conservatism, even at this early stage of American history, was permitted to prevail, and because slavery *was*, it was allowed *to be*. At a later period, the parent monarchy, impelled by the irresistible impetus communicated to its actions by the people, abolished slavery in all its forms and phases. The republic profiting, or fancying that it profited, by the evil thing, and not only tolerating, but loving it, because it was established, refused to follow the noble example. Thus it sowed dragons' teeth over more than half of the fairest dominion that ever in all recorded history fell to the lot of an energetic and intelligent race. The result is what we now see, and what all the friends of human liberty deplore. The dragons' teeth have grown up into giants. Frankenstein has made his monster, and the monster puts poison into the cup of prosperity, and keeps his master in constant terror of a day of retribution. Slavery, that might have been easily eradicated half a century ago, has assumed such formidable dimensions that it is hard to say which is the more difficult thing to do—to put up with it, or to abolish it; and which course is fraught with the most danger—to give the slaves their freedom, or to allow them to increase and multiply in bondage. But the history of such model states as Massachusetts—one of the most respectable and wise communities in the world—and, indeed, of all the New England States, together with New York and Pennsylvania, and the commonwealths of the West, which are gradually spreading themselves to the bases of the Rocky Mountains, is a proof not only of the far-sighted philanthropy, but of the worldly wisdom of the men who, at the earliest period of American history, washed their hands of the shame and guilt of slavery. The free states are not only the most populous, the most wealthy, and the most energetic in the Union; but by the activity of their intellect, the exuberance of their literature, and the general vigor—public and social, as well as private and commercial—of their citizens, they give the law and the tone to the whole of the Union. Massachusetts, Vermont, New Hampshire, Rhode Island, Connecticut, and Maine—small in extent, and, with the exception of Maine, as finely cultivated and almost as densely peopled as that Old England from whose shores their early founders emigrated, in disgust with the political and religious tyranny of their time—are the great hives that supply the fruitful and all but illimitable West.

The emigration from Ireland, from Germany, and from Norway, great as it is, would not keep the great West in healthful and progressive motion, were it not for the Yankees of New England. It is these who drift off from their parent establishments in these elderly states—for Massachusetts, as a commonwealth, is older than many European kingdoms, and not much more juvenile than Prussia—and who found mills, banks, stores, newspapers, churches, chapels, and universities in the wilderness of the Upper Mississippi and Missouri. Every now and then, when their numbers have sufficiently increased by European and other immigration, they "thunder at the gates of the capital," and claim admission for the new territory which they have wrested from desolation or from the Indians as a sovereign state and component part of the greatest confederation in the world. The non-existence of slavery within their bounds is one of the causes of their unparalleled growth and prosperity. The poor white man—the ragged, half-starved Irishman—with nothing to offer in exchange for his food, lodging, and raiment but the unskilled labor of his brawny arms; the frugal German and Norwegian, desirous to gain a few dollars by hard manual labor, and to invest the results of the purchase of an acre or two of the virgin earth—will not settle in large numbers in the slaveholding states. In the South they would enter into competition with the slave, and the slave, as far as mere labor goes, is master of the position. In the ruder operations of the field and plantation, where no particular intelligence is required, and where a horse is almost as good a laborer as a man, he is cheaper than the white race; and the white man, with higher aspirations than to be always a hewer of wood and a drawer of water, naturally betakes himself to regions where negro labor does not come into competition with his own, and where he will not be kept by capitalists, either of land or money, at a lower level than he believes to be his by right of his superior mind.

The free states are progressive, and, to use the regular Yankee word, "go-a-head-ative." They see far before them. They do not stand continually upon the ancient ways. Like Englishmen and Scotchmen, with whom they have many points of resemblance, they are "look-a-head-ative" as well as "go-a-head-ative," if I may imitate themselves so far as to coin an ugly but expressive word for the occasion; and, seeing that the whole continent requires to be settled and cut up into commonwealths; thinking little of distance and of time, and scarcely considering either as impediments to any work which they may undertake, or to any design on the accomplishment of which they have set their hearts; knowing no superiors to themselves, politically or socially, and being fired with the ambition not simply to become rich, but to be eminent and powerful, they manufacture states for the Union as well as fortunes for themselves. They give their names to towns, cities, and counties, and do, in this advanced age of the world, and by a different process, what the early Saxons and Danes did twelve hundred years ago for the British Isles. The people of the free states have an immense work yet before them. Maine is the only one of the six New England States that exists to any considerable extent in the condition of the primeval wilderness. The other five are finished. Their roads are made, the tree-stumps have been long ago removed, the original forest has disappeared, except where it has been allowed to remain, here and there, in small patches, for its beauty and amenity. The log hut is not often to be seen; but the neat, elegant, comfortable white house, the church, the chapel, the bank, are every where to be met with. There is no trace of squalor or of misery, but over the whole land there is an air of refinement and of high civilization. But the other free states have not yet arrived at the same high culture. Large portions of the "Empire State" of New York are still in a state of nature, and, though the Red Man has long ago disappeared, the bear and the wolf are in possession of districts not a day's journey by rail from the mighty city of Manhattan, and almost within sound of the paddle of the monster steam-boats that ply upon the Hudson. With capabilities of soil and climate, and with natural resources more than sufficient to feed a population of ten or twelve millions, the State of New York, though constantly invaded by the Saxon, Celtic, and Scandinavian immigration, has a resident population of less than four and a half millions. Though the most populous state in the Union, and absolutely much richer, both in wealth and in men, than England was in the days when Henry VIII first began to make England a power in the world, and almost as populous as when Cromwell first made his country to be feared and respected throughout Europe, still, New York is but half peopled. Pennsylvania, another large and flourishing commonwealth, with agricultural and mineral wealth all but inexhaustible in its soil, is not more populous than Scotland; and Ohio, one of the noblest of all the free states, and able to support as large a population as England, numbers upon its fruitful bosom little more than two millions of people, or a million less than London and its circumjacent boroughs.

Indiana—which an intelligent old Scotchman, who had cultivated his farm in it for upward of ten years, declared to me, with an expression of sorrow in his rough, honest countenance, to be an unwholesome place for a man of northern blood to live in—might contain and feed the whole population now existing in the United States, and be all the better for the burden, does not number above a million and a half of people. I asked the Scotchman what was his objection to Indiana? "Objection," he replied, with a strong Highland accent; "objection, did ye say? There is no objection but to its overfruitfulness. The soil is so rich, the climate so delicious, that the farmer has no adequate inducement to work. The earth produces its fruits too readily. The original curse presses too lightly. The sweat of a man's brow is to be read of, but not to be experienced here; and the very air is balmy and sleepy. Idleness is the affliction that we have to struggle against; and idleness leads to drinking, and to quarrelsomeness, and all other evil. Satan is to be fought with hard work, and that will conquer him better than preaching. Na, na," he added, shaking his head, "if I had my life to live over again, and know what I know now, I would settle in a ruder soil and in a colder climate. Men whose ancestors are from the cold North—the wholesome North, I say—require frost to bring out their virtues. Heat is fatal to the true Scotchman, and, for that matter, to the true Englishman also. Men of our blood thrive upon difficulties. We grow rich and fat upon toil and obstruction; but here, in Indiana, Illinois, and away to the West as far as you can go, man gains his bread too easily to remain virtuous. This is a matter," he continued, "which people do not sufficiently consider. The Southern and Middle States will in time deteriorate for these reasons, but the North—the North—*that* will be the country. And as for Canada, no one can describe, without being accused of extravagance, the greatness and the glory of which it may be made capable." In this respect, if my Highland friend was right—which I firmly believe he was—Wisconsin, Iowa, Kansas, and the large territories of Nebraska, Oregon, and Columbia, large enough to be made into fifty commonwealths of the extent of Massachusetts, may share with Canada the advantages of a climate that makes men hardy, enterprising, and strong. It certainly seems to have been of some effect in stimulating the energies of the "Yankees," and in making them, all things considered, the sharpest, smartest, and most eminent people in the Union—a people little loved, perhaps, but very much respected.

In the Southern States, partly, perhaps, from the influence of the climate, but more probably in a still greater degree from the operation of slavery upon the life, character, and feeling of the whites, there is nothing like the same social, commercial, and literary energy that exists in the North. The contrast between these two sections of the Union is in this respect most remarkable. Between Massachusetts and South Carolina, between Vermont and Arkansas, between Connecticut and Alabama, there exists almost as great a difference in every thing, except language and the style of dress and architecture, as there does between Scotland and Portugal, England and Naples, Wales and the Ionian Islands. The cities in the free "Far West" double, treble, and quadruple their population in twenty, sometimes in ten years. The cities of the slave states, and the slave states themselves, either remain stationary or increase disproportionately. In the free states all is bustle and activity; in the slave states there is elegant and drowsy stagnation. The railways in the North are well conducted. Populous towns, villages, and manufactories swarm and glitter along the line; but in the South the railways are for the most part ill-served and ill-regulated. The land is imperfectly cultivated, and the primeval forest is more extensive than the farms and plantations. The great rivers Missouri and Mississippi run for nearly two thousand miles through a comparative wilderness; the reclaimed land on either side occupies but a very narrow belt and border of the illimitable dominion that man has yet to rescue from the wild animals, and from the super-exuberant forest and the deadly swamp.

Even in Virginia, ancient enough to have been called by the same name when the empire now known as Russia was called Muscovy, and whence the swamp and the wilderness have long since disappeared, there is an air of non-progressiveness, if not decay and desolation.

The traveler from New England and the other free states no sooner penetrates into the slave-land than he sees all around him the proofs that slavery is omnipresent; not in the mere appearance of negroes at every turn and in all places, for they are to be found every where in America, but in the slovenly cultivation, the want of drainage, the absence of towns and villages in the rural districts, and the paucity of population even in the largest cities. Competition—the very soul of progress—is scarcely to be found. Where it exists at all it is only among the retail tradesmen. Thought is not free. You may talk of the dissolution of the Union as desirable and probable, abuse the president and his ministers, speak ill of Congress collectively and individually, be profane or immoral in your speech or life, but you must not say a word against the sanctity of the "Domestic Institution." Rome itself, with its *Index Expurgatorius,* does not act with an effect more blighting and deadly upon intellectual activity than the South does when it forbids the expression of opinion on this subject. No doubt it would be dangerous to allow of free discussion; as dangerous as it would be in Rome to allow Protestant divines to dispute publicly with priests and cardinals on the vital truths of Christianity, or the comparative merits of Luther and Pope Hildebrand. Slavery being an admitted fact and an established institution, it is not to be supposed that those who are educated in the belief that they profit by it can do otherwise than forbid, within their own jurisdiction, the calling of it in question, either by zealous and malignant philanthropists among themselves, or by interlopers from New or Old England, but the fact remains that thought is not free. Consequently, the wings of the Angel of Knowledge are clipped, so that he can not soar into the empyrean or sit upon the clouds. Literature, which can not attain its full development under any system of restriction or impediment whatsoever, whether it be theological, political, or social, attains but a stunted and imperfect growth. It loses its most generous inspiration, the sense of absolute liberty. It becomes conventional instead of natural. It "gives up to party what was meant for mankind;" and, as a necessary consequence of its thraldom, finds it impossible to compete with the universal literature which knows no such restrictions, and appeals to the wider audience of all humanity. The slave states have produced some excellent lawyers, some admirable orators, and some consummate politicians and statesmen, but they have produced no great poet, no great novelist, no great historian, no great philosopher or metaphysician; nay, as far as my knowledge extends, they have not brought forth even one great or eminent preacher. They have produced a few pleasant and fanciful rhymers and versifiers, both male and female, and one or two novelists and essayists of some ability, but no writer in any walk or department of literature whom the most adulatory partisanship or local preference can conscientiously compare with such names as Bryant, Longfellow, Whittier, Holmes, and Lowell in poetry; such historians as Prescott, Bancroft, and Motley; such novelists as Washington Irving and Hawthorne; or such a philosopher as Emerson—all of whom are Northern, and the greater number New England men or Yankees. The leading spirits in the slave states are aware of the deficiency without being aware of the cause, and can not as yet see that there are many things which can be obtained without liberty; but that a great, and wholesome, and fructifying literature, which can speak trumpet-tongued to all mankind, and move the universal heart of nations, is not among the number.

One characteristic of both the slave states and the free, which has been partially noticed by all travelers, though few, if any, have attempted to account for it on philosophical principles, is the intensely aristocratic sentiment, or, it may be called, instinct of the native-born Americans, of the Anglo-Saxon, and generally of the white race. It was the eminent statesman and orator, John C. Calhoun, who first enunciated the dogma, which has, since his time,

been openly accepted by the whole South, and more tacitly and partially by the North, that there is not such a thing as a democratic
republic; that there never was such a thing in ancient or modern
times; and that there must, of necessity, be an aristocracy of some
kind or other to keep the frame-work of society together, under a
form of government so delicate and so complicated as a republic.
That there may be a monarchy and a despotism without an aristocracy is proved by Asiatic as well as by European experience; and we
need not travel forty miles eastward from the English coast to find
a striking proof of it; but Mr. Calhoun held a strictly democratic
republic to be impossible, and appealed to Greece and Rome, to
Venice and Genoa, for corroboration. He declared that the only possible aristocracy in the United States was the aristocracy of color
and race. He may, to some extent, have undervalued or ignored the
aristocracy of wealth and genius, which always, in every society,
whatever may be its form of government, assert and maintain their
own claims to pre-eminence; but there can be no doubt that, as regards the aristocracy of color, avowed or unavowed, he was perfectly
right in the fact. As regards the political conclusions which he drew
from it, opinions will probably differ. The North, which will not
tolerate slavery, shows its participation in this aristocratic notion by
refusing to tolerate the social equality of the "nigger." "We shall not
make the black man a slave; we shall not buy him or sell him; but
we shall not associate with him. He shall be free to live, and to thrive
if he can, and to pay taxes and perform duties; but he shall not be
free to dine and drink at our board—to share with us the delibera-
tions of the jury-box—to sit upon the seat of judgment, however
capable he may be—to plead in our courts—to represent us in the
Legislature—to attend us at the bed of sickness and pain—to mingle
with us in the concert-room, the lecture-room, the theatre, or the
church, or to marry with our daughters. We are of another race, and
he is inferior. Let him know his place, and keep it." This is the
prevalent feeling, if not the language of the free North. A negro must
not ride in the public omnibuses nor in the railway cars; he must

not, however wealthy, sit in the boxes or in the pit of a theatre; and if he desires to go to church, he must worship with those of his own color, and not presume to taint the atmosphere of the pure whites by the odors that exhale from his impurer epidermis. The whites in the North object to a negro not alone for moral and political, but for physical reasons. They state that he smells, and that it is almost as offensive to come near him as it would be to fondle a skunk. The words of a pretended hymn—made for the negroes, but not by one of them, although it is sometimes asserted that the author had a dark skin—are often quoted to those who are incredulous as to the odors that exhale from the black man:

> "De Lord He lub de nigger well,
> He know de nigger by de smell;
> And when de nigger children cry,
> De Lord he gib 'em 'possum pie."

I attended a negro church, and heard a negro preacher at Richmond, in Virginia; and, though I have as sensitive a nose as most people, and a more sensitive one than many, I was quite unconscious of an unpleasant effluvium, or of any effluvium at all, proceeding from the persons of the seven or eight hundred black men and women there assembled to worship their Creator. I mentioned the fact to the Virginia gentleman who accompanied me. He replied that it was quite true that there was at that time no smell, "but then," said he, "the month is March. In June or July the odor would be perfectly intolerable, and I, for one, should not have ventured to have done myself the honor of accompanying you." But, whatever may be the fact as to the physical discomfort said to be produced by the odors of the black men on the olfactory nerves of the whites, it is evident that in the South, where, if any where, this peculiar unpleasantness would be more likely to be offensively demonstrative than in colder climates, there is no such repugnance to the persons of the black population as there is in the North. In the South, the slave-owner not only cohabits with the more youthful and beautiful of his female slaves, but seems to have no objection whatever to the close proximity of any negro, young or old, male or female; though the Northern men, who talk so much of liberty, and of the political equality of all men, turn up their scornful noses at the slightest possibility of contact with an African. Negro women are not only the favorite and most fondly-trusted nurses of white children, but often, and, indeed, generally, entertain for the infants of their masters and mistresses, whom they have reared and tended in their helplessness, a life-long and most devoted affection. They inspire the same feelings in the bosoms of their young charges. Black women nurse the little white girl in her babyhood—wash her, dress her, and adorn her— take her to school in her girlhood—and share in all the joys and sorrows of her youth. They are, besides, the honored, though humble confidants of their wedded life and maturity, and would scorn to accept of a freedom that would separate them from the objects of this disinterested and ungrudging affection. In the South, the negro may ride in the omnibus without offense; his proximity to the white creates neither alarm nor disgust; and the faithful slave, looked upon as a friend, receives the familiar and affectionate title of "uncle" or "aunt," as sex may dictate. If the master or mistress be young, and the "uncle" or "aunt" old, the negroes exercise the right of advice, authority, and control in every thing that relates to personal comfort and domestic ease; and the superior race is gratified by the control, and the interest which it presupposes. If the Northern states and the Northern people would only show half or a quarter as much social kindness to the negro as is shown in the South, the question of negro slavery would be deprived of one of its greatest difficulties. But, while Northern men talk of the political rights of the negro—while they oppress and degrade him socially, although they may neither buy nor sell him—their anti-slavery speeches, books, and resolutions savor of hypocrisy and false pretense. More than this, they harden the hearts of the slave-owners, who can see through a false pretense quite as readily as the Yankees, and tend to deprive the question of the abolition of slavery of the grace, the force, and the impetus that are derived from an uncompromising and thoroughly sincere conviction.

Another proof of the aristocratic feeling which pervades the white democracy of the United States is the repugnance which native-born Americans almost universally entertain to domestic service. As is well known, a domestic servant of American birth, and without negro blood in his or her veins, who condescends to help the mistress or master of a household in making the beds, milking the cows, cooking the dinner, grooming the horse, or driving the carriage, is not a servant, but a "help." "Help wanted," is the common heading of advertisements in the North, where servants are required. A native American of Anglo-Saxon lineage thinks himself born to lead and to rule, and scorns to be considered a "servant," or even to tolerate the name. Let negroes be servants, and, if not negroes, let Irishmen fill the place; but for an American, an Englishman, or a Scotchman to be a servant or a waiter is derogatory. Such people consider themselves of superior breed and blood. They are the aristocracy of the New World; and if poverty fall upon one of this class, as it may do upon many a noble-minded fellow, and compel him to tend sheep, wait in a shop, or, worse than all, to stand behind a chair at table, he is a help, not a servant. But the negro is not a help; he is emphatically a servant. And the Irishman is seldom long in America before he too begins to assert the supremacy of his white blood, and to come out of what he considers the degrading ranks of "service." The negroes, both free and slaves, have generally a great dislike for the Irish, whom they were the first to call "white niggers." A very poor white man—such as an Irishman generally is when he arrives in America, and struggles hard to compete with the negro for the lowest kinds of occupation—is looked upon with pity and hate by Sambo. "A white Buckra" is the most opprobrious epithet that a negro can make use of; for, in his eyes, wealth, authority, power, and white blood should always be found together. The Irish women fall willingly at first into domestic service, but the public opinion around them soon indoctrinates them with the aristocratic idea that black

men and women are the only proper servants; that white men ought
to trade and cultivate farms, and that white women are their proper
helpmates, and should scorn to serve, save in their own households,
and in behalf of their own husbands and children.

But to return to slavery, which is, in reality, far more of a white
man's than of a black man's question, and of which the aristocratic
tendency, as regards the white, is but one feather out of the multi-
farious plumage of the subject—it is well to consider what effect it
has upon the whole policy of the United States among men, both of
the North and South, who care no more for the negro, as a negro,
than they do for their horse or cow, but who use him, or abuse him,
as suits the higher political purpose which sways their actions. And *Pol.*
here we come to the very core of the political differences which
separate the free from the slave states of the Union. These differences
are many and serious, and are, besides, embarrassed and exasperated
by numerous complications of interest and policy quite unconnected *Political*
with slavery. Free America is ultra-protectionist, and Slave America
is strongly in favor of the widest freedom of trade. The free states are
alarmed at the increase of British manufactures, while the slave
states are not only not alarmed, but gratified, and desire to profit by
British industry to the fullest possible extent, in the cheapening of
clothes for themselves and their slaves, and of all articles of domestic
use and luxury, which Great Britain can furnish better and more
cheaply than the manufacturers of the North. But this is the least of
their differences. The unfortunate provision in the Constitution
which allows a slaveholder to possess votes for the House of Representatives—not one vote simply in his individual right as a free white *✗*
man, but several votes in proportion to the number of the black
population—makes a Southern white of more integral political importance than the Northern. He is a heavier weight in the political
scale, and, individually, is of more power and consequence than any
ordinary white man can be, unless the other add to his personal vote
the influence always derivable from eloquence and genius in swaying
the opinions of his fellow-men. The struggle between the North and

South, of which the negro is made the pretext, is, as all the world knows by this time, a struggle for political power and ascendancy—for the patronage of the republic, and of the several commonwealths which compose it. The men of the North and of the West—whether they be the old and staid conservatives of such states as Massachusetts and Connecticut, or the hardy pioneers of Michigan, Wisconsin, and Kansas, or those equally hardy and more adventurous and far-sighted "go-a-heads" who look to Nebraska, Oregon, Columbia, and even cast a longing look to the arable land of the Hudson's Bay Company, as the scene of their future operations in the art and industry of state-making—may ask why individually, and man for man, they should be of less account than the slave-owners and slave-breeders of the South, who vote in right of their slaves, but do nothing to extend the boundaries of the Union, unless by aggression upon the dominions of independent European and American powers? And this is the main difference between the two great sections. The Southern States desire to annex, and to increase the territories of the Union, but they have no means of doing so unless by war, just or unjust, against Mexico and Spain, and the effete, ridiculous, and perishing republics of Spaniards, half-breeds, and quadroons, that vegetate southward of Mexico as far as Panama. The Northern States, on the contrary, in sending out their pioneers, come into contact with no European powers. The wilderness is their natural inheritance, and neither to them nor to their forefathers has the Red Man been an invincible or even a formidable obstruction. It has always been possible to deal with him without doing much violence to the consciences of those who traded or fought with him. Philanthropy, very like misanthropy in its results, gave him trinkets and fire-water, that he might "civilize himself off the face of the earth;" and the Puritan or the peddler stepped into his broad acres, and made himself, like Alexander Selkirk or Robinson Crusoe, the autocrat of every circle bounded by the horizon. The North is compelled by nature, instinct, policy, and calculation to send forth its superabundant children to subdue and replenish the fruitful earth not otherwise preoccupied. The South has no such chances. It sees a territory farther south which is already subdued and replenished, though by an inferior race, and must either take that territory, *per fas aut nefas*, from its present possessors, or consent to be outnumbered, outweighed, and conquered by its rivals for power and office at Washington. To Europeans it sometimes appears strange that the United States—as an aggregate, already sufficiently large—should have such an insatiable lust of territory as to invade Mexican, Spanish, and other independent territories in this ruthless and unconscionable fashion; but, fairly and dispassionately looked upon, it seems as if the "manifest destiny" of which they speak were no dream, but a reality. They are doomed to "annex" by the necessities of their social politics. Like Robespierre, they must cut off heads or lose their own. Mexico is tempting, and Cuba is more tempting still; yet the prizes are costly. As for the little republics carved out of the weakness of Spain, which lengthen and spin out their useless lives in the latitudes between Mexico and Panama, no power on the earth, even if it can, will be so foolish as to interfere to prevent the inevitable consummation either of their absorption into the American Union, or of their annexation, in some more dependent form, to the great confederation. Were it not that the Constitution of the United States had made no provision for any increase except by the normal form and force of agglomeration and accretion, the Spanish republics or empires (for these moribund states change from one political condition to another with kaleidoscopic rapidity) would long ago have been absorbed into the ever-gaping and yawning maw of Uncle Sam. And herein exists a difficulty for the Union, all consequent upon slavery, and the antagonism which it excites at the North. Foreign conquest appears to be imperative; but, if it be undertaken, how will the North, which only wars with the Indian, with desolation, and the wild beasts of the forests, be affected by a state of affairs alien to the intentions of the founders of the Constitution, and to the whole spirit of the most populous and energetic portion of the republic? The answer to the question is in the future. No

SLAVERY IN THE SOUTH • 220

one can foresee the ultimate pattern which the moving of the shut-
tles and rollers will produce, or whether the whole machine will not
ultimately break into pieces. The strength of a chain cable is but the
strength of its weakest part. The strength of the American Union is
the strength of slavery. It is that question which bears the whole
strain of the mighty ship; and, if it prove strong enough, the ship
may defy all other dangers, and ride triumphantly upon all seas and
into all ports. But if that link be weak or broken, and have no sup-
ports in nature and necessity, and no links in the heart of humanity,
it will drop sooner or later, and then the world will see a new shift-
ing of the kaleidoscope. The focus may be symmetrical, but the
component parts will be differently disposed; and the Northern
States may make one pattern, the Southern a second, and the Cali-
fornian or Pacific sea-board a third. There is room enough and to
spare for all of them.

PART THREE

THE VIEW
OF THE
SOUTHERN WHITE

THOMAS JEFFERSON
(*1743-1826*)

Jefferson was one of the remarkable group of Virginia liberal slaveholders who hoped to free the slaves and colonize them in Africa. In *Notes on Virginia,* first published in 1782 shortly after his term of office as governor, Jefferson explained his legislative program for the emancipation of all slaves born after the passage of his law, providing for education at public expense "according to their geniuses," and thereafter to be colonized in a distant area under the protection of this country.

His arguments against permanently absorbing the Negroes into the general population emphasizes "Deep-rooted prejudices entertained by the whites; ten thousand recollections by the blacks of the injuries they have sustained; new provocations; the real distinctions nature has made . . ." Jefferson's *Notes* makes it clear that he shared the contemporary beliefs about the biological dangers of race mixture, the innate cultural differences, and the impression of undesirable physical characteristics. However, like William Byrd II, the enlightened planter of early eighteenth century Virginia, he believed that present environmental factors might, to some extent at least, account for the limited achievements of the Negro. Moreover, Jefferson urged caution and scientific investigation before anyone reached final conclusions on racial potentialities.

Jefferson, Monroe, and Madison were especially convinced that manumission without colonization meant race war after the Gabriel Prosser insurrection of 1800 near Richmond in which Gabriel had organized 1100 slaves for an attack in emulation of the current Haitian massacre of planters. The Virginian leaders thereupon turned to the organization of the American Colonization Society, which took form in 1816.

This selection is from *Notes on the State of Virginia* (Boston, 1829), pages 144-151, 169-171. It has often been quoted because of the eloquent appeal to end slavery as degrading to the Southern family and endangering the liberty of all.

. . . It will probably be asked, Why not retain and incorporate the blacks into the state, and thus save the expense of supplying, by importation of white settlers, the vacancies they will leave? Deep rooted prejudices entertained by the whites; ten thousand recollections, by the blacks, of the injuries they have sustained; new provocations; the real distinctions which nature has made; and many other circumstances, will divide us into parties, and produce convulsions, which will probably never end but in the extermination of the one or the other race.—To these objections, which are political, may be added others, which are physical and moral. The first difference which strikes us is that of colour.—Whether the black of the negro resides in the reticular membrane between the skin and scarf-skin, or in the scarf-skin itself; whether it proceeds from the colour of the blood, the colour of the bile, or from that of some other secretion, the difference is fixed in nature, and is as real as if its seat and cause were better known to us. And is this difference of no importance? Is it not the foundation of a greater or less share of beauty in the two races? Are not the fine mixtures of red and white, the expressions of every passion by greater or less suffusions of colour in the one, preferable to that eternal monotony, which reigns in the countenances, that immovable veil of black which covers all the emotions of the other race? Add to these, flowing hair, a more elegant symmetry of form, their own judgment in favour of the whites, declared by their preference of them, as uniformly as is the preference of the Oranootan for the black women over those of his own species. The circumstance of superior beauty, is thought worthy attention in the propagation of our horses, dogs, and other domestic animals; why not in that of man? Besides those of colour, figure, and hair, there are other physical distinctions proving a difference of race. They have less hair on

the face and body. They secrete less by the kidneys, and more by
the glands of the skin, which gives them a very strong and disagreeable odour. This greater degree of transpiration renders them more
tolerant of heat, and less so of cold than the whites. Perhaps too a
difference of structure in the pulmonary apparatus, which a late in-
genious* experimentalist has discovered to be the principal regulator
of animal heat, may have disabled them from extricating, in the act
of inspiration, so much of that fluid from the outer air, or obliged
them in expiration, to part with more of it. They seem to require less
sleep. A black after hard labour through the day, will be induced by
the slightest amusements to sit up till midnight, or later, though
knowing he must be out with the first dawn of the morning. They are
at least as brave, and more adventuresome. But this may perhaps
proceed from a want of forethought, which prevents their seeing a
danger till it be present.—When present, they do not go through it
with more coolness or steadiness than the whites. They are more
ardent after their female: but love seems with them to be more an
eager desire, than a tender delicate mixture of sentiment and sensation. Their griefs are transient. Those numberless afflictions, which
render it doubtful whether heaven has given life to us in mercy or in
wrath, are less felt, and sooner forgotten with them. In general, their
existence appears to participate more of sensation than reflection. To
this must be ascribed their disposition to sleep when abstracted from
their diversions, and unemployed in labour. An animal whose body is
at rest, and who does not reflect, must be disposed to sleep of course.
Comparing them by their faculties of memory, reason, and imagination, it appears to me that in memory they are equal to the whites;
in reason much inferior, as I think one could scarcely be found capable of tracing and comprehending the investigations of Euclid; and
that in imagination they are dull, tasteless, and anomalous. It would
be unfair to follow them to Africa for this investigation.We will consider them here, on the same stage with the whites, and where the

* Crawford.

facts are not apocryphal on which a judgment is to be formed. It will be right to make great allowances for the difference of condition, of education, of conversation, of the sphere in which they move. Many millions of them have been brought to, and born in America. Most of them indeed have been confined to tillage, to their own homes, and their own society: yet many have been so situated, that they might have availed themselves of the conversation of their masters; many have been brought up to the handicraft arts, and from that circumstance have always been associated with the whites. Some have been liberally educated, and all have lived in countries where the arts and sciences are cultivated to a considerable degree, and have had before their eyes samples of the best works from abroad. The Indians, with no advantages of this kind, will often carve figures on their pipes not destitute of design and merit. They will crayon out an animal, a plant, or a country, so as to prove the existence of a germ in their minds which only wants cultivation. They astonish you with strokes of the most sublime oratory; such as prove their reason and sentiment strong, their imagination glowing and elevated. But never yet could I find that a black had uttered a thought above the level of plain narration; never saw even an elementary trait of painting or sculpture. In music they are more generally gifted than the whites with accurate ears for tune and time, and they have been found capable of imagining a small catch.* Whether they will be equal to the composition of a more extensive run of melody, or of complicated harmony, is yet to be proved. Misery is often the parent of the most affecting touches in poetry. Among the blacks is misery enough, God knows, but no poetry. Love is the peculiar œstrum of the poet. Their love is ardent, but it kindles the senses only, not the imagination. Religion indeed has produced a Phyllis Whately;† but it

---

* The instrument proper to them is the Banjar, which they brought hither from Africa, and which is the original of the guitar, its chords being precisely the four lower chords of the guitar.

† [This misspelled reference to Phillis Wheatley (1753-1784) illustrates how illogical Jefferson could become on race analysis. Considering that she was an African slave and largely self-taught, the marvel is her intellectual

could not produce a poet. The compositions published under her name are below the dignity of criticism. The heroes of the Dunciad are to her, as Hercules to the author of that poem. Ignatius Sancho has approached nearer to merit in composition; yet his letters do more honour to the heart than the head. They breathe the purest effusions of friendship and general philanthropy, and show how great a degree of the latter may be compounded with strong religious zeal. He is often happy in the turn of his compliments, and his style is easy and familiar, except when he affects a Shandean fabrication of words. But his imagination is wild and extravagant, escapes incessantly from every restraint of reason and taste, and, in the course of its vagaries, leaves a tract of thought as incoherent and eccentric, as is the course of a meteor through the sky. His subjects should often have led him to a process of sober reasoning: yet we find him always substituting sentiment for demonstration. Upon the whole, though we admit him to the first place among those of his own colour who have presented themselves to the public judgment, yet when we compare him with the writers of the race among whom he lived and particularly with the epistolary class, in which he has taken his own stand, we are compelled to enrol him at the bottom of the column. This criticism supposes the letters published under his name to be genuine, and to have received amendment from no other hand; points which would not be of easy investigation. The improvement of the blacks in body and mind, in the first instance of their mixture with the whites, has been observed by every one, and proves that their inferiority is not the effect merely of their condition of life. We know that among the Romans, about the Augustan age especially, the condition of their slaves was much more deplorable than that of the blacks on the continent of America. The two sexes were confined in separate apartments, because to raise a child cost the master more than to buy one. Cato, for a very restricted indulgence to his slaves in this particular,

---

precocity not only as a poet, but as a fluent classicist and as a fascinating and brilliant conversationalist—all achieved before her death at the age of 31.—ED.]

took from them a certain price. But in this country the slaves multiply as fast as the free inhabitants. Their situation and manners place the commerce between the two sexes almost without restraint. The same Cato, on a principle of œconomy, always sold his sick and superannuated slaves. He gives it as a standing precept to a master visiting his farm, to sell his old oxen, old wagons, old tools, old and diseased servants, and every thing else become useless. . . . The American slaves cannot enumerate this among the injuries and insults they receive. It was the common practice to expose in the island *Æsculapius,* in the Tyber, diseased slaves, whose cure was like to become tedious. The emperor Claudius, by an edict, gave freedom to such of them as should recover, and first declared that if any person chose to kill rather than expose them, it should be deemed homicide. The exposing them is a crime of which no instance has existed with us; and were it to be followed by death, it would be punished capitally. We are told of a certain Vedius Pollio, who, in the presence of Augustus, would have given a slave as food to his fish, for having broken a glass. With the Romans, the regular method of taking the evidence of their slaves was under torture. Here it has been thought better never to resort to their evidence. When a master was murdered, all his slaves, in the same house, or within hearing, were condemned to death. Here punishment falls on the guilty only, and as precise proof is required against him as against a freeman. Yet notwithstanding these and other discouraging circumstances among the Romans, their slaves were often their rarest artists. They excelled too in science, insomuch as to be usually employed as tutors to their masters' children. Epictetus, Terence, and Phædrus, were slaves. But they were of the race of whites. It is not their condition then, but nature, which has produced the distinction. Whether further observation will or will not verify the conjecture, that nature has been less bountiful to them in the endowments of the head, I believe that in those of the heart she will be found to have done them justice. That disposition to theft with which they have been branded, must be ascribed to their situation, and not to any depravity of the moral sense. The man, in whose favour no laws of property exist, probably feels himself less bound to respect those made in favour of others. When arguing for ourselves, we lay it down as a fundamental, that laws, to be just, must give a reciprocation of right; that, without this, they are mere arbitrary rules of conduct, founded in force, and not in conscience: and it is a problem which I give to the master to solve, whether the religious precepts against the violation of property were not framed for him as well as his slave? And whether the slave may not as justifiably take a little from one, who has taken all from him, as he may slay one who would slay him? That a change in the relations in which a man is placed should change his ideas of moral right or wrong, is neither new, nor peculiar to the colour of the blacks. Homer tells us it was so 2600 years ago.

> Jove fix'd it certain, that whatever day
> Makes man a slave, takes half his worth away.

But the slaves of which Homer speaks were whites. Notwithstanding these considerations which must weaken their respect for the laws of property, we find among them numerous instances of the most rigid integrity, and as many as among their better instructed masters, of benevolence, gratitude and unshaken fidelity. The opinion, that they are inferior in the faculties of reason and imagination, must be hazarded with great diffidence. To justify a general conclusion, requires many observations, even where the subject may be submitted to the anatomical knife, to optical classes, to analysis by fire, or by solvents. How much more then where it is a faculty, not a substance, we are examining; where it eludes the research of all the senses; where the conditions of its existence are various and variously combined; where the effects of those which are present or absent bid defiance to calculation; let me add too, as a circumstance of great tenderness, where our conclusion would degrade a whole race of men from the rank in the scale of beings which their Creator may perhaps have given them. To our reproach it must be said, that though for a century and a half we have had under our eyes the races of black and of red men, they have never yet been viewed by us as subjects of natural history. I advance it therefore as a suspicion only, that the blacks, whether originally a distinct race, or made distinct by time and circumstances, are inferior to the whites in the endowments both of body and mind. It is not against experience to suppose, that different species of the same genus, or varieties of the same species, may possess different qualifications. Will not a lover of natural history then, one who views the gradations in all the races of animals with the eye of philosophy, excuse an effort to keep those in the department of man as distinct as nature has formed them? This unfortunate difference of colour, and perhaps of faculty, is a powerful obstacle to the emancipation of these people. Many of their advocates, while they wish to vindicate the liberty of human nature are anxious also to preserve its dignity and beauty. Some of these, embarrassed by the question 'What further is to be done with them?' join themselves in opposition with those who are actuated by sordid avarice only. Among the Romans emancipation required but one effort. The slave, when made free, might mix with, without staining the blood of his master. But with us a second is necessary, unknown to history. When freed, he is to be removed beyond the reach of mixture. . . .

The *particular* customs and manners that may happen to be received in that state?

It is difficult to determine on the standard by which the manners of a nation may be tried, whether *catholic,* or *particular*. It is more difficult for a native to bring to that standard the manners of his own nation, familiarized to him by habit. There must doubtless be an unhappy influence on the manners of our people produced by the existence of slavery among us. The whole commerce between master and slave is a perpetual exercise of the most boisterous passions, the most unremitting despotism on the one part, and degrading submissions on the other. Our children see this, and learn to imitate it; for man is an imitative animal. This quality is the germ of all education in him. From his cradle to his grave he is learning to do what he sees others do. If a parent could find no motive either in his philanthropy or his self love, for restraining the intemperance of passion towards his slave, it should always be a sufficient one that his child is present. But generally it is not sufficient. The parent storms, the child looks on, catches the lineaments of wrath, puts on the same airs in the circle of smaller slaves, gives a loose to the worst of passions, and thus nursed, educated, and daily exercised in tyranny, cannot but be stamped by it with odious pecularities. The man must be a prodigy who can retain his manners and morals undepraved by such circumstances. And with what execration should the statesman be loaded, who, permitting one half the citizens thus to trample on the rights of the other, transforms those into despots, and these into enemies, destroys the morals of the one part, and the amor patriæ of the other. For if a slave can have a country in this world, it must be any other in preference to that in which he is born to live and labour for another; in which he must lock up the faculties of his nature, contribute as far as depends on his individual endeavours to the evanishment of the human race, or entail his own miserable condition on the endless generations proceeding from him. With the morals of the people, their industry also is destroyed. For in a warm climate, no man will labour for himself who can make another labour for him. This is so true, that of the proprietors of slaves a very small proportion indeed are ever seen to labour. And can the liberties of a nation be thought secure when we have removed their only firm basis, a conviction in the minds of the people that these liberties are of the gift of God? That they are not to be violated but with his wrath? Indeed I tremble for my country when I reflect that God is just: that his justice cannot sleep for ever: that considering numbers, nature and natural means only, a revolution of the wheel of fortune, an exchange of situation is among possible events: that it may become probable by supernatural interference! The almighty has no attribute which can take side with us in such a contest.—But it is impossible to be temperate and to pursue this subject through the various considerations of policy, of morals, of history natural and civil. We must be contented to hope they will force their way into every one's mind. I think a change already perceptible, since the origin of the present revolution. The spirit of the master is abating, that of the slave rising from the dust, his condition mollifying, the way I hope preparing, under the auspices of heaven, for a total emancipation, and that this is disposed, in the order of events, to be with the consent of the masters, rather than by their extirpation.

THOMAS RODERICK DEW
(*1802-1846*)

The son of a prosperous planter and community leader of King and Queen County, Virginia, where he was born, Thomas R. Dew became one of the most influential proslavery propagandists. Although he graduated from the College of William and Mary, a liberal Jeffersonian school, and travelled two years abroad (where it is said he picked up a reactionary German philosophy), he took the "advanced" position that slavery was not merely a necessary evil but the soundest basis for a great civilization. As a professor of history and economics at his alma mater, he championed free trade against Northern protectionism and predicted secession if the trend toward higher tariffs continued.

After the Nat Turner insurrection of 1831 in Virginia had shocked the South, and Dew's state particularly, the legislature debated a resolution originating from the small western farming counties of Virginia that called for abolition. However, the large slaveholders of the eastern counties defeated it overwhelmingly. Professor Dew then wrote the lengthy justification of slavery given here, perhaps the first major defense of slavery written by a Southerner. As the reader will observe, he tried to refute the chief argument of the antislavery faction by minimizing the danger of slave insurrections and closing the door to other alternatives than perpetual slavery.

This abridgment of *Review of the Debate* . . . is taken from *The Proslavery Argument* (*1852*), pages 287-296, 462-472.

In looking to the texture of the population of our country, there is nothing so well calculated to arrest the attention of the observer, as the existence of negro slavery throughout a large portion of the confederacy. A race of people, differing from us in color and in habits, and vastly inferior in the scale of civilization, have been increasing and spreading, "growing with our growth, and strengthening with our strength," until they have become intertwined and intertwisted with every fibre of society. Go through our Southern country, and every where you see the negro slave by the side of the white man; you find him alike in the mansion of the rich, the cabin of the poor, the workshop of the mechanic, and the field of the planter. Upon the contemplation of a population framed like this, a curious and interesting question readily suggests itself to the inquiring mind:— Can these two distinct races of people, now living together as master and servant, be ever separated? Can the black be sent back to his African home, or will the day ever arrive when he can be liberated from his thraldom, and mount upwards in the scale of civilization and rights, to an equality with the white? This is a question of truly momentous character; it involves the whole framework of society, contemplates a separation of its elements, or a radical change in their relation, and requires, for its adequate investigation, the most complete and profound knowledge of the nature and sources of national wealth and political aggrandizement, an acquaintance with the elastic and powerful spring of population, and the causes which invigorate or paralyze its energies, together with a clear perception of the varying rights of man, amid all the changing circumstances by which he may be surrounded, and a profound knowledge of all the principles, passions, and susceptibilities which make up the moral nature of our species, and according as they are acted upon by ad-

ventitious circumstances, alter our condition, and produce all that
wonderful variety of character which so strongly marks and char-
acterizes the human family. Well, then, does it behoove even the
wisest statesmen to approach this august subject with the utmost
circumspection and diffidence; its wanton agitation even is pregnant
with mischief; but rash and hasty action threatens, in our opinion,
the whole Southern country with irremediable ruin. The evil of *yesterday's* growth may be extirpated *to-day,* and the vigor of society
may heal the wound; but that which is the growth of *ages,* may require ages to remove. The Parliament of Great Britain, with all its
philanthropic zeal, guided by the wisdom and eloquence of such
statesmen as Chatham, Fox, Burke, Pitt, Canning and Brougham,
has never yet seriously agitated this question, in regard to the West
India possessions. Revolutionary France, actuated by the most intemperate and phrenetic zeal for liberty and equality, attempted to
legislate the free people of color, in the Island of St. Domingo, into
all the rights and privileges of the whites; and, but a season afterwards, convinced of her madness, she attempted to retrace her steps.
But it was too late. The deed had been done. The bloodiest and most
shocking insurrection ever recorded in the annals of history had
broken out, and the whole Island was involved in frightful carnage
and anarchy, and France, in the end, has been stript "of the brightest
jewel in her crown," the fairest and most valuable of all her colonial
possessions. Since the revolution, France, Spain and Portugal, large
owners of colonial possessions, have not only not abolished slavery in
their colonies, but have not even abolished the slave trade in practice.

In our Southern slaveholding country, the question of emancipation has never been seriously discussed in any of our legislatures,
until the whole subject, under the most exciting circumstances, was,
during the last winter, brought up for discussion in the Virginia
Legislature, and plans of partial or total abolition were earnestly
pressed upon the attention of that body. It is well known that, during
the last summer, in the county of Southampton, in Virginia, a few
slaves, led on by Nat Turner, rose in the night, and murdered, in

the most inhuman and shocking manner, between sixty and seventy of the unsuspecting whites of that county. The news, of course, was rapidly diffused, and, with it, consternation and dismay were spread throughout the State, destroying, for a time, all feeling of security and confidence; and, even when subsequent development had proved that the conspiracy had been originated by a fanatical negro preacher, (whose confessions prove, beyond a doubt, mental aberration,) and that this conspiracy embraced but few slaves, all of whom had paid the penalty of their crimes, still the excitement remained, still the repose of the commonwealth was disturbed, for the ghastly horrors of the Southampton tragedy could not immediately be banished from the mind—and *rumor,* too, with her thousand tongues, was busily engaged in spreading tales of disaffection, plots, insurrections, and even massacres, which frightened the timid, and harassed and mortified the whole of the slaveholding population. During this period of excitement, when reason was almost banished from the mind, and the imagination was suffered to conjure up the most appalling phantoms, and picture to itself a crisis, in the vista of futurity, when the overwhelming numbers of the blacks would rise superior to all restraint, and involve the fairest portion of our land in universal ruin and desolation, we are not to wonder that, even in the lower part of Virginia, many should have seriously inquired if this supposed monstrous evil could not be removed from our bosom? Some looked to the removal of the free people of color, by the efforts of the Colonization Society, as an antidote to all our ills. Some were disposed to strike at the root of the evil: to call on the General Government for aid, and, by the labors of *Hercules,* to extirpate the curse of slavery from the land. Others again, who could not bear that Virginia should stand towards the General Government (whose unconstitutional action she had ever been foremost to resist) in the attitude of a suppliant, looked forward to the legislative action of the State, as capable of achieving the desired result. In this state of excitement and unallayed apprehension, the Legislature met, and plans for abolition were proposed, and earnestly advocated in debate.

Upon the impropriety of this debate, we beg leave to make a few observations. Any scheme of abolition, proposed so soon after the Southampton tragedy, would necessarily appear to be the result of that most inhuman massacre. Suppose the negroes, then, to be really anxious for their emancipation, no matter on what terms, would not the extraordinary effect produced on the Legislature by the Southampton insurrection, in all probability, have a tendency to excite another? And we must recollect, from the nature of things, no plan of abolition could act suddenly on the whole mass of slave population in the State. Mr. Randolph's was not even to commence its operation till 1840. Waiting, then, one year or more, until the excitement could be allayed, and the empire of reason could once more have been established, would surely have been productive of no injurious consequences; and, in the mean time, a Legislature could have been selected, which would much better have represented the views and wishes of their constituents, on this vital question. Virginia could have ascertained the sentiments and wishes of other slaveholding States, whose concurrence, if not absolutely necessary, might be highly desirable, and should have been sought after and attended to, at least, as a matter of State courtesy. Added to this, the texture of the Legislature was not of that character calculated to ensure the confidence of the people, in a movement of this kind. If ever there was a question debated in a deliberative body, which called for the most exalted talent, the longest and most tried experience, the utmost circumspection and caution, a complete exemption from prejudice and undue excitement, where both are apt to prevail, an ardent and patriotic desire to advance the vital interests of the State, uncombined with mere desire for vain and ostentatious display, and with no view to party or geographical divisions, that question was the question of the *abolition* of *slavery*, in the Virginia Legislature. "*Grave* and *reverend* seniors," "the very fathers of the Republic," were indeed required, for the settlement of a question of such magnitude. It appears, however, that the Legislature was composed of an unusual number of young and inexperienced members, elected in the month of April, previous to the Southampton massacre, and at a time of profound tranquillity and repose, when, of course, the people were not disposed to call from their retirement their most distinguished and experienced citizens.

We are very ready to admit, that in point of ability and eloquence, the debate transcended our expectations. One of the leading political papers in the State remarked, "We have never heard any debate so eloquent, so sustained, and in which so great a number of speakers had appeared, and commanded the attention of so numerous and intelligent an audience." . . . . . "Day after day, multitudes throng to the capital, and have been compensated by eloquence which would have illustrated Rome or Athens." But, however fine might have been the rhetorical display, however ably some isolated points may have been discussed, still we affirm, with confidence, that no enlarged, wise and practical plan of operations was proposed by the abolitionists. We will go farther, and assert that their arguments, in most cases, were of a wild and intemperate character, based upon false principles, and assumptions of the most vicious and alarming kind, subversive of the rights of property and the order and tranquillity of society, and portending to the whole slaveholding country —if they ever shall be followed out in practice—the most inevitable and ruinous consequences. Far be it, however, from us, to accuse the abolitionists in the Virginia Legislature of any settled or malevolent design to overturn or convulse the fabric of society. We have no doubt that they were acting conscientiously for the best; but it often happens that frail, imperfect man, in the too ardent and confident pursuit of imaginary good, runs upon his utter destruction.

We have not formed our opinion lightly upon this subject; we have given to the vital question of abolition the most mature and intense consideration which we are capable of bestowing, and we have come to the conclusion—a conclusion which seems to be sustained by facts and reasoning as irresistible as the demonstration of the mathematician—that every plan of emancipation and deportation which we can possibly conceive, is *totally* impracticable. We shall endeavor to prove that the attempt to execute these plans can only have a tendency to increase all the evils of which we complain, as resulting from slavery. If this be true, then the great question of abolition will necessarily be reduced to the question of emancipation, with a permission to remain, which, we think, can easily be shown to be utterly subversive of the interests, security and happiness of both the blacks and whites, and consequently, hostile to every principle of expediency, morality, and religion. We have heretofore doubted the propriety, even, of too frequently agitating, especially in a public manner, the question of abolition, in consequence of the injurious effects which might be produced on the slave population. But the Virginia Legislature, in its zeal for discussion, boldly set aside all prudential considerations of this kind, and openly and publicly debated the subject, before the world. The seal has now been broken—the example has been set from a high quarter; we shall, therefore, waive all considerations of a prudential character, which have hitherto restrained us, and boldly grapple with the abolitionists and this great question. We fear not the result, so far as truth, justice and expediency alone are concerned. But we must be permitted to say that we do most deeply dread the effects of misguided philanthropy, and the marked, and, we had like to have said, impertinent intrusion in this matter, of those who have no interest at stake, and who have not intimate and minute knowledge of the whole subject, so absolutely necessary to wise action.

Without further preliminary, then, we shall advance to the discussion of the question of abolition, noticing not only the plans proposed in the Virginia Legislature, but some others, likewise. And, as the subject of slavery has been considered in every point of view, and pronounced, in the *abstract,* at least, as entirely contrary to the law of nature, we propose taking, in the first place, a hasty view of the origin of slavery, and point out the influence which it has exerted on the progress of civilization, and to this purpose it will be necessary to look back to other ages—cast a glance at nations differing from us in civilization and manners, and see whether it is possible to mount to the source of slavery.

1. *Origin of Slavery, and its Effects on the Progress of Civilization.*

Upon an examination of the nature of man, we find him to be almost entirely the creature of circumstances—his habits and sentiments are, in a great measure, the growth of adventitious causes—hence the endless variety and condition of our species. We are almost ever disposed, however, to identify the course of nature with the progress of events in our own narrow contracted sphere; we look upon any deviation from the constant round in which *we* have been spinning out the thread of our existence, as a departure from nature's great system, and, from a known principle of our nature, our first impulse is to condemn. It is thus that the man born and matured in the lap of freedom, looks upon slavery as unnatural and horrible; and, if he be not instructed upon the subject, is sure to think that so unnatural a condition could never exist, but in few countries or ages, in violation of every law of justice or humanity; and he is almost disposed to implore the divine wrath, to shower down the consuming fire of heaven on the Sodoms and Gomorrahs of the world, where this unjust practice prevails.

But, when he examines into the past condition of mankind, he stands amazed at the fact which history develops to his view. "Almost every page of ancient history," says Wallace, in his Dissertation on the Numbers of Mankind, "demonstrates the great multitudes of slaves; which gives occasion to a melancholy reflection, that the world, when best peopled, was not a world of freemen, but of slaves." "And in every age and country, until times comparatively recent," says Hallam, "personal servitude appears to have been the lot of a large, perhaps the greater portion of mankind."

Slavery was established and sanctioned by divine authority, among even the elect of heaven, the favored children of Israel. Abraham, the founder of this interesting nation, and the chosen servant of the Lord, was the owner of *hundreds* of slaves. That magnificent shrine, the Temple of Solomon, was reared by the hands of slaves. Egypt's venerable and enduring piles were reared by similar hands. Slavery existed in Assyria and Babylon. The ten tribes of Israel were carried off in bondage to the former by Shalmanezar, and the two tribes of Judah were subsequently carried in triumph by Nebuchadnezzar, to beautify and adorn the latter. Ancient Phœnicia and Carthage had slaves. The Greeks and Trojans, at the siege of Troy, had slaves. Athens, and Sparta, and Thebes, indeed the whole Grecian and Roman worlds, had more slaves than freemen. And in those ages which succeeded the extinction of the Roman empire in the West, *"servi,* or slaves," says Dr. Robertson, "seem to have been the most numerous class." Even in this day of civilization, and the regeneration of governments, slavery is far from being confined to our hemisphere alone. The serf and labor rents prevalent throughout the whole of Eastern Europe, and a portion of Western Asia, and the ryot rents throughout the extensive and over populated countries of the East, and over the dominions of the Porte in Europe, Asia and Africa, but too conclusively mark the existence of slavery over these boundless regions. And when we turn to the continent of Africa, we find slavery, in all its most horrid forms, existing throughout its whole extent, the slaves being at least three times more numerous than the freemen; so that, looking to the whole world, we may, even now, with confidence assert, that slaves, or those whose condition is infinitely worse, form by far the largest portion of the human race!

Well, then, may we here pause, and inquire a moment—for it is surely worthy of inquiry—how has slavery arisen and thus spread over our globe? We shall not pretend to enumerate accurately, and in detail, all the causes which have led to slavery; but we believe the principal may be summed up under the following heads: 1st. Laws of War; 2d. State of Property and Feebleness of Government; 3d. Bargain and Sale; and 4th. Crime. . . .

Color alone is here [in the South] the badge of distinction, the true mark of aristocracy, and all who are white are equal in spite of the variety of occupation. The same thing is observed in the West Indies. "Of the character common to the white resident of the West Indies, it appears to me," says Edwards, "that the leading feature is an independent spirit, and a display of *conscious equality* throughout all ranks and conditions. The poorest white person seems to consider himself nearly on a level with the richest; and emboldened by this idea, approaches his employer with extended hand, and a freedom which, in the countries of Europe, is seldom displayed by men in the lower orders of life towards their superiors." And it is this spirit of equality which is both the generator and preserver of the genuine spirit of liberty.

Insecurity of the whites, arising from plots, insurrections, &c., among the blacks. This is the evil, after all, let us say what we will, which really operates most powerfully upon the schemers and emancipating philanthropists of those sections where slaves constitute the principal property. Now, if we have shown, as we trust we have, that the scheme of deportation is utterly impracticable, and that emancipation, with permission to remain, will produce all these horrors *in still greater degree,* it follows that this evil of slavery, allowing it to exist in all its latitude, would be no argument for legislative action, and therefore we might well rest contented with this issue; but as we are anxious to exhibit this whole subject in its true bearings, and as we do believe that this evil has been most strangely and causelessly exaggerated, we have determined to examine it a moment, and point out its true extent. It seems to us that those who insist most upon it, commit the enormous error of looking upon every slave in the whole slaveholding country as actuated by the most deadly enmity to the whites, and possessing all that reckless, fiendish temper, which would lead him to murder and assassinate the moment the opportunity occurs. This is far from being true; the slave, as we

---

* [This section may be contrasted with the discussions in Herbert Aptheker, *American Negro Slave Revolts* (New York, 1943), and Harvey Wish, "American Slave Insurrections Before 1861," *Journal of Negro History,* XXII (1937), pp. 299-320.—ED.]

have already said, generally loves the master and his family;* and few indeed there are, who can coldly plot the murder of men, women and children; and if they do, there are fewer still who can have the villany to execute. We can sit down and imagine that all the negroes in the south have conspired to rise on a certain night, and murder all the whites in their respective families; we may suppose the secret to be kept, and that they have the physical power to exterminate, and yet we may say the whole is morally impossible. No insurrection of this kind can ever occur where the blacks are as much civilized as they are in the United States. Savages and Koromantyn slaves can commit such deeds, because their whole life and education have prepared them; and they glory in the achievement; but the negro of the United States has imbibed the principles, the sentiments, and feelings of the white; in one word, he is civilized—at least, comparatively; his whole education and course of life are at war with such fell deeds. Nothing, then, but the most subtle and poisonous principles, sedulously infused into his mind, can break his allegiance, and transform him into the midnight murderer. Any man who will attend to the history of the Southampton massacre, must at once see, that the cause of even the partial success of the insurrectionists, was the very circumstance that there was no extensive plot, and that Nat, a demented fanatic, was under the impression that heaven had enjoined him to liberate the blacks, and had made its manifestations by loud noises in the air, an eclipse, and by the greenness of the sun. It was these signs which determined *him,* and ignorance and superstition, together with implicit confidence in Nat, determined a few others, and thus the bloody work began. So fearfully and reluctantly did they proceed to the execution, that we have no doubt that if Travis, the first attacked, could have waked whilst they were getting into his house, or could have shot down Nat or Bill, the rest would have fled, and the affair would have terminated *in limine.*

---

* We scarcely know a single family, in which the slaves, especially the domestics, do not manifest the most unfeigned grief at the deaths which occur among the whites.

We have read with great attention the history of the insurrections in St. Domingo, and have no hesitation in affirming, that to the reflecting mind, that whole history affords the most complete evidence of the difficulty and almost impossibility of succeeding in these plots, even under the most favorable circumstances. It would almost have been a moral miracle, if that revolution had not succeeded. The French revolution had kindled a blaze throughout the world. The society of the *Amis des Noirs,* (the friends of the blacks,) in Paris, had educated and disciplined many of the mulattoes, who were almost as numerous as the whites in the island. The National Assembly, in its mad career, declared these mulattoes to be equal in all respects to the whites, and gave them the same privileges and immunities as the whites. During the ten years, too, immediately preceding the revolution, more than 200,000 negroes were imported into the island from Africa. It is a well known fact, that newly imported negroes are always greatly more dangerous than those born among us; and of those importations a very large proportion consisted of Koromantyn slaves, from the Gold Coast, who have all the savage ferocity of the North American Indian.* And lastly, the whites themselves, disunited and strangely inharmonious, would nevertheless have suppressed the insurrections, although the blacks and mulattoes were nearly *fifteen-fold* their numbers, if it had not been for the constant and too fatal interference of France. The great sin of that revolution rests on the National Assembly, and should be an awful warning to every legislature to beware of too much tampering with so delicate and difficult a subject, as an alteration of the fundamental relations of society.

But there is another cause which will render the success of the

* It was the Koromantyns who brought about the insurrection in Jamaica, in 1760. They are a very hardy race, and the Dutch, who are a calculating, money-making people, and withal the most cruel masters in the world, have generally preferred these slaves, because they might be forced to do most work; but the consequence of their avarice has been that they have been more cursed with insurrections than any other people in the West Indies.

blacks forever impossible in the South, as long as slavery exists. It is, that in modern times, especially, wealth and talent must ever rule over mere physical force. During the feudal ages, the vassals never made a settled concerted attempt to throw off the yoke of the lord or landed proprietor, and the true reason was, they had neither property nor talent, and consequently the power, under these circumstances, could be placed no where else than in the hands of the lords; but so soon as the *tiers etat* arose, with commerce and manufactures, there was something to struggle for, and *le crise des revolutions,* (the crisis of revolutions,) was the consequence. No connected, persevering, and well concerted movement, ever takes place, in modern times, unless for the sake of property. Now, the property, talent, concert, and we may add, habit, are all with the whites, and render their continued superiority absolutely certain, if they are not meddled with, no matter what may be the disproportion of numbers. We look upon these insurrections in the same light that we do the murders and robberies which occur in society, and in a slaveholding State,—they are a sort of substitute for the latter; the robbers and murderers in what are called free States, are generally the poor and needy, who rob for money; negro slaves rarely murder or rob for this purpose; they have no inducement to do it—the fact is, the whole capital of the South is pledged for their maintenance. The present Chief Magistrate of Virginia has informed us that he has never known of but one single case in Virginia where negroes murdered for the sake of money. Now, there is no doubt, but that the common robberies and murders for money, take off, in the aggregate, more men, and destroy more property, than insurrections among the slaves; the former are the result of fixed causes eternally at work, the latter of occasional causes which are rarely, *very rarely,* in action. Accordingly, if we should look to the whole of our southern population, and compare the average number of deaths, by the hands of assassins, with the numbers elsewhere, we would be astonished to find them perhaps as few, or fewer, than in any other population of equal amount on the globe. In the city of London there is, upon an average, a murder, or a house-breaking and robbery, every night in the year, which is greater than the amount of deaths by murders, insurrections, &c., in our whole southern country; and yet the inhabitant of London walks the streets, and sleeps in perfect confidence, and why should not we, who are in fact in much less danger?* These calamities in London very properly give rise to the establishment of a police, and the adoption of precautionary measures; and so they should in our country, and every where else. And if the Virginia Legislature had turned its attention more to this subject during its last session, we think, with all due deference, it would have redounded much more to the advantage of the State than the intemperate discussion which was gotten up.

But it is agreed on almost all hands, that the danger of insurrection now is not very great; but a time must arrive, it is supposed by many, when the dangers will infinitely increase, and either the one or the other race must necessarily be exterminated. "I do believe," said one in the Virginia Legislature, "and such must be the judgment of every reflecting man, that unless something is done in time to obviate it, the day must arrive when scenes of inconceivable horror must inevitably occur, and one of these two races of human beings will have their throats cut by the other." Another gentleman anticipates the dark day when a negro Legislature would be in session in the capital of the Old Dominion! Mr. Clay, too, seems to be full of gloomy anticipations of the future. In his colonization speech of 1830, he says, "Already the slaves may be estimated at two millions, and the free population at ten; the former being in the proportion of one to five of the latter. Their respective numbers will probably double in periods of thirty-three. In the year 1863, the number

---

* We wish that accurate accounts could be published of all the deaths which had occurred from insurrections in the United States, West Indies, and South America, since the establishment of slavery; and that these could be compared to the whole population that have lived since that epoch, and the number of deaths which occur in other equal amounts of population from popular sedition, robberies, &c., and we would be astonished to see what little cause we have for the slightest apprehension on this score.

of the whites will probably be twenty, and of the blacks four millions. In 1896, forty and eight; and in the year 1929, about a century, eighty and sixteen millions. What mind is sufficiently extensive in its reach—what nerve sufficiently strong—to contemplate this vast and progressive augmentation, without an awful foreboding of the tremendous consequences." If these anticipations are true, then may we in despair sit quietly down by the waters of Babylon, and weep over our lot, for we can never remove the blacks—*"Hæret lateri lethalis arundo."*

But we have none of these awful forebodings. We do not look to the time when the throats of one race must be cut by the other; on the contrary, we have no hesitation in affirming, and we think we can prove it, too, that in 1929, taking Mr. Clay's own statistics, we shall be much more secure from plots and insurrections than we are at this moment. It is an undeniable fact that, in the increase of population, the power and security of the dominant party always increases much more than in proportion to the relative augmentation of their numbers. One hundred men can much more easily keep an equal number in subjection than fifty, and a million would rule a million more certainly and securely than any lesser number. The dominant can only be overturned by concert and harmony among the subject party, and the greater the relative numbers on both sides, the more impossible does this concert on the part of the subjected become. A police, too, of the same relative numbers, is much more efficient amid a numerous population than a sparse one. We will illustrate by example, which cannot fail to strike even the most sceptical. Mr. Gibbon supposes that the hundredth man in any community is as much as the people can afford to keep in pay for the purposes of a police. Now suppose the community be only one hundred, then one man alone is the police. Is it not evident that the ninety-nine will be able at any moment to destroy him, and throw off all restraint? Suppose the community one thousand, then ten will form the police, which would have rather a better chance of keeping up order among the nine hundred and ninety, than the one in the one hundred—but still this would be insufficient. Let your community swell to one million, and ten thousand would then form the police, and ten thousand troops will strike terror in any city on the face of the globe. Lord Wellington lately asserted in the British Parliament, that Paris, containing a population of a million of souls, (the most boisterous and ungovernable,) never required, before the reign of Louis Philippe, more than forty-five hundred troops to keep it in the most perfect subjection. It is this very principle which explains the fact so frequently noticed, that revolutions are effected much more readily in small states than in large ones. The little republics of Greece underwent revolution almost every month; the dominant party was never safe for a moment. The little states of modern Italy have undergone more changes and revolutions than all the rest of Europe together, and if foreign influence were withdrawn, almost every ship from Europe, even now, would bring the news of some new revolution in those states. If the standing army will remain firm to the government, a successful revolution in most large empires, as France, Germany, and Russia, is almost impossible. The two revolutions in France have been successful, in consequence of the disaffection of the troops, who have joined the popular party.

Let us apply these principles to our own case; and for the sake of simplicity, we will take a county of a mixed population of twenty thousand, viz., blacks ten thousand, and whites as many:—the patrol which they can keep out, would, according to our rule, be two hundred; double both sides, and the patrol would be four hundred; quadruple, and it would be eight hundred—now, a patrol of eight hundred would be much more efficient than the two hundred, though they were, relatively to the numbers kept in order, exactly the same; and the same principle is applicable to the progress of population in the whole slaveholding country. In 1929, our police would be much more efficient than now, if the two estates preserve anything like the same relative numbers. We believe it would be better for the whites that the negro population should double, if they added only one-half more to their numbers, than that they should remain stationary on both sides. Hence, an insuperable objection to all these deporting schemes—they cannot diminish the relative proportion of the blacks to the whites, but on the contrary increase it, while they check the augmentation of the population as a whole, and consequently lessen the security of the dominant party. We do not fear the increase of the blacks, for that very increase adds to the wealth of society, and enables it to keep up the police. This is the true secret of the security of the West Indies and Brazil. In Jamaica, the blacks are eight-fold the whites; throughout the extensive empire of Brazil they are three to one. Political prophets have been prophesying for fifty years past, that the day would speedily arrive, when all the West Indies would be in possession of the negroes; and the danger is no greater now than it was at the commencement. We sincerely believe the blacks never will get possession, unless through the mad interference of the mother countries, and even then we are doubtful whether they can conquer the whites. Now, we have nowhere in the United States the immense disproportion between the two races observed in Brazil and the West Indies, and we are not like to have it in all time to come. We have no data, therefore, upon which to anticipate that dreadful crisis, which so torments the imagination of some. The little islands of the West Indies, if such crisis were fated frequently to arrive, ought to exhibit one continued series of massacres and insurrections, for their blacks are relatively much more numerous than with us, and a small extent of territory is, upon the principle just explained, much more favorable to successful revolution than a large one. Are we not, then, most unphilosophically and needlessly tormenting ourselves with the idea of *insurrection*—seeing that the West India Islands, even so much worse off than ourselves, are, nevertheless, but rarely disturbed? It is well known that where the range is sufficiently extensive, and the elements sufficiently numerous, the calculation of chances may be reduced to almost a mathematical certainty; thus, although you cannot say what will be the profit or loss of a particular gambling house in Paris on any one night, yet you may, with great accuracy, calculate upon the profits for a whole year, and with still greater accuracy, for any longer period, as ten, twenty, or one hundred years. Upon the same principle we speculate with much greater certainty upon masses of individuals, than upon single persons. Hence, bills of mortality, registers of births, marriages, crimes, &c., become very important statistics, when calculated upon large masses of population, although they prove nothing in families or among individuals. Proceeding upon this principle, we cannot fail to derive the greatest consolation from the fact, that although slavery has existed in our country for the last two hundred years, there have been but three attempts at insurrection—one in Virginia, one in South Carolina, and, we believe, one in Louisiana—and the loss of lives from this cause has not amounted to one hundred persons in all. We may then calculate in the next two hundred years, upon a similar result, which is incomparably smaller than the number which will be taken off in free States by murders for the sake of money.

But our population returns have been looked to, and it has been affirmed that they show a steady increase of blacks, which will finally carry them in all proportion beyond the whites, and that this will be particularly the case in Eastern Virginia. We have no fears on this score either; even if it were true, the danger would not be very great. With the increase of the blacks, we can afford to enlarge the police; and we will venture to say, that with the hundredth man at our disposal, and faithful to us, we would keep down insurrection in any large country on the face of the globe. But the speakers in the Virginia Legislature, in our humble opinion, made most unwarrantable inferences from the census returns. They took a period between 1790 and 1830, and judged exclusively from the aggregate results of the whole time. Mr. Brown pointed out their fallacy, and showed that there was but a small portion of the period in which the blacks had rapidly gained upon the whites, but during the residue they were most rapidly losing their high relative increase, and would, perhaps, in 1840, exhibit an augmentation less than the whites. But let us go a little back. In 1740, the slaves in South-Carolina, says Marshall,

were three times the whites; the danger from them was greater then
than it ever has been since, or ever will be again. There was an insurrection in that year, which was put down with the utmost ease, although instigated and aided by the Spaniards. The slaves in Virginia,
at the same period, were much more numerous than the whites. Now,
suppose some of those *peepers* into futurity could have been present,
would they not have predicted the speedy arrival of the time when
the blacks, running ahead of the whites in numbers, would have destroyed their security? In 1763, the black population of Virginia
was 100,000, and the white 70,000. In South-Carolina, the blacks
were 90,000, and the whites 40,000. Comparing these with the returns of 1740, our prophets, could they have lived so long, might
have found some consolation in the greater relative increase of the
whites. Again, when we see in 1830, that the blacks in both States
have fallen in numbers below the whites, our prophets, were they
alive, might truly be pronounced *false*.

JAMES HENRY HAMMOND
(*1807-1864*)

Born in Newberry District, South Carolina, the son of a Massachusetts teacher, farmer, and merchant, James Hammond graduated in 1825 from South Carolina College, which was popular with the planter class. He studied law, passed the bar, and enjoyed a lucrative practice at Columbia. He also became interested in journalism and published the *Southern Times,* which advocated nullification and extreme state's rights. After he married the daughter of a very wealthy planter, he dropped law to operate a large cotton plantation, thus becoming a substantial slaveholder.

He then turned to politics, beginning as a congressman and urging Southern states to unite in resistance to high tariffs by seceding from the Union. In 1842 he was elected governor and served two terms. His fire-eating speeches called for American expansionism from Panama to the North Pole. He was active in the Southern Convention of 1850 at Nashville, where he hoped to convince the entire South to join South Carolina in secession during that national crisis over the Wilmot Proviso. In 1857, he was elected to the Senate, where he advocated proslavery propaganda to win over Northern opinion. He is best remembered for his much-quoted proslavery speech in which he argued the necessity of Northern wage slaves and Southern plantation slaves as "the very mudsills of society." Defiantly, he declared, "You dare not make war on cotton . . . No power on earth dares make war upon it. Cotton is king." When Lincoln was elected president, Hammond resigned from the Senate and supported the Southern Confederacy.

As this selection shows, Hammond's answers to antislavery charges, though not factually irreproachable, were more plausible than those of most proslavery propagandists. "Letters on Slavery," *The Pro-Slavery Argument* (Philadelphia, 1853), pages 119-135.

Stability and peace are the first desires of every slave-holder, and the true tendency of the system. It could not possibly exist amid the eternal anarchy and civil broils of the ancient Spanish dominions in America. And for this very reason, domestic Slavery has ceased there. So far from encouraging strife, such scenes of riot and bloodshed, as have within the last few years disgraced our Northern cities, and as you* have lately witnessed in Birmingham and Bristol and Wales, not only never have occurred, but I will venture to say, never will occur in our slave-holding States. The only thing that can create a mob (as you might call it) here, is the appearance of an abolitionist, whom the people assemble to chastise. And this is no more of a mob, than a rally of shepherds to chase a wolf out of their pastures would be one.

But we are swindlers and repudiators! Pennsylvania is not a slave State. A majority of the States which have failed to meet their obligations punctually are non-slave-holding; and two-thirds of the debt said to be repudiated is owed by these States. Many of the States of this Union are heavily encumbered with debt—none so hopelessly as England. Pennsylvania owes $22 for each inhabitant—England $222, counting her paupers in. Nor has there been any repudiation definite and final, of a lawful debt, that I am aware of. A few States have failed to pay some installments of interest. The extraordinary financial difficulties which occurred a few years ago will account for it. Time will set all things right again. Every dollar of both principal and interest, owed by any State, North or South, will be ultimately paid, *unless the abolition of Slavery overwhelms us all in one common ruin.* But have no other nations failed to pay? When

* [This letter was addressed by Hammond to the English.—ED.]

were the French Assignats redeemed? How much interest did your National Bank pay on its immense circulation, from 1797 to 1821, during which period that circulation was inconvertible, and for the time *repudiated?* How much of your national debt has been incurred for money borrowed to meet the interest on it, thus avoiding delinquency in detail, by insuring inevitable bankruptcy and repudiation in the end? And what sort of operation was that by which your present Ministry recently expunged a handsome amount of that debt, by substituting, through a process just not compulsory, one species of security for another? I am well aware that the faults of others do not excuse our own, but when failings are charged to Slavery, which are shown to occur to equal extent where it does not exist, surely Slavery must be acquitted of the accusation.

It is roundly asserted, that we are not so well educated nor so religious here as elsewhere. I will not go into tedious statistical statements on these subjects. Nor have I, to tell the truth, much confidence in the details of what are commonly set forth as statistics. As to education, you will probably admit that slave-holders should have more leisure for mental culture than most people. And I believe it is charged against them, that they are peculiarly fond of power, and ambitious of honors. If this be so, as all the power and honors of this country are won mainly by intellectual superiority, it might be fairly presumed, that slave-holders would not be neglectful of education. In proof of the accuracy of this presumption, I point you to the facts, that our Presidential chair has been occupied for forty-four out of fifty-six years, by slave-holders; that another [Pierce] has been recently elected to fill it for four more, over an opponent who was a slave-holder also; and that in the Federal Offices and both Houses of Congress, considerably more than a due proportion of those acknowledged to stand in the first rank are from the South. In this arena, the intellects of the free and slave States meet in full and fair competition. Nature must have been unusually bountiful to us, or we have been at least reasonably assiduous in the cultivation of such gifts as she has bestowed—unless indeed you refer our superiority to moral qualities, which I am sure *you* will not. More wealthy we are not; nor would mere wealth avail in such rivalry.

The piety of the South is unobtrusive. We think it proves but little, though it is a confident thing for a man to claim that he stands higher in the estimation of his Creator, and is less a sinner than his neighbor. If vociferation is to carry the question of religion, the North, and probably the Scotch, have it. Our sects are few, harmonious, pretty much united among themselves, and pursue their avocations in humble peace. In fact, our professors of religion seem to think—whether correctly or not—that it is their duty "to do good in secret," and to carry their holy comforts to the heart of each individual, without reference to class *or color,* for his special enjoyment, and not with a view to exhibit their zeal before the world. So far as numbers are concerned, I believe our clergymen, when called on to make a showing, have never had occasion to blush, if comparisons were drawn between the free and slave States. And although our presses do not teem with controversial pamphlets, nor our pulpits shake with excommunicating thunders, the daily walk of our religious communicants furnishes, apparently, as little food for gossip as is to be found in most other regions. It may be regarded as a mark of our want of excitability—though that is a quality accredited to us in an eminent degree—that few of the remarkable religious *Isms* of the present day have taken root among us. We have been so irreverent as to laugh at Mormonism and Millerism, which have created such commotions farther North; and modern prophets have no honor in our country. Shakers, Rappists, Dunkers, Socialists, Fourierists and the like, keep themselves afar off. Even Puseyism has not yet moved us. You may attribute this to our domestic Slavery if you choose. I believe you would do so justly. There is no material here for such characters to operate upon.

But your grand charge is, that licentiousness in intercourse between the sexes, is a prominent trait of our social system, and that it necessarily arises from Slavery. This is a favorite theme with the abolitionists, male and female. Folios have been written on it. It is a common observation, that there is no subject on which ladies of eminent virtue so much delight to dwell, and on which in especial learned old maids, like Miss Martineau, linger with such an insatiable relish. They expose it in the slave States with the most minute observance and endless iteration. Miss Martineau, with peculiar gusto, relates a series of scandalous stories, which would have made Boccaccio jealous of her pen, but which are so ridiculously false as to leave no doubt, that some wicked wag, knowing she would write a book, has furnished her materials—a game too often played on tourists in this country. The constant recurrence of the female abolitionists to this topic, and their bitterness in regard to it, cannot fail to suggest to even the most charitable mind, that

"Such rage without betrays the fires within."

Nor are their immaculate coadjutors of the other sex, though perhaps less specific in their charges, less violent in their denunciations. But recently in your Island, a clergyman has, at a public meeting, stigmatized the whole slave region as a "brothel." Do these people thus cast stones, being "without sin?" Or do they only

"Compound for sins they are inclined to
By damning those they have no mind to."

Alas that David and Solomon should be allowed to repose in peace—that Leo should be almost canonized, and Luther more than sainted—that in our own day courtezans should be formally licensed in Paris, and tenements in London rented for years to women of the town for the benefit of the Church, with the knowledge of the Bishop—and the poor slave States of America alone pounced upon, and offered up as a holocaust on the altar of immaculateness, to atone for the abuse of natural instinct by all mankind; and if not actually consumed, at least exposed, anathematized and held up to scorn, by those who

"Write,
Or with a rival's or an eunuch's spite."

But I do not intend to admit that this charge is just or true. Without meaning to profess uncommon modesty, I will say that I wish the topic could be avoided. I am of opinion, and I doubt not every right-minded man will concur, that the public exposure and discussion of this vice, even to rebuke, invariably does more harm than good; and that if it cannot be checked by instilling pure and virtuous sentiments, it is far worse than useless to attempt to do it, by exhibiting its deformities. I may not, however, pass it over; nor ought I to feel any delicacy in examining a question, to which the slaveholder is invited and challenged by clergymen and virgins. So far from allowing, then, that licentiousness pervades this region, I broadly assert, and I refer to the records of our courts, to the public press, and to the knowledge of all who have ever lived here, that among our white population there are fewer cases of divorce, separation, crim. con. [adultery], seduction, rape and bastardy, than among any other five millions of people on the civilized earth. And this fact I believe will be conceded by the abolitionists of this country themselves. I am almost willing to refer it to them and submit to their decision on it. I would not hesitate to do so, if I thought them capable of an impartial judgment on any matter where Slavery is in question. But it is said, that the licentiousness consists in the constant intercourse between white males and colored females. One of your heavy charges against us has been, that we regard and treat these people as brutes; you now charge us with habitually taking them to our bosoms. I will not comment on the inconsistency of these accusations. I will not deny that some intercourse of the sort does take place. Its character and extent, however, are grossly and atrociously exaggerated. No authority, divine or human, has yet been found sufficient to arrest all such irregularities among men. But it is a known fact, that they are perpetrated here, for the most part, in the cities. Very few mulattoes are reared on our plantations. In the cities, a large proportion of the inhabitants do not own slaves. A still larger proportion are natives of the North, or foreigners. They should share, and justly, too, an equal part in this sin with the slave-holders. Facts cannot be ascertained, or I doubt not, it would appear that they are the chief offenders. If the truth be otherwise, then persons from abroad have stronger prejudices against the African race than we have. Be this as it may, it is well known, that this intercourse is regarded in our society as highly disreputable. If carried on habitually, it seriously affects a man's standing, so far as it is known; and he who takes a colored mistress—with rare and extraordinary exceptions—loses caste at once. You will say that *one* exception should damn our whole country. How much less criminal is it to take a white mistress? In your eyes it should be at least an equal offence. Yet look around you at home, from the cottage to the throne, and count how many mistresses are kept in unblushing notoriety, without loss of caste. Such cases are nearly unknown here, and down even to the lowest walks of life, it is almost invariably fatal to a man's position and prospects to keep a mistress openly, whether white or black. What Miss Martineau relates of a young man's purchasing a colored concubine from a lady, and avowing his designs, is too absurd even for contradiction. No person would dare to allude to such a subject, in such a manner, to any decent female in this country.

After all, however, the number of the mixed breed, in proportion to that of the black, is infinitely small, and out of the towns next to nothing. And when it is considered that the African race has been among us for two hundred years, and that those of the mixed breed continually intermarry—often rearing large families—it is a decided proof of our continence, that so few comparatively are to be found. Our misfortunes are two-fold. From the prolific propagation of these mongrels among themselves, we are liable to be charged by tourists with delinquencies where none have been committed, while, where one has been, it cannot be concealed. Color marks indelibly the offence, and reveals it to every eye. Conceive that, even in your virtuous and polished country, if every bastard, through all the circles of your social system, was thus branded by nature and known to all, what shocking developments might there not be! How little indignation might your saints have to spare for the licentiousness of the slave region. But I have done with this disgusting topic. And I think I may justly conclude, after all the scandalous charges which tea-table gossip, and long-gowned hypocrisy have brought against the slave-holders, that a people whose men are proverbially brave, intellectual and hospitable, and whose women are unaffectedly chaste, devoted to domestic life, and happy in it, can neither be degraded nor demoralized, whatever their institutions may be. My decided opinion is, that our system of Slavery contributes largely to the development and culture of these high and noble qualities.

In an economical point of view—which I will not omit—Slavery presents some difficulties. As a general rule, I agree it must be admitted, that free labor is cheaper than slave labor. It is a fallacy to suppose that ours is *unpaid labor*. The slave himself must be paid for, and thus his labor is all purchased at once, and for no trifling sum. His price was, in the first place, paid mostly to your countrymen, and assisted in building up some of those colossal English fortunes, since illustrated by patents of nobility, and splendid piles of architecture, stained and cemented, if you like the expression, with the blood of kidnapped innocents; but loaded with no heavier curses than abolition and its begotten fanaticisms have brought upon your land—some of them fulfilled, some yet to be. But besides the first cost of the slave, he must be fed and clothed, well fed and well clothed, if not for humanity's sake, that he may do good work, retain health and life, and rear a family to supply his place. When old or sick, he is a clear expense, and so is the helpless portion of his family. No poor law provides for him when unable to work, or brings up his children for our service when we need them. These are all heavy charges on slave labor. Hence, in all countries where the denseness of the population has reduced it to a matter of perfect certainty, that labor can be obtained, whenever wanted, and the laborer be forced, by sheer necessity, to hire for the smallest pittance that will keep soul and body together, and rags upon his back while in actual employment—dependent at all other times on alms or poor rates—in all such countries it is found cheaper to pay this pittance, than to clothe, feed, nurse, support through childhood, and pension in old age, a race of slaves. Indeed, the advantage is so great as speedily to compensate for the loss of the value of the slave. And I have no hesitation in saying, that if I could cultivate my lands on these terms, I would, without a word, resign my slaves, provided they could be properly disposed of. But the question is, whether free or slave labor is cheapest to us in this country, at this time, situated as we are. And it is decided at once by the fact that we cannot avail ourselves of any other than slave labor. We neither have, nor can we procure, other labor to any extent, or on anything like the terms mentioned. We must therefore, content ourselves with our dear labor, under the consoling reflection that what is lost to us, is gained to humanity; and that, inasmuch as our slave costs us more than your free man costs you, by so much is he better off. You will promptly say, emancipate your slaves, and then you will have free labor on suitable terms. That might be if there were five hundred where there now is one, and the continent, from the Atlantic to the Pacific, was as densely populated as your Island. But until that comes to pass, no labor can be procured in America on the terms you have it.

While I thus freely admit that to the individual proprietor slave labor is dearer than free, I do not mean to admit as equally clear that it is dearer to the community and to the State. Though it is certain that the slave is a far greater consumer than your laborer, the year round, yet your pauper system is costly and wasteful. Supported by your community at large, it is not administered by your hired agents with that interested care and economy—not to speak of humanity—which mark the management of ours, by each proprietor, for his own non-effectives; and is both more expensive to those who pay, and less beneficial to those who receive its bounties. Besides this, Slavery is rapidly filling up our country with a hardy and healthy race, peculiarly adapted to our climate and productions, and conferring signal political and social advantages on us as a people, to which I have already referred.

I have yet to reply to the main ground on which you and your coadjutors rely for the overthrow of our system of Slavery. Failing in all your attempts to prove that it is sinful in its nature, immoral to its effects, a political evil, and profitless to those who maintain it, you appeal to the sympathies of mankind, and attempt to arouse the world against us by the most shocking charges of tyranny and cruelty. You begin by a vehement denunciation of "the irresponsible power of one man over his fellow men." The question of the responsibility of power is a vast one. It is the great political question of modern times. Whole nations divide off upon it and establish different fundamental systems of government. That "responsibility," which to one set of millions seems amply sufficient to check the government, to the support of which they devote their lives and fortunes, appears to another set of millions a mere mockery of restraint. And accordingly as the opinions of these millions differ, they honor each other with the epithets of "serfs" or "anarchists." It is ridiculous to introduce such an idea as this into the discussion of a mere domestic institution; but since you have introduced it, I deny that the power of the slave-holder in America is "irresponsible." He is responsible to God. He is responsible to the world—a responsibility which abolitionists do not intend to to allow him to evade—and in acknowledgment of which, I write you this letter. He is responsible to the community in which he lives, and to the laws under which he enjoys his civil rights. Those laws do not permit him to kill, to maim, or to punish beyond certain limits, or to overtask, or to refuse to feed and clothe his slave. In short, they forbid him to be tyrannical or cruel. If any of these laws have grown obsolete, it is because they are so seldom violated, that they are forgotten. You have disinterred one of them, from a compilation by some Judge Stroud of Philadelphia, to stigmatize its inadequate penalties for killing, maiming, &c.

Your object appears to be—you can have no other—to produce the impression, that it must be often violated on account of its insufficiency. You say as much, and that it marks our estimate of the slave. You forget to state that this law was enacted by *Englishmen,* and only indicates *their* opinion of the reparation due for these offences. Ours is proved by the fact, though perhaps unknown to Judge Stroud or yourself, that we have essentially altered this law; and the murder of a slave has for many years been punishable with death in this State. And so it is, I believe, in most or all the slave States. You seem well aware, however, that laws have been recently passed in all these States, making it penal to teach slaves to read. Do you know what occasioned their passage, and renders their stringent enforcement necessary? I can tell you. It was the abolition agitation. If the slave is not allowed to read his bible, the sin rests upon the abolitionists; for they stand prepared to furnish him with a key to it, which would make it, not a book of hope, and love, and peace, but of despair, hatred and blood; which would convert the reader, not into a christian, but a demon. To preserve him from such a horrid destiny, it is a sacred duty which we owe to our slaves, not less than to ourselves, to interpose the most decisive means. If the Catholics deem it wrong to trust the bible to the hands of ignorance, shall we be excommunicated because we will not give it, and with it the corrupt and fatal commentaries of the abolitionists, to our slaves! Allow our slaves to read your writings, stimulating them to cut our throats! Can you believe us to be such unspeakable fools?

I do not know that I can subscribe in full to the sentiment so often quoted by the abolitionists, and by Mr. Dickinson in his letter to me: *"Homo sum humani nihil a me alienum puto,"* as translated and practically illustrated by them. Such a doctrine would give wide authority to every one for the most dangerous intermeddling with the affairs of others. It will do in poetry—perhaps in some sorts of philosophy—but the attempt to make it a household maxim, and introduce it into the daily walks of life, has caused many a "homo" a broken crown; and probably will continue to do it. Still, though a slaveholder, I freely acknowledge my obligations as a man; and that I am bound to treat humanely the fellow-creatures whom God has entrusted to my charge. I feel, therefore, somewhat sensitive under the accusation of cruelty, and disposed to defend myself and fellow-slaveholders against it. It is certainly the interest of all, and I am convinced that it is also the desire of every one of us, to treat our slaves with proper kindness. It is necessary to our deriving the greatest amount of profit from them. Of this we are all satisfied. And you snatch from us the only consolation we Americans could derive from the opprobrious imputation of being wholly devoted to making money, which your disinterested and gold-despising countrymen delight to cast upon us, when you nevertheless declare that we are ready to sacrifice it for the pleasure of being inhuman. You remember that Mr. Pitt could not get over the idea that self-interest would ensure kind treatment to slaves, until you told him your woeful stories of the middle passage. Mr. Pitt was right in the first instance, and erred, under your tuition, in not perceiving the difference between a temporary and permanent ownership of them. Slaveholders are no more perfect than other men. They have passions. Some of them, as you may suppose, do not at all times restrain them. Neither do husbands, parents and friends. And in each of these relations, as serious suffering as frequently arises from uncontrolled passions, as ever does in that of master and slave, and with as little chance of indemnity. Yet you would not on that account break them up. I have no hesitation in saying that our slaveholders are kind masters, as men usually are kind husbands, parents and friends —as a general rule, kinder. A bad master—he who overworks his slaves, provides ill for them, or treats them with undue severity—loses the esteem and respect of his fellow-citizens to as great an extent as he would for the violation of any of his social and most of his moral obligations. What the most perfect plan of management would be, is a problem hard to solve. From the commencement of Slavery in this country, this subject has occupied the minds of all slaveholders, as much as the improvement of the general condition of mankind has those of the most ardent philanthropists; and the greatest progressive amelioration of the system has been effected. You yourself acknowledge that in the early part of your career you were exceedingly anxious for the *immediate* abolition of the slave trade, lest those engaged in it should so mitigate its evils as to destroy the force of your arguments and facts. The improvement you then *dreaded* has gone on steadily here, and would doubtless have taken place in the slave trade, but for the measures adopted to suppress it.

Of late years we have been not only annoyed, but greatly embarrassed in this matter, by the abolitionists. We have been compelled to curtail some privileges; we have been debarred from granting new ones. In the face of discussions which aim at loosening all ties between master and slave, we have in some measure to abandon our efforts to attach them to us, and control them through their affections and pride. We have to rely more and more on the power of fear. We must, in all our intercourse with them, assert and maintain strict mastery, and impress it on them that they are slaves. This is painful to us, and certainly no present advantage to them. But it is the direct consequence of the abolition agitation. We are determined to continue masters, and to do so we have to draw the rein tighter and tighter day by day to be assured that we hold them in complete check. How far this process will go on, depends wholly and solely on the abolitionists. When they desist, we can relax. We may not before. I do not mean by all this to say that we are in a state of actual alarm and fear of our slaves; but under existing circumstances we should be ineffably stupid not to increase our vigilance and strengthen our hands. You see some of the fruits of your labors. I speak freely and candidly—not as a colonist, who, though a slaveholder, has a master; but as a free white man, holding, under God, and resolved to hold, my fate in my own hands; and I assure you that my sentiments, and feelings, and determinations, are those of every slaveholder in this country.

The research and ingenuity of the abolitionists, aided by the invention of runaway slaves—in which faculty, so far as improvising falsehood goes, the African race is without a rival—have succeeded in shocking the world with a small number of pretended instances of our barbarity. The only wonder is, that considering the extent of our country, the variety of our population, its fluctuating character, and the publicity of all our transactions, the number of cases is so small. It speaks well for us. Yet of these, many are false, all highly colored, some occurring half a century, most of them many years ago; and no doubt a large proportion of them perpetrated by foreigners. With a few rare exceptions, the emigrant Scotch and English are the worst masters among us, and next to them our Northern fellow-citizens. Slaveholders born and bred here are always more humane to slaves, and those who have grown up to a large inheritance of them, the most so of any—showing clearly that the effect of the system is to foster kindly feelings. I do not mean so much to impute innate inhumanity to foreigners, as to show that they come here with false notions of the treatment usual and necessary for slaves, and that newly acquired power here, as everywhere else, is apt to be abused. I cannot enter into a detailed examination of the cases stated by the abolitionists. It would be disgusting, and of little avail. I know nothing of them. I have seen nothing like them, though born and bred here, and have rarely heard of anything at all to be compared to them. Permit me to say that I think most of *your* facts must have been drawn from the West Indies, where undoubtedly slaves were treated much more harshly than with us. This was owing to a variety of causes, which might, if necessary, be stated. One was, that they had at first to deal more extensively with barbarians fresh from the wilds of Africa; another, and a leading one, the absenteeism of proprietors. Agents are always more unfeeling than owners, whether placed over West Indian or American slaves, or Irish tenantry. We feel this evil greatly even here. You describe the use of *thumb screws,* as one mode of punishment among us. I doubt if a thumb screw can be found in America. I never saw or heard of one in this country. Stocks are rarely used by private individuals, and confinement still more seldom, though both are common punish-

ments for whites, all the world over. I think they should be more frequently resorted to with slaves, as substitutes for flogging, which I
consider the most injurious and least efficacious mode of punish-
ing them for serious offences. It is not degrading, and unless excessive occasions little pain. You may be a little astonished, after all the
flourishes that have been made about "cart whips," &c., when I say
flogging is not the most degrading punishment in the world. It may
be so to a white man in most countries, but how is it to the white
boy? That necessary coadjutor of the schoolmaster, the "birch," is
never thought to have rendered infamous the unfortunate victim of
pedagogue ire; nor did Solomon in his wisdom dream that he was
counselling parents to debase their offspring, when he exhorted them
not to spoil the child by sparing the rod. Pardon me for recurring to
the now exploded ethics of the Bible. Custom, which, you will perhaps agree, makes most things in this world good or evil, has removed all infamy from the punishment of the lash to the slave.
Your blood boils at the recital of stripes inflicted on a man; and
you think you should be frenzied to see your own child flogged.
Yet see how completely this is ideal, arising from the fashions of
society. You doubtless submitted to the rod yourself, in other years,
when the smart was perhaps as severe as it would be now; and you
have never been guilty of the folly of revenging yourself on the
Preceptor, who, in the plenitude of his "irresponsible power,"
thought proper to chastise your son. So it is with the negro, and the
negro father.

As to chains and irons, they are rarely used; never, I believe, except in cases of running away. You will admit that if we pretend to
own slaves, they must not be permitted to abscond whenever they
see fit; and that if nothing else will prevent it, these means must be
resorted to. See the inhumanity necessarily arising from Slavery,
you will exclaim. Are such restraints imposed on no other class of
people, giving no more offence? Look to your army and navy. If
your seamen, impressed from their peaceful occupations, and your
soldiers, recruited at the gin-shops—both of them as much kid-

napped as the most unsuspecting victim of the slave trade, and doomed to a far more wretched fate—if these men manifest a propensity to desert, the heaviest manacles are their mildest punishment. It is more commonly death, after summary trial. But armies and navies, you say, are indispensable, and must be kept up at every sacrifice. I answer, that they are no more indispensable than Slavery is to us—and to *you;* for you have enough of it in your country, though the form and name differ from ours.

Depend upon it that many things, and in regard to our slaves, most things which appear revolting at a distance, and to slight reflection, would, on a nearer view and impartial comparison with the customs and conduct of the rest of mankind, strike you in a very different light. Remember that on our estates we dispense with the whole machinery of public police and public courts of justice. Thus we try, decide, and execute the sentences, in thousands of cases, which in other countries would go into the courts. Hence, most of the acts of our alleged cruelty, which have any foundation in truth. Whether our patriarchal mode of administering justice is less humane than the Assizes, can only be determined by careful enquiry and comparison. But this is never done by the abolitionists. All our punishments are the outrages of "irresponsible power." If a man steals a pig in England, he is transported—torn from wife, children, parents, and sent to the antipodes, infamous, and an outcast forever, though probably he took from the superabundance of his neighbor to save the lives of his famishing little ones. If one of our well-fed negroes, merely for the sake of fresh meat, steals a pig, he gets perhaps forty stripes. If one of your cottagers breaks into another's house, he is hung for burglary. If a slave does the same here, a few lashes, or it may be a few hours in the stocks, settles the matter. Are our courts or yours the most humane? If Slavery were not in question, you would doubtless say ours is mistaken lenity. Perhaps it often is; and slaves too lightly dealt with sometimes grow daring. Occasionally, though rarely, and almost always in consequence of excessive indulgence, an individual rebels. This is the highest crime he can commit. It is treason. It strikes at the root of our whole system. His life is justly forfeited, though it is never intentionally taken, unless after trial in our public courts. Sometimes, however, in capturing, or in self-defence, he is unfortunately killed. A legal investigation always follows. But, terminate as it may, the abolitionists raise a hue and cry, and another "shocking case" is held up to the indignation of the world by tender-hearted male and female philanthropists, who would have thought it all right had the master's throat been cut, and would have triumphed in it.

I cannot go into a detailed comparison between the penalties inflicted on a slave in our patriarchal courts, and those of the Courts of Sessions, to which freemen are sentenced in all civilized nations; but I know well that if there is any fault in our criminal code, it is that of excessive mildness.

Perhaps a few general facts will best illustrate the treatment this race receives at our hands. It is acknowledged that it increases at least as rapidly as the white. I believe it is an established law, that population thrives in proportion to its comforts. But when it is considered that these people are not recruited by immigration from abroad, as the whites are, and that they are usually settled on our richest and least healthy lands, the fact of their equal comparative increase and greater longevity, outweighs a thousand abolition falsehoods, in favor of the leniency and providence of our management of them. It is also admitted that there are incomparably fewer cases of insanity and suicide among them than among the whites. The fact is that among the slaves of the African race these things are almost wholly unknown. However frequent suicide may have been among those brought from Africa, I can say that in my time I cannot remember to have known or heard of a single instance of deliberate self-destruction, and but of one of suicide at all. As to insanity, I have seen but one permanent case of it, and that twenty years ago. It cannot be doubted that among three millions of people there must be some insane and some suicides; but I will venture to say that more cases of both occur annually among every hundred thousand of the population of Great Britain, than among all our slaves. Can it be possible, then, that they exist in that state of abject misery, goaded by constant injuries, outraged in their affections, and worn down with hardships, which the abolitionists depict, and so many ignorant and thoughtless persons religiously believe?

With regard to the separation of husbands and wives, parents and children, nothing can be more untrue than the inferences drawn from what is so constantly harped on by abolitionists. Some painful instances perhaps may occur. Very few that can be prevented. It is, and it always has been, an object of prime consideration with our slaveholders, to keep families together. Negroes are themselves both perverse and comparatively indifferent about this matter. It is a singular trait, that they almost invariably prefer forming connexions with slaves belonging to other masters, and at some distance. It is, therefore, impossible to prevent separations sometimes, by the removal of one owner, his death, or failure, and dispersion of his property. In all such cases, however, every reasonable effort is made to keep the parties together, if they desire it. And the negroes forming these connexions, knowing the chances of their premature dissolution, rarely complain more than we all do of the inevitable strokes of fate. Sometimes it happens that a negro prefers to give up his family rather than separate from his master. I have known such instances. As to wilfully selling off a husband, or wife, or child, I believe it is rarely, very rarely done, except when some offence has been committed demanding "transportation." At sales of estates, and even at Sheriff's sales, they are always, if possible sold in families. On the whole, notwithstanding the migratory character of our population, I believe there are more families among our slaves, who have lived and died together without losing a single member from their circle, except by the process of nature, and in the enjoyment of constant, uninterrupted communion, than have flourished in the same space of time, and among the same number of civilized people in modern times. And to sum up all, if pleasure is correctly defined to be the absence of pain—which, so far as the great body of mankind is concerned, is undoubtedly its true definition—I believe our slaves are the happiest three millions of human beings on whom the sun shines. Into their Eden is coming Satan in the guise of an abolitionist.

As regards their religious condition, it is well known that a majority of the communicants of the Methodist and Baptist churches of the South are colored. Almost everywhere they have precisely the same opportunities of attending worship that the whites have, and, besides special occasions for themselves exclusively, which they prefer. In many places not so accessible to clergymen in ordinary, missionaries are sent, and mainly supported by their masters, for the particular benefit of the slaves. There are none I imagine who may not, if they like, hear the gospel preached at least once a month—most of them twice a month, and very many every week. In our thinly settled country the whites fare no better. But in addition to this, on plantations of any size, the slaves who have joined the church are formed into a class, at the head of which is placed one of their number, acting as deacon or leader, who is also sometimes a licensed preacher. This class assembles for religious exercises weekly, semi-weekly, or oftener, if the members choose. In some parts, also, Sunday schools for blacks are established, and Bible classes are orally instructed by discreet and pious persons. Now where will you find a laboring population possessed of greater religious advantages than these? Not in London, I am sure, where it is known that your churches, chapels, and religious meeting houses, of all sorts, cannot contain one-half of the inhabitants.

I have admitted, without hesitation, what it would be untrue and profitless to deny, that slaveholders are responsible to the world for the humane treatment of the fellow-beings whom God has placed in their hands. I think it would be only fair for you to admit, what is equally undeniable, that every man in independent circumstances, all the world over, and every government, is to the same extent responsible to the whole human family, for the condition of the poor and laboring classes in their own country, and around them, wherever they may be placed, to whom God has denied the advantages he has given themselves. If so, it would naturally seem the duty of true humanity and rational philanthropy to devote their time and labor, their thoughts, writings and charity, first to the objects placed as it were under their own immediate charge. And it must be regarded as a clear evasion and skilful neglect of this cardinal duty, to pass from those whose destitute situation they can plainly see, minutely examine and efficiently relieve, to enquire after the condition of others in no way entrusted to their care, to exaggerate evils of which they cannot be cognizant, to expend all their sympathies and exhaust all their energies on these remote objects of their unnatural, not to say dangerous, benevolence; and finally, to calumniate, denounce, and endeavor to excite the indignation of the world against their unoffending fellow-creatures for not hastening, under their dictation, to redress wrongs which are stoutly and truthfully denied, while they themselves go but little farther in alleviating those chargeable on them than openly and unblushingly to acknowledge them. There may be indeed a sort of merit in doing so much as to make such an acknowledgment, but it must be very modest if it expects appreciation.

Now I affirm, that in Great Britain the poor and laboring classes of your own race and color, not only your fellow-beings, but your *fellow-citizens,* are more miserable and degraded, morally and physically, than our slaves; to be elevated to the actual condition of whom, would be to these, *your fellow-citizens,* a most glorious act of *emancipation.* And I also affirm, that the poor and laboring classes of our older free States would not be in a much more enviable condition, but for our Slavery. One of their own Senators has declared in the United States Senate, "that the repeal of the Tariff would reduce New-England to a howling wilderness." And the American Tariff is neither more nor less than a system by which the slave States are plundered for the benefit of those States which do not tolerate Slavery. . . .

GEORGE FITZHUGH
(*1806-1881*)

The son of an army surgeon and planter, George Fitzhugh was born in Prince William County, Virginia. Apparently, he devoted much more of his time to writing proslavery propaganda than to his career as a lawyer or as a planter, which he pursued unenthusiastically. Largely self-educated—his father died during George's youth and the estate was sold—he read conventional books, preferring book reviews on analytical topics, and displayed markedly conservative political and social tastes. Most of his life was spent in the quiet village of Port Royal, not far from Fredericksburg, and while he began as a liberal Jeffersonian Democrat, he was soon advocating such causes as the re-enslaving of free Negroes through a system of peonage.

During 1854, he was a contributing editor to the Richmond *Examiner*, one of the largest newspapers of the South, then headed by a fire-eating editor. Many of Fitzhugh's articles for the *Examiner* were re-published in a book, *Sociology for the South* (1854) which shared honors with Henry Hughes' *A Treatise on Sociology* (1854) as the first American book to use the new word "sociology" in its title. Obviously, it was pure proslavery propaganda rather than social science, and in it Fitzhugh argued, as the selection below shows, that the innate inferiority of the Negro required a slave system. The novel element in Fitzhugh's text was his argument that free society in all its manifestations—free trade, democratic equality, individualism, feminism, and the other liberal "isms"—was a failure. He later elaborated this indictment in *Cannibals All! Or Slaves Without Masters* (1857) in which he compared the happy state of the slave with that of the exploited British and Northern wage worker.

His intemperate attack aroused Republican congressmen to charge that Fitzhugh represented the Southern determination to enslave workers of both races. (Fitzhugh had written, "Slavery is the natural and normal condition of the laboring man whether white or black".) Lincoln, according to his law partner, was so disturbed by the argument that he used Fitzhugh's House Divided antithesis about the struggle between slavery and freedom for his own famous speech on that subject, although he reversed the conclusion. The selection below includes the Fitzhugh version of the (Hegelian) struggle between slavery and freedom in history.

After the Civil War, Fitzhugh served as an associate judge in the local Freedmen's Court and continued to write on racial and economic issues. He died in 1881 in Huntsville, Texas.

This short selection from *Cannibals All!* actually reflects Fitzhugh's chief ideas: "The Counter Current, or Slavery Principle," *De Bow's Review* 21 (1856), 90-95.

THE COUNTER CURRENT, OR
SLAVERY PRINCIPLE

The tendency of modern civilization is to beget one public opinion throughout christendom. This civilization is itself the outgrowth and result of christianity grafted on Greek, Roman, and Hebrew institutions, slightly modified by remnants of feudalism. In the past, all recur to the same fountains of thought, on the subjects of law, politics, morality, and religion. In the fine arts, as well as the moral sciences, the highest authorities are also found two thousand years back. This derivation of all thought from a common source would, of itself, in time, wear off national distinctions, and bring about sameness of character, of purpose, and of progress. The attainment of such conclusion is greatly facilitated and hastened by the general freedom of intercourse and of trade, which distinguishes the group of christian peoples.

Men derive the principles of science and the rudiments of thought, in their youth, from the common fountains of antiquity, and when they arrive at manhood flock to the schools of France, Germany, and Italy, to learn over again the lessons of youth put into modern forms.

The moral, religious, social, and political wants of a people thus educated, must be very similar, and even if they were not, common thoughts and belief, radiating from a few centres, will in time wear off all marked institutional distinctions. From these considerations we conclude, that the south, if she continue to belong to the family of christian peoples, must eventually model her institutions in conformity with the practices and opinions of those peoples.

Since the period of the Crusades, when all Europe seemed emptying itself into the lap of Asia, no spirit of propagandism so intense and so wide spread, has been witnessed among men, as that of the anti-slavery movement. Thirty years ago, it had fastened convictions on the minds of all, and the question of universal emancipation had ceased to be one of principle, and become one only of time, conveniency, and expediency. In little more than a century the public opinion, which begat the intense self-sacrificing zeal that distinguished the crusades, gave place to apathy, and soon thereafter to condemnation. Now, the same European christian peoples, who once considered a fillibustering expedition to Palestine sufficient atonement for the blackest crimes, look upon those expeditions as greatly adding to the crimes, which they even often intended to expiate. From this, and thousands [of] other similar changes of public sentiment to be found in history, the south will find room to gather hope for the future. Indeed, the abolition movement has occupied men's minds quite long enough to suggest the expectation that it will soon give way to other optimist and perfectionist theories and pursuits. We think we perceive already unmistakable evidence that a counter current of thought has already originated. Like all reactions of opinion, it has been occasioned by experimental demonstration of the fallacy and inadequacy of existing theories, and of practices founded on those theories. The great socialist and communist movement of the day, which is co-extensive with free society, whilst it has not yet invoked the re-establishment of domestic slavery, asserts, in a thousand forms, the utter failure of existing social institutions, which have arisen from the ruins of feudal servitude. The socialists are generally abolitionists, who propose to improve the condition of mankind by the adoption of institutions unlike any to be found in the past.

Despite of their intentions, they became the highest authority in favor of slavery, by their admissions that no other known and tested forms of social organization are even tolerable. So far as their doctrines are destructive, they are sustained by unanswerable theories and equally unanswerable facts. They show "that capital, skill, and competition, are calculated to place the masses of the, so called, free laborers, at the mercy of the rich, professional, and skilful, without any obligation to protection on the part of the latter, or valuable right of any sort on the part of the former. That men emancipated, without property, are relieved from the dominion of humane masters to be remitted to the more heartless and less responsible despotism of skill and capital." It is needless to inquire whether their theories are correct, since the results have always been such as they anticipated. The condition of emancipated laborers has, at all times and in all places, been far worse than their previous condition as slaves. But these socialists are all optimists and perfectionists, and none, except Mr. Carlyle, will sacrifice their theoretical Utopias for that practical amelioration of condition which slavery would be sure to produce. The extent of the socialist movement, so far as it is destructive, is little understood at the south. Beside professing socialists, who embrace a large majority of the writers on social, political, and moral subjects, beside the poor, who are generally chartists and red republicans, the moralists, the poets, the play writers, the clergy, and the press, are all largely imbued with the conviction of the necessity of organic social change. Indeed, except Mr. Macaulay, we know of no distinguished man who adheres to the philosophy of free society, and who believes that, in practice, it has meliorated the condition of the laboring masses. We have, then, the almost unanimous testimony of men of all conditions, that free society is a failure, is intolerable, and requires total subversion and reconstruction. This is, of itself, a mighty reactionary movement in favor of slavery. Another effective argument and fact in its favor is deducible from the consideration, that whilst there is this great *destructive* movement, no two agree in their constructive philosophy. Each one has his favorite Utopia; and thousands of Fourierite, Owenite, and similar schemes are tested annually, all eventuating in ridiculous failure.

But their remains to be exhibited much stronger evidence of a reactive and counter current of thought on this subject.

Until within the last few years, the abolition argument has been conducted on the postulate that "slavery was a great sin, and therefore should be abolished." The south yielding to the universal sentiment and opinion of the christian world, agreed to the premises, and vainly endeavored to escape, or ward off, the conclusion. Some, admitting all other kinds of slavery to be wrong, stuck up for negro slavery as an exceptional and justifiable institution. Others, and by far the greater number, admitted negro slavery too to be wrong in principle, and looked forward to gradual emancipation as the remedy. Very recently the south has taken stronger and bolder grounds. It maintains that domestic slavery is right in principle and practice. That it is authorised by the almost universal usage of mankind, and expressly and continually recognised, enjoined, and approved by the Bible. That the present and past condition, moral, social, political, religious, and economic of free society, demonstrates the rationalness and necessity of slavery as the only cure or preventive of the crime, hunger, pauperism, mendicity, infidelity, anarchy, and agrarianism, which beget frequent famines, riots, and revolutions in western Europe, and which threaten and disturb our north. The south maintains that form of society to be best which is attended with fewest evils, and challenges the abolitionists to a comparison of the evils of the opposing systems. This exhibits thorough and decided change of opinion at least at the south. We do not know what course the abolitionists mean to pursue under this changed aspect of the controversy. So far they are dumb. As socialists, for all radical and theoretical abolitionists are socialists, they are estopped from denying the intolerable evils of their own existing system. The only alternative left to them is to invite us to give up our slaves and join the Mormons of Utah, the Saints of Oneida, the fraternity of Shakers, or the saloons of Free Love. The controversy is absolutely narrowed down to a choice between society like ours at the south, and some fanatical, sensual, or infidel form of socialism.

All men attempt to justify their acts by the faith that is in them, to justify their practices by their principles. Until the rise of so-

cialism, political economy was the philosophy and the attempted justification of universal liberty. Hobbes understood and described correctly the boiling and seething cauldron of free society. Its antagon-
isms and competition he represented as an internecine war, fatal
to the weak and unfortunate. Had the society around him exhibited
man in his usual and normal state, he would have been right in as-
serting "the state of war to have been the natural state of man."
Hobbes told the truth, and his memory has been blasted for so
doing. Adam Smith, a more superficial observer and thinker, only
saw the good effects resulting to the strong, wise, and fortunate, from
liberty and free competition, and attempted to justify and recom-
mend what Hobbes had condemned and deplored.

His philosophy is the only one to which free society can appeal for
justification and defence. Its maxims, of "let alone," of "little of
government," and "freedom from restriction," are directly at war
with the system of slavery, and if carried out to their ultimate consequences, equally at war with all kinds of subordination and of
government. The socialists all see that this philosophy stands in the
way of their proposed organic changes, and concur in denouncing
the philosophy as well as the form of society which it justifies. To
free competition and laissez-faire, they justly attribute the deplorable condition of the masses. This presents another point of agreement between us of the south and the socialists, for slavery cannot be justified on principle, short of the denial and refutation of
political economy. Mr. Carlyle, in his Latter Day Pamphlets, admirably demonstrates the tendency of political economy to beget universal misrule and anarchy. The opposite, or slavery principle, is inculcated throughout those eloquent pamphlets, as necessary to save
society from universal wreck and overthrow. Mr. Carlyle is the pro-
foundest thinker who writes the English language. He concurs with
the other socialists, that "we must have a new world, if we are to
have any world at all!" But instead of a world of "no government
and free-love," he maintains the necessity of much and rigorous

government, and of slavery, for the lazy, reprobate and idle.

We have arrived at this point: we have exhibited a reaction in public opinion which utterly ignores and repudiates the present organization of free society, as right, or even tolerable. We have further shown, that the same opinion not only repudiates existing social forms, but also the principles, or philosophy, which justify those forms. And, further, we show that the foremost mind of English thought, adopts slavery as the substitute and remedy for existing social and political evils.

We think conclusive evidence of the necessity of domestic slavery is furnished by citing the facts of the universal discontent, famines, revolutions, infidelity, agrarianism, crime, mendicity, and socialism of free society, and the quiet, contentment, abundance, comfort, conservatism, and religious faith of slave society; but we invite those who are not satisfied with this and other proof which we have suggested, to explore English history. The first experiment of liberating the laboring class was made in England. In France, and most of the continent, much of feudal slavery remained till the French revolution of 1792. All writers concur that pauperism and beggary were unknown in England until the liberation of the serfs, and that crime was vastly increased by their liberation. The history of the English poor is to be found in her so-called poor laws. These laws, from the days of Edward the Third to those of Elizabeth, present the most cruel and bloody code to be found in the annals of history. No provision, during that time, was made for the poor, except stripes, branding, and hanging. They were confined to their parish, and punished severely for charging or receiving good wages. The preambles of the various statutes, with regard to them, always denominate them as "rogues, robbers, vagrants, or vagabonds;" yet, bad as their condition was then, it is much worse now, because excess of numbers or competition has reduced their wages to the starving point. Half the time of the British Parliament is occupied in vain attempts to regulate and diminish their hours of labor, to provide for their education, and to keep them from starving. But, nevertheless, their condition daily becomes worse; and yet, perhaps, they are better off than any free laboring class in western Europe. The history of the English poor is the only history of free society, and to that we appeal, to prove the necessity of the more general and active adoption into practise of the slavery principle.

Let us now inquire what is slavery, or the slavery principle? We would define it to be "a social status or condition in which the will of the superior stands for law to the inferior." If this be a correct definition, then have all peoples recognized and approved it, as well in theory as in practice. The wives, the children, the soldiers, the sailors, the lunatics, the idiots, and the convicts, the world over, throughout all time, have been subjected to this "status." That slavery is the appropriate social status of far the larger portion of the human family, admits of no dispute, because the practice and theories of all mankind, in all ages, and in all countries, have concurred in assigning them to that condition. The slavery principle is a necessary and universal principle of government, and is the opposite of the let alone, or Laissez faire doctrine, of the political economists. The only difference that can exist between us and the abolitionists is this: are the negroes, as a class, weak, helpless, improvident or dependent, like women and children, and therefore, as a class, to be subjected to slavery; or are they fitted generally for the offices and functions of masters? We presume very few will not be willing to admit that negroes are not fitted for the unrestricted liberties of white men. All men, whose opinions are worth considering, will agree, that more of the slavery principle should be adopted in the government of negroes than of white men. The question, then, as to the status of the negroes, is narrowed down to this: is the kind of slavery to which he is subjected the proper and necessary one, looking to his moral and intellectual wants and capacities? He is certainly improving, and his bonds relax everywhere as he improves. We believe that nature best adapts and modifies slavery to suit its subjects, but are quite willing to see the question discussed, how far it would be proper to define by law the obligations of the master and the rights of the slave?

NOTE.—Without further explanation, it might appear that we hold the opinion that woman is naturally, in intellect and morality, the inferior of man. We do not think so, however. Their intellectual and moral qualities differ in character rather than in degree. The man has more audacity and physical courage, and is fitter to command. The woman is more observant and impressible, possesses a calmer and more correct judgment, has more moral fortitude, and is better fitted to counsel and advise. The relations usually subsisting between the sexes, are the true and natural ones. Woman is oftener, as she should be, "the power behind the throne greater than the throne itself."

HINTON ROWAN HELPER
(*1829-1909*)

Among the nonslaveholding majority of western North Carolina who contested power with the Eastern planters, Hinton R. Helper was born on a small farm in what is now Davie County. His family belonged to the Henry Clay Whig Nationalists who resisted the planters' demands for extreme state's rights if not outright secession. Helper attended a small academy and became a facile writer. After working as a Salisbury clerk (and lifting money from an employer's till), he left for New York, sailed to California, and spent three years there vainly searching for gold. He wrote a trivial, bad-tempered book, *The Land of Gold* (1855), which showed marked prejudices against Chinese, the Irish, Indians, Jews, Negroes, and other allegedly inferior races.

Returning to Salisbury in 1854, he sensed the enormous demand for antislavery books that had grown since *Uncle Tom's Cabin* and was encouraged by antislavery leaders to try one of his own. Thus he published *The Impending Crisis of the South* (1857) which he dedicated to the nonslaveholding Southern whites. Using and abusing Census figures to prove that Southern backwardness economically and culturally was due to the Lords of the Lash (as he put it), he called for the end of slavery.

With the aid of Republicans who gladly capitalized on a Southern defector from Dixie, he was guaranteed a first edition of 100,000 copies of the book. So popular did *The Impending Crisis* become that in the Congressional session of 1859-60, the House of Representatives heatedly rejected John B. Sherman of Ohio as Speaker because he had endorsed the sentiments of the Helper book. Democrats vainly countered with an anti-Helper literature. Thereafter, the author was rewarded with a consulship to Buenos Aires, a post which started him off to decades of business as well as political contacts with Latin America. During Reconstruction, he published several violently anti-Negro books "to write the Negro out of America." Eventually, his grandiose promotional plans outstripped realities and he committed suicide.

This selection is from pages 405-413 of *The Impending Crisis.*

What has produced this literary pauperism of the South? One single word, most pregnant in its terrible meanings, answers the question. That word is—SLAVERY! But we have been so long accustomed to the ugly thing itself, and have become so familiar with its no less ugly fruits, that the common mind fails to apprehend the connection between the one, as cause, and the other as effect; and it therefore becomes necessary to give a more detailed answer to our interrogatory.

Obviously, then, the conditions requisite to a flourishing literature are wanting at the South. These are—

I. Readers. The people of the South are not a reading people. Many of the adult population never learned to read; still more, do not care to read. We have been impressed, during a temporary sojourn in the North, with the difference between the middle and laboring classes in the Free States, and the same classes in the Slave States, in this respect. Passing along the great routes of travel in the former, or taking our seat in the comfortable cars that pass up and down the avenues of our great commercial metropolis, we have not failed to contrast the employment of our fellow-passengers with that which occupies the attention of the corresponding classes on our various Southern routes of travel. In the one case, a large proportion of the passengers seem intent upon mastering the contents of the newspaper, or some recently published book. The merchant, the mechanic, the artizan, the professional man, and even the common laborer, going to or returning from their daily avocations, are busy with their morning or evening paper, or engaged in an intelligent discussion of some topic of public interest. This is their leisure hour, and it is given to the acquisition of such information as may be of immediate or ultimate use, or to the cultivation of a taste for elegant literature. In the other case, newspapers and books seem generally ignored, and noisy discussions of village and State politics, the tobacco and cotton crops, filibusterism in Cuba, Nicaragua, or Sonora, the price of negroes generally, and especially of "fine-looking wenches," the beauties of lynch-law, the delights of horse-racing, the excitement of street fights with bowie-knives and revolvers, the "manifest destiny" theory that justifies the stealing of all territory contiguous to our own, and kindred topics, constitute the warp and woof of conversation. All this is on a level with the general intelligence of the Slave States. It is true, these States have their educated men,—the majority of whom owe their literary culture to the colleges of the North. Not that there are no Southern colleges—for there are institutions, so called, in a majority of the Slave States—Some of them, too, are not deficient in the appointments requisite to our higher educational institutions; but as a general thing, Southern colleges are colleges only in *name*, and will scarcely take rank with a third-rate Northern academy, while our academies, with a few exceptions, are immeasurably inferior to the public schools of New York, Philadelphia, and Boston. The truth is, there is a vast inert mass of stupidity and ignorance, too dense for individual effort to enlighten or remove, in all communities cursed with the institution of slavery. Disguise the unwelcome truth as we may, slavery is the parent of ignorance, and ignorance begets a whole brood of follies and of vices, and every one of these is inevitably hostile to literary culture. The masses, if they think of literature at all, think of it only as a costly luxury, to be monopolized by the few.

The proportion of white adults over twenty years of age, in each state, who cannot read and write, to the *whole* white population, is as follows:

Connecticut,	1 to every	568	Louisiana,	1 to every	38½
Vermont,	1 "	473	Maryland,	1 "	27
N. Hampshire,	1 "	310	Mississippi,	1 "	20
Massachusetts,	1 "	166	Delaware,	1 "	18

Maine,	1	"	108	South Carolina	1	"	17
Michigan,	1	"	97	Missouri,	1	"	16
Rhode Island,	1	"	67	Alabama,	1	"	15
New Jersey,	1	"	58	Kentucky,	1	"	13½
New York	1	"	56	Georgia,	1	"	13
Pennsylvania,	1	"	50	Virginia,	1	"	12½
Ohio,	1	"	43	Arkansas,	1	"	11½
Indiana,	1	"	18	Tennessee,	1	"	11
Illinois,	1	"	17	North Carolina,	1	"	7

In this table, Illinois and Indiana are the only Free States which, in point of education, are surpassed by any of the Slave States; and this disgraceful fact is owing, principally, to the influx of foreigners, and to immigrants from the Slave States. New-York, Rhode Island, and Pennsylvania have also a large foreign element in their population, that swells very considerably this percentage of ignorance. For instance, New-York shows, by the last census, a population of 98,722 who cannot read and write, and of this number 68,052 are foreigners; Rhode Island, 3,607, of whom 2,359 are foreigners; Pennsylvania, 76,272, of whom 24,989 are foreigners. On the other hand, the ignorance of the Slave States is principally *native* ignorance, but comparatively few emigrants from Europe seeking a home upon a soil cursed with "the peculiar institution." North Carolina has a foreign population of only 340, South Carolina only 104, Arkansas only 27, Tennessee only 505, and Virginia only 1,137, who cannot read and write; while the aggregate of *native* ignorance in these five States (exclusive of the *slaves,* who are debarred all education by *law*) is 278,948! No longer ago than 1837, Governor Clarke, of Kentucky, in his message to the Legislature of that State, declared that "by the computation of those most familiar with the subject, *one-third of the adult population of the State are unable to write their names";* and Governor Campbell, of Virginia, reported to the Legislature, that "from the returns of ninety-eight clerks, it appeared that of 4,614 applications for marriage licenses in 1837, no less than 1,047 were made by men unable to write."

In the Slave States the proportion of free white children between the ages of five and twenty, who are found at any school or college, is not quite *one-fifth* of the whole; in the Free States, the proportion is more than *three-fifths*.

We could fill our pages with facts like these to an almost indefinite extent, but it cannot be necessary. No truth is more demonstrable, and, no truth has been more abundantly demonstrated, than this: that Slavery is hostile to general education; its strength, its very life, is in the ignorance and stolidity of the masses; it naturally and necessarily represses general literary culture. To talk, therefore, of the "creation of a purely Southern Literature," without *readers* to demand, or *writers* to produce it, is the mere babble of idiocy.

II. Another thing essential to the creation of a literature is MENTAL FREEDOM. How much of *that* is to be found in the region of Slavery? We will not say that there is *none;* but if it exists, is exists as the outlawed antagonist of human chattelhood. He who believes that the despotism of the accursed institution expends its malignant forces upon the *slave,* leaving intact the white and (so called) free population, is the victim of a most monstrous delusion. One end of the yoke that bows the African to the dust, presses heavily upon the neck of his Anglo-Saxon master. The entire mind of the South either stultifies itself into acquiescence with Slavery, succumbs to its authority, or chafes in indignant protest against its monstrous pretensions and outrageous usurpations. A free press is an institution almost unknown at the South. Free speech is considered as treason against slavery: and when people dare neither speak nor print their thoughts, free thought itself is well nigh extinguished. All that can be said in *defence* of human bondage, may be spoken freely; but question either its morality or its policy, and the terrors of lynch law are at once invoked to put down the pestilent heresy. The legislation of the Slave States for the suppression of the freedom of speech and the press, is disgraceful and cowardly to the last degree, and can find its parallel only in the meanest and bloodiest despotisms of the Old World. No institution that could bear the light would thus sneakingly seek to burrow itself in utter darkness. Look, too, at the mobbings, lynchings, robberies, social and political proscriptions, and all manner of nameless outrages, to which men in the South have been subjected, simply upon the suspicion that they were the enemies of Slavery. We could fill page after page of this volume with the record of such atrocities. But a simple reference to them is enough. Our countrymen have not yet forgotten why John C. Underwood was, but a few months since, banished from his home in Virginia, and the accomplished Hedrick driven from his College professorship in North Carolina. They believed Slavery inimical to the best interest of the South, and for daring to give expression to this belief in moderate yet manly language, they were ostracised by the despotic Slave Power, and compelled to seek a refuge from its vengeance in States where the principles of freedom are better understood. Pending the last Presidential election, there were thousands, nay, tens of thousands of voters in the Slave States, who desired to give their suffrages for the Republican nominee, John C. Fremont himself a Southron, but a nonslaveholder. The Constitution of the United States guaranteed to these men an expression of their preference at the ballot-box. But were they permitted such an expression? Not at all. They were denounced, threatened, overawed, by the Slave Power—and it is not too much to say that there was really no *Constitutional election,*— that is, no such free expression of political preferences as the Constitution aims to secure—in a majority of the Slave States.

From a multiplicity of facts like these, the inference is unavoidable, that Slavery tolerates no freedom of the press—no freedom of speech—no freedom of opinion. To expect that a whole-souled, manly literature can flourish under such conditions, is as absurd as it would be to look for health amid the pestilential vapors of a dungeon, or for the continuance of animal life without the aid of oxygen.

III. Mental activity—force—enterprise—are requisite to the creation of literature. Slavery tends to sluggishness—imbecility—inertia. Where free thought is treason, the masses will not long take the trouble of thinking at all. Desuetude begets incompetence—the *dare-not* soon becomes the *cannot*. The mind thus enslaved necessarily loses its interests in the processes of other minds; and its tendency is to sink down into absolute stolidity or sottishness. Our remarks find melancholy confirmation in the abject servilism in which multitudes of the non-slave-holding whites of the South are involved. In them, ambition, pride, self-respect, hope, seem alike, extinct. Their slaveholding fellows are, in some respects, in a still more unhappy condition—helpless, nerveless, ignorant, selfish; yet vain-glorious, self-sufficient and brutal. Are these the chosen architects who are expected to build up "a purely Southern literature?"

The truth is, slavery destroys, or vitiates, or pollutes, whatever it touches. No interest of society escapes the influence of its clinging curse. It makes Southern religion a stench in the nostrils of Christendom—it makes Southern politics a libel upon all the principles of Republicanism—it makes Southern literature a travesty upon the honorable profession of letters. Than the better class of Southern authors themselves, none will feel more keenly the truth of our remarks. They write books, but can find for them neither publishers nor remunerative sales at the South. The executors of Calhoun seek, for his works, a Northern publisher. Benton writes history and prepares voluminous compilations, which are given to the world through a Northern publisher. Simms writes novels and poems, and they are scattered abroad from the presses of a Northern publisher. Eighty per cent of all the copies sold are probably bought by Northern readers.

When will Southern authors understand their own interests? When will the South, as a whole, abandoning its present suicidal policy, enter upon that career of prosperity, greatness, and true renown, to which God by his word and his providences, is calling it? "If thou take away from the midst of thee the yoke, the putting forth of the finger and speaking vanity; and if thou draw out thy soul to the hungry and satisfy the afflicted soul; then shall thy light rise in obscurity and thy darkness be as the noonday: And the Lord shall guide thee continually and satisfy thy soul in drought, and make fat thy bones; and thou shalt be like a watered garden, and like a spring of water, whose waters fail not. And they that shall be of thee shall build the old waste places; thou shalt raise up the foundations of many generations; and thou shalt be called, The repairer of the breach, The restorer of paths to dwell in.

Our limits, not our materials, are exhausted. We would gladly say more, but can only, in conclusion, add as the result of our investigations in this department of our subject, that *Literature and Liberty are inseparable; the one can never have a vigorous existence without being wedded to the other.*

Our work is done. It is the voice of the non-slaveholding whites of the South, through one identified with them by interest, by feeling, by position. That voice, by whomsoever spoken, must yet be heard and heeded. The time hastens—the doom of slavery is written —the redemption of the South draws nigh. . . .

DATE DUE

OCT 1 4 '86			
OCT 2 7 '86			
FEB 1 5 '87			
MAR 3 '87			
MAR 2 4 '87			
FEB 8 '88			
APR 3 '89			
			PRINTED IN U.S.A.